WILL TO ARGUE

WILL TO ARGUE

Studies in Late Colonial and Postcolonial Controversies

Sumanyu Satpathy

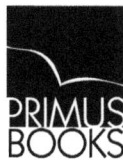

PRIMUS
BOOKS

PRIMUS BOOKS
An imprint of Ratna Sagar P. Ltd.
Virat Bhavan
Mukherjee Nagar Commercial Complex
Delhi 110 009

Offices at CHENNAI   LUCKNOW
AGRA AHMEDABAD BANGALORE COIMBATORE DEHRADUN GUWAHATI
HYDERABAD JAIPUR KANPUR KOCHI KOLKATA MADURAI MUMBAI PATNA
RANCHI VARANASI

First published 2017

ISBN: 978–93–86552–28–0 (hardback)
ISBN: 978–93–86552–29–7 (POD)

Published by Primus Books
Lasertypeset by Sai Graphic Design
Arakashan Road, Paharganj, New Delhi 110055

Printed and bound in India by Replika Press P. Ltd.

Contents

Acknowledgements

Any book, almost a decade in the making, often owes its eventual appearance to several friends, colleagues, and institutions; so much so, it can safely be called a work of collaboration. *Will to Argue* is no exception.

The book was conceived—and work on it begun—during the period of my stay at the Michael J. Osborne Centre of the Institute for Advance Studies, La Trobe University, where I was a Distinguished Fellow (February–June 2007). I was able to accept and make use of this Fellowship only because my then parent institution, University of Delhi, had granted me a year's sabbatical for which I am grateful to the University administration. I not only presented two of the chapters in their earliest draft form, but was also able to conceptualize and draft the entire overarching Introduction to the book while affiliated to La Trobe. I continued to work on the book until my appointment as Head of Department of English for two successive terms slowed down my research (2008–11; 2012–15). The administrative responsibilities also took me away from the excellent South Asian Studies section of the La Trobe library. While this in part explains the long period of gestation, the hiatus resulted in the work taking a form that is different from its original structure.

I have made extensive use of archival material available at the Odisha State Archives, Bhubaneswar and the Natonal Archives of India, Delhi; Utkal Sahitya Samaj, Cuttack, thanks to their officials. During the last couple of years of my research, the initiative taken by a private enterprise, Srujanika, equipped me with a portable digital archive comprising numerous periodicals and books which were impossible to lay hands on because they had become brittle, and at places indecipherable. To the officials and rich resources of the library of Sahitya Akademi, the Central Reference Library (Arts) at University of Delhi, and the small but invaluable library of the

Department of English at University of Delhi, I owe a debt of gratitude.

I have been lucky to share the work in progress with colleagues and research students, both in India and abroad. However, my primary debt of gratitude is to someone who has nothing to do with this book directly, but who first helped me cut my scholarly teeth way back in the early 1980s at the University of Hyderabad. It was he who first taught me the value of archival research: Professor S. Viswanthan. I am also grateful to my very dear friend Jatin K. Nayak of Utkal University. I first met him one ambient Oxford morning at Merton College, during my brief visit to the ancient seat of learning in connection with my research on T.S. Eliot's *Criterion* in the Anglo-American poet's centenary year. In fact, several controversial aspects of Eliot's life threatened to mar the occasion. Jatin assigned himself the onerous task of impressing upon a scholar, who then used to feel the ghostly presence of his research subject, Eliot, to study and translate Odia literature. That was way back in 1988, and since then Jatin has been a constant source of inspiration. Harish Trivedi, who was my colleague and Chair at the Department of English, University of Delhi—at the time of my joining—had already cleared the ground for scholars of English literature to engage in research in their respective 'vernacular' language-literatures with a clear conscience. His work by 1997 had, especially his justly famous *Colonial Transactions*, provided us with a model and a line of enquiry that was far too tempting to not emulate. Moreover, by then I had had the extraordinary good fortune of making the acquaintance of Sisir Kumar Das (at the University of Delhi) and Meenakshi Mukherjee (at the University of Hyderabad). I had actually seen the latter working on her book, *Realism and Reality* in one of the carrels of the American Studies Research Center (ASRC). Later, both these scholars encouraged me to work in the field of Odia literary culture. It is through Mukherjee that I was introduced to J.P. Das, the eminent Odia writer, whose novel *Desh, Kaal, Patra* (now available in English translation by Jatin as *Time Elsewhere*) is the result of painstaking archival work, and is often cited by, ironically enough, scholars of nineteenth-century Odisha's history. The vast body of extensive and pioneering archival work done by one of the finest Indian scholars, Natabar Samantaray has acted as a beacon light and made my task a lot easier, and has given me scholarly direction.

I owe a debt of gratitude to Samantaray's acolytes, Gaganendra Dash, Sudarshan Acharya, and Debendra Dash for their encyclopedic knowledge of Indian/Odia/Hindi/Sanskrit classics. I also wish to acknowledge the contribution of generations of my students who have kept alive my interest in the subject. Very late in the day, I found in Priya Kumar, a scholar-colleague, who gave crucial advice on trimming the manuscript to a manageable length.

I am also grateful to Sue Thomas, the late Terry Collits, Kay Souter (Professors at La Trobe University during my time there as a Fellow), Regenia Gagnier (Exeter University), Adrian Pable, and Harshana Rambukwella (both then at The University of Hong Kong), Swapan Chakravarty and his friend Ashim Mukhopadhyay in the National Library, Udaya Kumar, Gautam Chakravarty, Shubhas Chandra, Raj Kumar, Phanindra Bhusan Nanda, Judith Misrahi-Barak, Isabel Hoffmeyer, Ira Raja, Amritjit Singh, and Malashri Lal for practical and scholarly help. I am also happy to acknowledge the research assistance I received from Animesh Mohapatra. I have often used him as a sounding board, when he would respond with the maturity of a seasoned scholar. I am grateful to him too for bringing other scholars, of immense potential like him, who helped me bring in fresh perspectives and new archival material—Lalit Kumar, Gautam Chaubey, Umasankar Patra, Indira Prasad, Ashokan, Narender, Loiya, Shaswat Panda and Mohammad Afzal. Of these scholars, the academic world will hear much in the near future. If readers find the book rich in terms of its use of a range of obscure archives in Odisha, I owe it to Bigyan Ranjan Das, who turns into a veritable worm as soon as he enters libraries and archives, with his uncanny understanding of what the investigation demands. I am equally grateful to Nikhil Patnaik (who launched and currently heads Srujanika), Padmanavanji, and Ashok Choudhury (both of Sahitya Akademi, New Delhi) for their invaluable help. I am grateful to members of the non-teaching staff of University of Delhi during the difficult days of my headship, whose indirect contribution to the book cannot be underestimated—Archana Mehta, Asha Rani, Satbir, Yogesh, Vinita and Pratap. I fondly recall my former friends and colleagues at North Eastern Hill University, Shillong and Aizawl (Noorul Hasan, Robin S. Ngangom, Nobonita Ganguly, E.N. Lal, D.V. Kumar and K.C. Baral), fellow researchers and friends from our ASRC, Hyderabad days; Sukhbir Singh, K. Narayana Chandran, Yugendranath, and Venkataswerulu.

Members of my family, especially my wife, Aparna, have stood by me during the demanding years of my 'headship' at the Department, frequent and long absences from home, my cranky moods when I would lose the plot of the essays and the book.

Earlier versions of some of the chapters appeared in the following journals or books: Chapter 1 in Comparative Literature Studies; Chapter 4 in Debashish Banerjee, ed., *Rabindranath Tagore in the Twenty-first Century: Theoretical Renewals*; Chapter 5 in *Economic and Political Weekly*. I would like to thank the editors and/or publishers for permission to draw on those versions.

New Delhi   SUMANYU SATPATHY

1

Uses of Controversy
Texts, Identities and the Nation

These trophies . . . are known to the world under several names;
as disputes, arguments, rejoinders, brief considerations, answers,
replies, remarks, reflections, objections, confutations. For a very
few days they are fixed up all in public places . . . for passengers
to gaze at; whence the chiefest and largest are removed to certain
magazines they call libraries, there to remain in a quarter purposely
assigned them, and thenceforth begin to be called books of
controversy.

—JONATHAN SWIFT, *Battle of the Books*

Katherine Mayo's notorious book *Mother India*, which appeared in
the same year as M.K. Gandhi's *An Autobiography or the Story of
my Experiments with Truth* (1927), may have been welcomed by the
British colonialists but it provoked angry reactions among Indians.
It led to the publication of over fifty books and pamphlets, and
Gandhi's comment that it was a 'drain inspector's report'. Thirty-
seven years later, V.S. Naipaul's *An Area of Darkness* (1964), with
an equally negative portrayal of India and its people, similarly
angered many Indian intellectuals. There was a similarity in the
pattern of reactions to the two texts as well. For instance, if one of
the responses to Mayo's work was called *My Mother India*, Nissim
Ezekiel's response to Naipaul came under the title 'Naipaul's India
and Mine'. Much more obscure and localized, though no less lively,
a contentious issue cropped up in Odisha's literary circles in the
1950s about the authenticity of the definitive edition of the fifteenth-
century vernacular classic, the Odia *Mahabharata* by Sarala Das,
Odisha's 'national' poet. The periodical press was filled with claims
and counterclaims made about both the poet and the text.[1] For

better or worse, all these and similar cultural expressions are referred to by the broad rubric, 'controversy' (*tark-bitark* or *vaad-vivaad*). What do such controversies do to a culture? Do they interpret it? Can one conceive of them as a genre? Do they offer serious diagnostic tools to the social scientist or cultural historian? The following chapters address these and similar questions. Though they deal with diverse and often seemingly unconnected subjects and periods, each of the chapters focuses, directly or indirectly, on major controversies at the local or national level. The present volume seeks to examine if and how certain kinds of uncontainable controversies contribute to an understanding of the strategies in which any form of nationalism or identity formation—during colonial and postcolonial times—imagines, shapes, and constructs itself. For, though numerous controversies have arisen in postcolonial India, many of them can be traced back, albeit in less sophisticated and less developed forms, to an earlier era when colonialism clashed with nationalist ideologies. As Arif Dirlik says:

Decolonization was a process fraught with the violence of colonialism, where anticolonialism could achieve its goals only by turning against the colonizers their weapons of violence. Under the circumstances, the contradictions of anticolonialism had to be suppressed if the struggle were to have any chance of success. This was the tragedy of decolonization, which now appears as its futility. Its results have been the reverse of what it intended: the contradictions, emerging to the surface, call into question both earlier understandings of colonialism and the anticolonial struggles they informed.[2]

However, as we shall see, not all controversies are momentous nation-forming discourses. The controversies that are taken up in the five chapters break out around moments of crucial political crises in their respective locations, but by no means stay circumscribed by those locations, and therefore, help us understand the way identities and communities of various kinds are formed in those locations vis-à-vis much larger contexts. Many of them could be well-known and well-defined; many others could be obscure and discrete, limited to the communities affected by them. But if the former seem to be meaningful in the larger context of nation formation, the others provide social scientists with a key to understanding local phenomena at a micro level, which nonetheless might have implications for the larger communities of which the local one is a part. The literary controversies over Naipaul's or Salman Rushdie's comments affected writers from across India, whereas the controversy over Sarala Das and his *Mahabharata* was limited to the Odia speaking people. The Urdu-Hindi controversy is pan-Indian, whereas the Bengali-Odia controversy is limited to the erstwhile Bengal Presidency, and continues to be invoked only by the Odias even now. Through the chapters, I shall endeavour to suggest how these larger controversies are not entirely unaffected by the seemingly trivial local issues and vice versa; the crisscrossing of apparently unrelated discourses can be discerned through studies, such as the one that follows, of controversies, in some detail.

Undoubtedly, a controversy qua controversy is discursive, and like all discourses, it might reveal more about the culture in which it erupts than its purported aims of proving or disproving something, somebody or some idea to be conclusively right or wrong, using the power of logic. Their value for understanding a given culture in a given time is independent of whether they succeed in doing so. However, certain kinds of controversies might prove to be more useful for a student of literary culture than the others. I contend through these chapters, citing instances mostly from the Indian context, that it might be possible to see how discourses of nationalism and such other ideologies (mostly identity-related) arise from and give rise to some of the most irresolvable literary-cultural controversies. For, though the nation is seen as, in phenomenological terms, the coming into consciousness of a community, it has also been viewed, in constructionist terms, as an 'imagined community',[3] and following Antonio Gramsci, as a 'rhetorical prejudice' or 'an intellectual conceit'.[4] The imagining that goes into the making of a modern nation can be better understood through many of these controversies by viewing them in terms of a genre or discursive field, through which nationalism attempts to sort out the self-other binary. Per contra, one of the ways in which postcolonial cultures willy-nilly seek to acquire identities (which then might proceed to claim nationhood) is through controversies which, more often than not, continue to have a subterranean life even after the event of the 'nation'. In fact, controversies related to nationalist questions have seldom died a natural death, and if the contentious issues were prematurely buried—through state coercion, tactically elicited consent or mass amnesia—they have returned, as in many of Edgar Allen Poe's tales, to haunt the imagination of the post-colony,[5] for the simple reason that both nation and its concomitant, nationalism, are processes[6] rather than ontologically finished products. And certain discourses, which may have originally powered nationalism, abide in the popular imagination of the nation, overstaying their

welcome, and perpetually threatening the body politic of the nation-
state until, logically progressing, they materialize in fatal forms,
leading even to dismemberment.

Thus, rather than focusing on the colonialism-nationalism
binary, in fact moving away from it, I have concentrated on the
contradictions within the nationalist framework. For, these internal
contradictions which generate the controversies replicate in diverse
ways through the disequilibrium in the power-culture pact.[7] This can
be seen in the way Indian nationalists were divided along several
binaries vis-à-vis language, religion, sexuality, literature/culture,
caste, and on their attitude towards nationalism itself (moderates *v.*
extremists). As a result, several controversies broke out; and one
might say, the latter generated further differences, which continued
to redefine nationalist alliances, issues, and strategies. In the late-
nineteenth century, the controversy on the Urdu/Hindi divide
continued for some decades, until it gave rise to another binary, the
Urdu/Hindustani as well as the Urdu-Muslim *v.* Hindi-Hindu vis-à-
vis Hindustani-Muslim/Hindu controversies. As leaders like Gandhi
kept underplaying these in the larger interest of the anti-colonial
struggle, the elision did not naturally put an end to the Hindi-Urdu
controversy, but allowed it to fester, leading to Partition. I am not
saying that the controversy caused the Partition in a teleological
sense, but rather that within the fact of the controversy's resilience—
since the controversy was treated as non-negotiable on either side/s
in the context of the other givens of a liberal-democratic framework
within which nationalism fought its battles—inhered the historical
compulsions of the Partition. The same has been the case with the
Gandhi-Ambedkar debate around the issue of caste. It may have
been underplayed and left unresolved during the nationalist struggle,
but it came alive at the time of the framing of the Constitution. It
refused to die down even after the 'solution' to the controversy was
found in the form of the reservation policy, creating fresh controversies
such as the ones during the two Mandal-related legislations.

Gandhi seems to be the point of reference almost everywhere,
to the point of being ubiquitous, in the sense that for over two
decades after his return from South Africa, every controversy seems
to have been taken to him for a resolution—be it the question of
caste, language, women, widowhood or sexuality. Some of these,
like non-violence and khadi were, of course, of his own making. In
the mid-1920s, he would speak about same-sex desire, a subject that
one of the chapters (on Rabindranath Tagore's *Chitrangada*) will
address, without directly invoking Gandhi. The subject had by then

induced major controversies, especially following the work of Pandey Bechan Sharma 'Ugra', someone who deeply admired him. The protagonists as well as adversaries in the entire episode were all nationalists of diverse ideological hues.[8] Gandhi was to publish articles on the subject of male homosexuality, condemning the practice, in *Young India*, 9 September 1926. Whether it was following the storm of controversy that arose when Ugra published 'Chocolate' in the periodical he was editing, or he wrote it suo moto is difficult to figure out at this stage. What is beyond doubt and is on record is that one of Ugra's detractors, Banarasidas Chaturvedi, editor of the literary monthly *Vishal Bharat* (the invocation of nationalist sentiment in the naming of the journal may be noticed here) sent an article to Gandhi in which writings like Ugra's were attacked on account of their obscenity, and the article was duly published in *Young India*. The other Ugra detractors and those who opposed his *Matvala* wrote self-righteously on questions of 'deviant sexuality' as and when it was represented in literature. One belonging to Banarasidas's group, Ramnath Lal aka Suman, argued in 1924 that 'boy-worship' was the biggest problem facing India—more important than untouchability, oppression of widows, or Hindu-Muslim conflicts—since it pervaded all castes, communities, and religions.[9] Gandhi's article, already referred to, was innocuously entitled 'Plight of School Children', where he decried masturbation and homosexuality among boys. This clearly shows how nationalists were concerned that the practice of homosexuality would confirm the perception among colonialists that the Indians were effete. Even Suryakant Tripathi 'Nirala' and Munshi Premchand joined the fray, arguing from opposite perspectives, with Premchand opposing 'bad desires': 'I consider the naked portrayal of bad desires in literature very harmful. The best way to control "Chocolate", etc. is by publishing pamphlets.'[10] Gandhi was close to being dragged into the controversy, had he not refrained from going openly public over 'Chocolate'. He had made his position clear in a private letter to Banarasidas, which the latter had suppressed. When Banarasidas revealed the contents of the letter in 1953, well after Gandhi's death, it revived the controversy albeit in a different form. Due to his prevarications, Gandhi changed his view on the subject and congratulated himself by admitting that he wisely limited his approval of 'Chocolate' in a letter, 'If I had published my opinion it would have done great harm'.[11] In 1952, Mohansingh Sengar, editor of *Naya Samaj*, wrote an article entitled 'Ek Sahityik Anarth' ('A Literary Mischief' inaccurately translated by Ruth Vanita as 'A

Literary Injustice'). The entire episode is indicative of how controversies related to sexuality also got embroiled in questions of nationalism.[12]

Yet, there might arise from time to time, interesting controversies which are nonetheless inconsequential or remotely connected to the larger issues of identity do not come within the purview of my argument here. Whereas, instances as the ones cited below were rare during the heyday of nationalist print journalism, scurrility having been conspicuous by its near-total absence, in the late capitalist era, a distinction needs to be made with regard to nationalism at the time of colonialism and during our postcolonial times. In order to do this, I would like to cite instances from the realm of popular culture, for it is not as if discourses in the public sphere are only about weighty matters emanating from serious politics, art, and literature. Popular culture also sometimes makes its presence felt in the domain of public sphere. In fact, sometimes controversies around films, TV shows, as well as film and TV personalities might dominate the public sphere. The twin cases of Shilpa Shetty and Rakhi Sawant[13] might clarify the point I have just made with regard to my understanding of the specific genre of controversy. In the British reality show 'Celebrity–Big Brother', housemates Goody, Danielle Lloyd, and Jo O'Meara allegedly ganged up against Shilpa. She claimed to have been subjected to humiliation through snide and biting comments. Reported and repeated on electronic and print media, the comments caused outrage, both in India and Britain, with the issue figuring in the House of Commons, and the feminist Germaine Greer and two Indian ministers demanding corrective action. Around the same time, a small time media personality, Rakhi Sawant dramatically alleged that she had been forcibly kissed by her colleague Mika Singh. The 'controversy arising out of Mika Singh allegedly kissing Sawant', according to gossip magazines, 'refuses to die down'. Limited to gossip columns, it remained a low-key affair. On closer scrutiny, it becomes clear that this controversy is too limited and self-serving to be of any interest to anyone on the basis of communal or gender affiliations; though at one point Girija Vyas, Chairperson, National Commission for Women, took cognizance of the complaint.[14] Depending on the aim of the cultural critics, both the controversies could prove to be valuable, though for my purposes, the case of Shilpa alone qualifies to the generic description of a controversy, and might prove to be more valuable to a social scientist than the one involving Rakhi. The reason is that the Shilpa controversy fulfils the most important definitional criterion in that it affects the community's or the putative nation's (in this case, India's) self-image. Though some commentators have highlighted the issue as that of the South-Asian diaspora, why for some reason the question of gender/sex has been elided, for example, whether the sex issue would have arisen and not that of race (after all she was called all kinds of names, including one that was slang for the female genitalia that was blipped out, thus prompting people to assume that the blipped term was racist and not sexist) if a white male had made the same or similar remarks, is a moot point. Thus, not all controversies are forms of cultural entertainment, but have deeper consequences for the post-colony, and affect national lives.

Towards a Definition

Under the circumstances, might we evolve a working definition of controversy treating it as a genre? Though the *Oxford English Dictionary* locates the first usages of the term from the late-fourteenth century onward, it then referred to small, private disagreements—either personal or legal—and was mostly confined to narrow circles.[15] The term is sometimes still used in this sense, but my use of the term is more specific. For my purposes, I see this certain kind of controversy as a cultural text—verbal or non-verbal—where members of the public participate in, argue, and debate, by making use of various organs of the media, any issue arising out of the utterance or action of an individual or group of individuals within or outside the community, but which directly or indirectly affect the community's self-image and identity. Needless to say, the term 'members of the public' includes non-specialists within the discursive field in which the controversy occurs.[16] It will soon become apparent that I have a fundamental disagreement with the *interpretation* of Jürgen Habermas's formulation regarding the public sphere (not with the formulation itself) that both Nancy Fraser and Francesca Orsini offer.[17]

Habermas is silent on the question as to whether or how the 'public sphere' yields consensus or public opinion, whereas Fraser and Orsini see the role of the public sphere as generating opinions through debates and controversies, and conclude by saying that, '[p]ublic opinion becomes the result of such discussions, a consensus about the common good'.[18] For me, consensus is either secured or is at best temporary and unstable. What Habermas quite clearly avoids is the possible collusion between the public sphere and the state apparatus; and allows for the possibility of a lack of consensus in the public sphere. On the other hand, the interpretation of the two critics of Habermas clears the ground for 'hegemony'. Gramsci speculates the possibility of hegemony, as Raymond Williams has clarified, 'its internal structures are highly complex, and have continually to be renewed, recreated and defended; and by the same token, that they can be continually challenged and in certain respects modified'.[19] However, it is also not wholly that consensus or hegemony is not imposed from without, as Raymond Williams argues. In many cases it is. Thus, contestation, which is what my definition of controversy contributes to, resists the completion/ closure of consensus. Hence, Habermas takes care to define public sphere as a realm where 'something *approaching* public opinion can be formed' [emphasis mine].[20]

Sumit Sarkar enumerates a large number of controversies in the public sphere citing innumerable newspaper and magazine articles with opposite viewpoints, 'Swadeshi and revivalism versus "progress"';[21] he also narrates a second set within the Swadeshi movement 'between constructive Swadeshi' and 'political extremism'.[22] Orsini, too, deals with several controversies with regard to the Hindi public sphere. Some other revisionist historiographers like Ashis Nandy tend to take sides in an attempt to resolve, once and for all, certain controversies. Nandy describes the *Jana Gana Mana* controversy in terms of 'claims [which] have occasionally been made that the song was written in honour of King George V' and explains this in terms of 'the hostility [that] Tagore's concept of nationalism aroused in the expanding middle-class culture of Indian politics'.[23] The controversy dogged Tagore all his life, and even until the year of his death, he kept responding to the questions on the subject,[24] though many commentators have noted Tagore's earlier mendicancy and the so-called Universalist leanings for which he was criticized by many extremists such as Bipin Chandra Pal, Brahmabandhav Upadhyay and Aurobindo Ghosh.[25] In spite of the brilliance of his argument, Nandy seems to be brushing aside the growing suspicion among a few Swadeshi adherents that Tagore was being ambivalent about India's nationalist aspirations. Mrinalini Sinha also argues how nationalism had to cope with pressure from within *c.*1920; '. . . official Indian nationalism was under increasing pressure to renegotiate its own relation to various competing agendas emanating from caste, class, gender, and communal (sectarian) politics within India'.[26]

It should have been clear by now that if two or more truths are being claimed or contested by the warring parties in any given controversy, the historian is not always expected/called upon to adjudicate. Should she support one of them through supplying what she thinks is incontrovertible fact, she does not necessarily put an end to the controversy, rather contributes to its afterlife. Given the historical aporia integral to such controversies, the cultural critic prefers to study the meaning and interpret, in the Clifford Geertz sense of the term, the text of the controversy.[27] But in praxis, nationalism tries to resolve controversies in its search for homogeneity, an essential condition for constructing a nation and identity.[28] Instead of being taken to a resolution, the controversy, during the process of such construction, was temporarily swept under the carpet, as it were, at the altar of transient needs of nationalism; but it, like other controversies, reappeared either in the same or a mutant version later in history. One of the propositions in the dialectic set of a controversy is contained by the dominant, as it were in the interest of nationalism. Non-violence and violent struggle; Hindu/ Muslim; Hindi/Urdu; Hindi/English, and so on, when the power of Gandhian rhetoric tilts the balance in favour of one. But this is hardly a resolution: witness Chauri Chaura, and all the violence that culminated in the Partition and the trauma that ensued.[29]

Returning to the definitional aspect of controversy, especially in the context of my use of the term here, I feel tempted here to slightly rephrase T.S. Eliot's caveat in an entirely unrelated context, and say that I do not 'aim to supersede or to outlaw any use of the word [controversy] which precedence has made permissible. The word has, and will continue to have, several meanings in several contexts: I am concerned with one meaning in one context. In defining the term in this way, I do not bind myself, for the future, not to use the term in any of the other ways in which it has been used.'[30] The way I define the term controversy, locating it as I do among typical products of the era of print capitalism and mass media, and therefore, of modernity, enables me to see it as being coeval with the emergent discourses of nationalism. It further enables me to count such controversies, as I have already hinted earlier, among the broad rubric of what Partha Chatterjee so felicitously calls the 'Nationalist Text', and I provisionally give it a further subgeneric status. It may originally have been used in the private domain, but, as a social force, it realizes its full potential only by the end of the eighteenth century and beginning of the nineteenth century. The following instances, two to begin with, might clarify the point. Ezra Pound supplied his version of Tagore's explanation regarding the occasion of *Jana Gana Mana*, to his correspondent, Homer Pound:

There is a charming tale of the last durbar anent. One Bengali here in London was wailing to W.B.Y. 'How can we speak of patriotism of Bengal

when our greatest poet has written this ode to the king?' And Yeats taxing
one of Rabindranath's students elicited this response. 'Aah! I will tell you
about that poem. The national committee came to Mr. Tagore and asked
him to write something for the reception. And as you know Mr. Tagore is
very obliging. And all that afternoon he tried to write them a poem, and
he *could* not. And that evening the poet as usual retired to his meditation.
And in the morning he descended with a sheet of paper. He said, 'Here is
a poem I have written. It is addressed to the deity. But you may give it to
the national committee. Perhaps it will content them.'[31]

At the end of his version, Ezra Pound told his correspondent that
'The joke, which is worthy of Voltaire, is for private consumption
only, as it might be construed politically *if it were to be printed'*
[emphasis mine].[32] How was he to know that the joke was printed,
and it was indeed misconstrued politically, and that eventually when
the song was preferred over other songs as India's national anthem,
it became even more controversial, and has remained so ever since!
Going further back to an earlier phase of Indian nationalism, the
following seemingly innocuous episode that figures in Gandhi's
Autobiography might serve to further illustrate my point:

The question of wearing the turban had great importance in this state of
things. Being obliged to take off one's Indian turban would be pocketing
an insult. So I thought I had better bid good-bye to the Indian turban and
begin wearing an English hat, which would save me from the insult and
the unpleasant controversy. But Abdulla Sheth disapproved of the idea. He
said, 'If you do anything of the kind, it will have a very bad effect. You will
compromise those insisting on wearing Indian turbans. And an Indian
turban sits well on your head. If you wear an English hat, you will pass for
a waiter.' There was practical wisdom, patriotism and a little bit of
narrowness in this advice.

The wisdom was apparent, and he would not have insisted on the
Indian turban except out of patriotism; the slighting reference to the waiter
betrayed a kind of narrowness. Amongst the indentured Indians there were
three classes: Hindus, Musalmans and Christians. The last were the
children of indentured Indians who became converts to Christianity. Even
in 1893 their number was large. They wore the English costume, and the
majority of them earned their living by service as waiters in hotels. Abdulla
Sheth's criticism of the English hat was with reference to this class. It was
considered degrading to serve as a waiter in a hotel. The belief persists even
today among many. On the whole I liked Abdulla Sheth's advice. I wrote
to the press about the incident and defended the wearing of my turban in
the court. The question was very much discussed in the papers, which
described me as an 'unwelcome visitor'. Thus the incident gave me an
unexpected advertisement in South Africa within a few days of my arrival

there. Some supported me while others severely criticized my temerity. My turban stayed with me practically until the end of my stay in South Africa.[33]

It is worth noting that as the narrative progresses, different kinds of headgear begin to acquire cultural significations as markers of national identity: '*Indian* turban' (repeated five times), '*English* hat', (repeated three times), and so on. And also, on different Indian heads, the hat acquires a class marker along with that of community affiliations—Hindu, Muslim, and Christian. The hat sits comfortably on the English head and the turban on the Indian, whereas the hat on an Indian's head, because it is used by the Indian Christian labour class in South Africa, signifies a waiter. Thus, there are several nationalist subtexts in this episode that Gandhi is at pains to explain. It is another matter that in trying to highlight the patriotic aspect of the semiotic of the dress, he exposes another prejudice, that of class. Be that as it may, by the time we come to the end of the paragraph, we realize that what he has described through the concluding sentences of his little narrative constitutes, by the terms of my definition, a controversy (he even allows the use of the term), 'The question was very much discussed in the papers, which described me as an "unwelcome visitor", "unexpected advertisement", and finally, "Some supported me while others severely criticized my temerity".' What is important here for our purposes is that the controversy contributes to the construction and strengthening of national identities. This would not have been possible without the mediation of the papers.

The use of print media for nationalist purposes could well have begun with Raja Rammohun Roy, who was one of the first Indians to use 'the printing press for public controversy'.[34]As he himself tells us, 'My continued controversies with the Brahmans on the subject of their idolatry and superstition, and my interference with their custom of burning widows, and other pernicious practices, revived and increased their animosity against me. . . .'[35] We ought to remind ourselves here that even though he is writing this to an English friend, he is repositioning India's 'spiritual' or inner aspect of which Chatterjee speaks.[36] As an aside, one might point out how this case does not fit into Chatterjee's schema of the inner/outer dichotomy, as pointed out by Sumit Sarkar (which Chatterjee uses to theorize nationalist historiography in the first of the trilogy)—also ends up shedding his (Rammohun's) 'prejudice' against the British.[37] As Rammohun Roy further goes on to say, how, 'availing myself of the art of printing, now established in India, I published various works and pamphlets against their errors, in the native and foreign languages'. 'The ground which I took in all my *controversies* was, not that of opposition to *Brahminism*, but to a *perversion* of it; and I endeavoured to show that the idolatry of the Brahmans was contrary to the practice of their ancestors, and the principles of the ancient books and authorities which they profess to revere and obey' [emphasis mine].[38]

The last point that he makes in the sentence above, regarding the need he felt to go into the past to clinch the issue of corruption or perversion, takes me to my next point that I make in my definition about why controversies are distinctly a by-product of modernity. It is the post-Enlightenment emphasis on proof and evidence for truth claims that makes the phenomenon a modern one. Cartography, archaeology, and such other new sciences and scientific methods which strengthened history writing projects, ensured that in communities like India's—notorious for poor record-keeping—with a strong belief system and alternative knowledge systems which were so firmly ensconced, and were now challenged or discarded by the newly emergent intelligentsia, controversies arose in any number. A text that goes radically against the grain of public perception, causing a sense of outrage in a large number of people affected by the subject, can be christened as a genre of controversy. Such primary texts which meet with vehement opposition could be verbal or non-verbal, could be briefly or elaborately argued, and their authors could be called controversialists.

During the nineteenth century, in Europe especially, the rise of rationalists resulted in a spurt in controversies, well supported by a burgeoning print media. These rationalists often chose to offer revisionist versions and critiques of faith and dogma. Hence, the frequent deployment of the term, 'dogmatist' to run down a traditional argument. But dogma soon turns into a secular metaphor for any 'irrational' defence of a belief; and even a non-rationalist could be dogmatic by virtue of holding an ideological position. In this book, the controversialists range from Thomas B. Macaulay, Anthony MacDonnell, Rajendralal Mitra, Babu Kantichandra Bhattacharya, Radhanath Ray, Tagore, Biswanath Kar, Gopinath Mohanty, Naipaul, Rushdie, Vikram Chandra or Chinua Achebe, who began by attacking commonly held ideas and perceptions.

We presently return to the second distinction regarding colonial and postcolonial nationalisms, as some of the chapters move away from considerations of nationalism during colonial times to that in the postcolonial times, i.e. from what Chatterjee calls 'the moment of arrival' until contemporary times. 'Has the history of colonialism then exhausted itself?' Chatterjee asks and says, 'Such a conclusion will be unwarranted. For hardly anywhere in the postcolonial world has it been possible for the nation-state to fully appropriate the life of the nation into its own. Everywhere the intellectual-moral leadership of the ruling classes is based on a spurious ideological unity. The fissures are clearly marked on the surface.'[39] Seven years later, Chatterjee begins his next set of essays on colonial and postcolonial histories by saying, 'Nationalism has once more appeared on the agenda of world affairs'.[40] The iterability of the ideology of nationalism in post-nationalist times raises questions about the temporal prefix 'post' in the term post-nationalist if not the postcolonial phase of the modern nation state. The recent controversies following the sloganeering in the campus of Jawaharlal Nehru University and the dubbing of the sloganeers as 'anti-nationalist' is a case in point.

It might as well be useful to approach the same issue from the perspective of Raymond Williams's convenient distinction between dominant, residual, and emergent forms in a system of practices and values in any given culture. Following Williams, one might say that, in spite of the broad disagreements within nationalist ideologies, during the three phases of nationalism in Chatterjee's schema, nationalism itself remained the dominant form of ideology. But after the moment of arrival and state formation, the residuum of nationalism continues to work. Thus, it might not be accurate to think of the revival of nationalism—Hindi/Hindu or any other—as if it had disappeared at the time of nation formation. The residual nationalist issues such as those of racism continue to coexist with the dominant, and opportunistically haunt postcolonial India. As Williams, while talking about how 'whatever the degree of internal conflict or internal variation, [the modes of real oppositions] do not in practice go beyond the limits of the central effective and dominant definitions', says, 'This is true, for example, of the practice of parliamentary politics, though its internal oppositions are real'. Then, of course, he goes on to say that 'whatever the degree of internal controversy and variation, they do not exceed the limits of the central corporate definitions', though my argument here breaks away from this position of his from now on. Be that as it may.[41]

Controversy as a Source of Narrativizing Nationalist History

Having seen a nexus between controversies and questions of nation, nationalism and identity, one is not surprised to come across recent historiographies referring to controversies and drawing important conclusions regarding Indian nationalism. But we must remind ourselves that controversies are the very obverse of consensus, obtained through state coercion or appropriation; and by their very nature, might be resistant to any attempt to 'find the truth'. They share the two propositions in a Hegelian dialectic, without ensuring a synthesis, unlike in the case of the standard modes of enquiry, seeking after philosophical truth, whether the Socratic method of *elenchus*, or the Hegelian/Marxist method of synthesis (there are exceptions in the form of the symbolic victory in favour of one of the two warring propositions when the hegemonic state intervenes, as in the case of the Indian national anthem). But generally, in all instances of cultural controversy, any attempt to quell a controversy only prolongs it, as we shall see.

The source of the recurrence of controversies can be divined from the way difference is contained in what grows into an apparent consensus, or nationalist ideology, in which thesis inheres its own antithesis.[42] The following formulation is helpful for Chatterjee. For the methodology that he adopts in some of his later essays too involves the use of several pairs of binaries in dialectic tension. In fact, he does make it clear in the first of his trilogy, that 'Our approach in this study admits an even stronger formulation: nationalist ideology . . . is inherently polemical, shot through tension . . . it is part of the ideological content of nationalism which takes as its adversary a contrary discourse—the discourse of colonialism'.[43] Here, Chatterjee considers two broad oppositional discourses— colonialism and nationalism. But later on, he focuses on resolutions rather than contradictions within nationalist polemics. For example, in the second volume, he argues that the Indian nation emerged out of an attempt to resolve several conflicts/controversies: tradition/ modernity; Hindu/Muslim; Hindi/Urdu; elite/subaltern; material/ spiritual; inner/outer; home/world; communal/secular; men/ women; traditional woman/modern women and so on. Though he has earlier criticized Benedict Anderson for not 'pursuing the varied, and often contradictory, *political* possibilities inherent in this process [and sealing up his theme with a sociological determinism]',[44] insofar as his own methodology is concerned, Chatterjee tends to favour resolutions of ideological conflicts and conflicting ideas. Though non-determinist in nature, these are resolutions nonetheless. For example, while dealing with the contradiction between the national and the modern during the high tide of nationalism in India, Chatterjee asks, 'how are we to sort out these contradictory elements in nationalist discourse?'[45] However, after marking out these binaries and the premises on which issues were debated, the contradictions, Chatterjee invariably goes on to posit that chooses to resolve. A typical formulation would be the following or its variant:

This was the central principle by which nationalism resolved the women's [*sic*] question in terms of its own historical project. The details were not, of course, worked out immediately. In fact, from the middle of the nineteenth century right up to the present day, there have been many controversies about the precise application of the home/world, spiritual/ material, feminine/masculine dichotomies in various matters concerning the everyday life of the 'modern' woman—her dress, food, manners, education, her role in organizing life at home, her role outside the home. . . . the specific solutions were drawn from a variety of sources. . . . The content of the resolution was neither predetermined nor unchanging, but its form had to be consistent with the system of dichotomies that shaped and *contained* the nationalist project [emphasis mine].[46]

For his overall argument, this is impeccable. But the problem arises due to the contradictions in matters of some details which are inconsequential for the efficacy of the argument, but which strengthen the case for the argument in these essays. If we say that '. . . from the middle of the nineteenth century right up to the present day, there have been many controversies', we cannot at the same time insist on the past perfect nature of the nationalist project and its resolution of the controversies, nor on the category, 'A Genealogy of the Resolution'. Similarly, in the chapter 'Histories and Nations', he considers two models of historiographies—the national and the regional (*'bharatavarshiya'* and 'Bengalis of many *jati'*) and concludes that the question would no longer be national and regional but confederal.[47] These contradictions, if an ailment, surface as symptoms in the form of controversies. Though Chatterjee does not deal with specific controversies at the empirical level, these latter can be seen as having been generated by the binaries he deals with in the context of nationalism in the ideal/theoretical domain.

Enunciatory Site

In most controversies, usually two or more fundamental points of view are shared by two or more groups of opponents, but they do not necessarily represent those exclusive/different identities. Were that the case, the genre of controversy would have yielded itself to easy theorization. Interestingly enough, controversies, more often than not, bind the two parties arguing for and against with a stronger bond around a cultural symbol. The controversies around the song that Tagore composed whether in praise of George V or the motherland do not mean that one of the two groups is anti-nationalist (though one argues that Tagore's song was anti-nationalist in its original inspiration, and the other believes quite the contrary). Similarly, the more local controversy over Sarala Das's biographical specificities is suggestive of the strong bond of the two warring groups. These two instances are cases in point. Bengalis and Indians (two broad communities/nations) in the case of the first one, Odias in general in the latter case, have argued endlessly; but neither against a real or imagined dominant/hegemonic group. They have argued as if any resolution would result in some momentous victory or defeat and have any impact on their national destiny, whereas Ezra Pound could afford to call the whole controversy in its nascent stage, 'a joke'. But these controversies do have a hold on their sense of belonging to a community or a nation. Some controversies, on the other hand, do contribute actively to sustain the identity and result in the ideology of pride, and are against the dominant 'other'. The controversy over Jayadeva's identity or Sri Chaitanya's conferment of the title 'Atibadi' to Jagannatha Das can be grouped under this. In this case, the Odias imagine themselves to be overridden by the more dominant (historically) Bengalis, and such controversies help them to regroup under the banner of one identity. Communities can be seen to imagine themselves into beings and non-existent entities, consolidating ideas of nationhood. The more threatened and fluid the notion of a homogeneous community or of nation, the greater is the pressure to redefine and hold onto newer ideas of communal identities. For, modern nations (nation states) have been formed using diverse strategies of homogenization, controversies constituting one such strategy. Bipin Chandra Pal said in utter puzzlement about the Odisha for Odia Movement:

When I first went to Cuttack fifty years ago. Neither the classes nor the masses there had developed any separatist provincial consciousness. Orissa formed then a part of Bengal Administration. The Administration of Bengal was composed of three provinces of Bengal, Bihar and Orissa. Bihar, though inside the administrative province of Bengal, had a distinct linguistic and cultural individuality of its own.[48]

This puzzlement can only be explained in terms of the invasion of new ways of knowing one's past. Much has been said about how the nationalists/intellectuals craved for a history.[49] As we have seen, the zeal with which *jatis* scanned the putative glorious past also produced the anxiety to claim glory. Thus, most controversies, which are nation-forming discourses, arise from disagreements over the past. It is like a round of the card-game of Bridge, when the losing partners argue over how the other ought to have played the last round. It is the way memory works selectively to recall the momentous events of the past few minutes. There is no serious argument between the winners. Even the claim that Bengal had no history and that even the Odias have a history could create a controversy. Ironically enough, Bipin Chandra's recollection itself is debatable, for if there was no history of the rivalry, it was either because there was no record of the history or because there was no motive for either travellers from the neighbourhood settling down in Odisha or if they did, for the Odias to protest, as the divide itself was non-existent.

The chapters here do not always directly study or interpret the controversies; in fact, more often than not, a controversy might merely provide the starting point for analysing a range of larger questions, mostly and not always ideological, which the warring parties often lose sight of due to their specific concerns. Yet, it will be seen that each has something or the other to do with the identity of a community at various points of time since the time of the advent of modernity. They erupt around crucial political flashpoints in their respective histories. The controversies studied here also seem to contribute to an understanding of formation of identities of various kinds: from local, religious, communal, and linguistic identities to racial, sexual, and national ones. The interpenetrating grids that tie up the studies are as follows:

Hegemonic Languages, Texts, and their Subversion

These are textual-political controversies in three sets: in each case a local narrative(s) is in an interface with its national counterpart, the latter being the dominant of the two, and also acting as a master text that would be used as a signifier of a latter-day ontological entity categorized 'Indian'. Since its inception, each of the master texts had a spread that was broadly Hindu, brahmanical and Sanskritic, and not necessarily 'Indian' but maybe of a fuzzy Bharat. The local one is confined to the geopolitic of fluid (shrinking or expanding) territoriality, variously and at different times called Utkal, Odra, Kalinga, and so on. The gigantic shadow of the

Mahabharata straddles three sets of controversies taken up, but they also touch on the issue of the relative dominance or subjugation of one language or the other—one chapter being exclusively about linguistic controversies in India. The chapters explore the interconnections between the historical-textual event and the historical political implications that set in motion the controversy in question which in turn infuse newer significations for the text. For example, during what Sheldon Pollock calls the vernacular millennium, the Odia *Mahabharata* was composed by Sarala Das around the 1450s.[50] This is generally seen as a tacit agenda on the part of a community to diffuse the Sanskrit cosmopolis,[51] so as to forge for itself a language for purposes of cultural expression. As a lower caste Odia, Sarala Das is also seen to have tried to resist the brahmanical order by composing in the then current and accessible Odia idiom, a local version of *Mahabharata*, thus succeeding in resisting the high-brahmanical upper-caste text of the Sanskrit *Mahabharata*. Centuries later, during the late-colonial period, the text becomes a subject of sporadic debate. But, later in the mid-twentieth century, a fresh controversy erupts over the identity of the author, his place of birth and the authenticity of his text.

In the late-nineteenth century, again, there is yet another complex web of ideological moment calling for the reinvention of the *Mahabharata* when Radhanath Ray publishes his unfinished epic *Mahayatra*. This too becomes a major subject of debate soon after its publication mainly due to the representation of caste, especially Brahmanism.

Episodes in the epic have forever been seen in newer contexts, and new meanings read into them. For example, the episode involving Chitrangada, during the late colonial period, stands for a new signified. Accordingly, seeing new meanings in the character of Chitrangada, Tagore reinvented her not once but three times over, if not more. The concerned chapter is on this reinvention of the Chitrangada episode by Tagore cast in different versions by the poet himself from 1892 to 1931. In contrast to Gandhi, Jawaharlal Nehru endorsed Tagore's idea that Indian women ought to look up to Chitrangada. The intrepid Manipur princess was unorthodox and epitomized equality. Nehru, who often found himself closer to Tagore's thinking than with Gandhi's, echoed similar sentiments. Talking about his deceased wife Kamala, Nehru wrote in his book *Discovery of India*, 'Like Chitra in Tagore's plays, she [Kamala] seemed to say to me: I am Chitra. No goddess to be worshipped, nor yet the object of common pity to be brushed aside. If you design to keep me by your side in the path of danger and daring, if you allow me to share the great duties of your life, then you will know myself. . . .'

The other theme moves away from the Sanskrit cosmopolis to the gradual emergence of newer hegemonic languages such as Persian, Urdu, English, Hindi, and Bangla. In fact, a whole chapter is exclusively devoted to the linguistic controversies from the mid-nineteenth century onward. Linguistic controversies in India are often treated as discrete units as if such controversies in various languages and regions never had any bearing on other languages and regions. Cultural expressions within different linguistic groups inherit and share these derivative discourses while employing linguistic strategies as part of their linguistic-identarian aesthetics.

Gandhi and National Texts

Gandhi's position on various issues, from sexuality to tropes such as the charkha and khadi and the language question have posed their own set of challenges to Gandhian Swadeshi politics and their relationship with the Indian National Congress (INC), and caused controversies. Outlining the first of the controversies relating to the Gandhian trope of khadi, Lisa Trivedi says, 'But the spinning franchise promptly drew controversy'.[52] She further shows how industrialists like Birla challenged khadi proponents in newspaper articles and pamphlets. Tagore and critic Anil Baran Roy, among others, too attacked the notion of khadi's viability as an economic rejoinder to foreign goods. Given his national prominence, Tagore's views were picked up in a variety of publications, both in the English and vernacular press. Tagore had two concerns. He accused Gandhi of being unrealistically anti-industrial and promoting a programme that was incapable of addressing the enormous problem of Indian poverty. More troubling than this, however, was Tagore's view that the khadi movement had been adopted without serious reason or reflection. Later in life, Tagore was somewhat sceptical of nationalism in all its forms and urged Gandhi not to promote nationalism through his politics.

National and Literary History

Issues related to history—political or literary—entered the realm of public discourse along with nationalism in the nineteenth century. This was necessitated by the call for anti-colonial as well as nationalist struggles, invoked in key moments of identity struggle. Whether it was language or the definitiveness of iconic cultural texts and their authors, whether it was the caste system or clashes around communal symbols, history posed a serious epistemic challenge to claimants on either side of the divide. Sometimes, languages, idioms, religious or linguistic identities inextricably get entangled in many of the controversies. It is again the new disciplinary-knowledge of history that becomes a major player.

Thus, the idea behind organizing a whole book around a series of controversies is to try and explore the ideologies driving people's will to argue, and to understand the way many of these controversies have contributed to and have been a part of, even while being determined by, the ideologies of community/identity/nation formation.

Notes

1. Katherine Mayo, *Mother India,* London: Jonathan Cape,1927; Mrinalini Sinha, 'Introduction', in *Selections from Mother India,* ed. Mrinalini Sinha, New Delhi: Women's Press, 1998, pp. 1–74; V.S. Naipaul, *An Area of Darkness,* London: A. Deutsch, 1964; Nissim Ezekiel's rejoinder was among the earliest salvo fired against Naipaul, originally published in *Imprint* and subsequently reprinted in Adil Jussawalla, *New Writing in India,* Harmondsworth: Penguin, 1974; Adil Jussawalla and Eunice de Souza, eds., *Statements,* Bombay: Orient Longman, 1977. Countering generally agreed upon dates among scholars, Gopinath Mohanty stirred the hornet's nest with 'Sarala Dasnka Ghara Keunthi?', *Jhankara,* vol. 8, no. 2, 1957, pp. 249–58. Krishnachandra Panigrahi embarked on the project soon after with 'Sarala Sahityara Rachannakala O Aitihashika Chitra', *Jhankara,* vol. 8, no. 9, 1956, pp. 1–10. The debate continued for almost a decade.

Apart from the controversies which will be in focus across the following chapters, one might also refer to Chinua Achebe, 'An Image Of Africa: Racism in Conrad's *Heart of Darkness*', *Massachusetts Review,* vol. 18, 1977, pp. 782–94. Edward Said goes on to say that Achebe's criticism does not go far enough, see Edward Said, *Culture and Imperialism,* London: Chatto & Windus, 1993, p. 200. Many Third World scholars, including Afro-Americans, have defended *Heart of Darkness.* Salman Rushdie, 'Damme, This is the Oriental Scene for You', first published in *The New Yorker;* subsequently reprinted as 'Introduction', in *The Vintage Book of Indian Writing, 1947-1997,* ed. Salman Rushdie and Elizabeth West, London: Vintage, 1997, pp. ix–xxii; repr. in *Step Across the Line: Collected Non-Fiction 1992–2002,* London: Jonathan Cape, 2002, pp. 159–73. Amit Chaudhuri, ed., 'Introduction', in *The Picador Book of Modern Indian Literature*, London: Picador, 2001, pp. xvii–xxxii; Kamala Das, 'Foreword', in *Our Favourite Indian Stories*, ed. Khushwant Singh and Neelam Kumar, Delhi: Jaico Publishing, 2002, pp. 17–20; Leela N. Gandhi, 'Indo-Anglian Fiction: Writing India, Elite Aesthetics, and the Rise of the "Stephanian" Novel', *Australian Humanities Review*, no. 8, November 1997. Also see, 'A Major Literary Event', *The Hindu*, 19 August 2001.

2. Arif Dirlik, 'Rethinking Colonialism: Globalisation, Postcolonialism and the Nation', *Interventions*, vol. 4, no. 30, 2002, p. 434.

3. Benedict Anderson, *Imagined Communities: Reflections on the Origin and Spread of Nationalism*, London: Verso, 1983.

4. The 'rhetorical prejudice (originating in literature) according to which the Italian nation has always existed, from ancient Rome to the present day. This and other totems and intellectual conceits, although politically "useful" in the period of national struggle as a means of stirring up and concentrating energies, are critically inept and become, ultimately, a weakness'; Antonio Gramsci, quoted in Aijaz Ahmad, *Lineages of the Present*, London: Verso, 2000, p. 145.

5. Among many examples of the return of the 'dead', one can cite just a few. The issue of Maithili and Mithilakshar of the late-nineteenth and early-twentieth century Mithila was 'settled' by the policymakers with Anthony MacDonnell in the colonial period (as we shall see in Chapter 4 of the first section). As late as 2010, here is a report in *The Times of India* under the caption: 'C[hief] M[inister] is anti-Maithili', 'The state Congress chairman of its media department Prem Chandra Mishra on Friday dubbed CM Nitish Kumar's interest in Mithila and its cultural icon Vidyapati as phoney. . . . Mishra alleged that the CM . . . had no interest in the promotion of Maithili language. He also said that the Nitish government, in 2007, removed Maithili language and literature from the curriculum of Bihar Secondary Examination Board (BSEB), and placed it as an optional subject.' See, <http://timesofindia. indiatimes.com/city/patna/CM-is-anti-Maithili/articleshow/6239108. cms>, accessed 2 May 2016. Similarly, during the reorganization of states in 1948, Odisha had tried hard and continued to agitate for the inclusion of Sadheikala and Kharasuan, as we shall see in Chapter 1 of the first section. But as late as 2008, the chief minister of Odisha, Naveen Patnaik, in a strong reaction (to a move by the Jharkhand supremo, Sibu Soren), said if the United Progressive Alliance government accepted Soren's demand, it would be treated as 'anti-Orissa'. He said Orissa's long-standing demand had been for inclusion of Oriya-speaking Sadheikala and Kharasuan areas of Jharkhand in the state, <http://archive.indianexpress.com/news/orissa-bengal-react-sharply-to-soren-s-demands/338681/>, accessed 2 May 2016.

6. Horace B. Davis, *Towards a Marxist Theory of Nationalism*, New York: Monthly Review Press, 1978, p. 31.

7. Ernest Gellner, quoted in G. Aloysius, *Nationalism without a Nation in India*, Delhi: OUP, 1997, p. 14.

8. Ruth Vanita, 'Introduction', in *Chocolate and Other Writings on Male Homoeroticism*, ed. Pandey Bechan Sharma 'Ugra', Delhi: OUP, 2009, pp. 1–30.

9. Ibid., p. 8.

10. Ibid., p. 10.

11. Ibid.

12. Ugra, *Chocolate and Other Writings*. For 'Assertion of Masculinity', see, among others, Partha Chatterjee, *The Partha Chatterjee Omnibus: Comprising Nationalist Thought and the Colonial World, The Nation and its Fragments, and A Possible India* (II), New Delhi: OUP, 1985; repr. 1999, pp. 65–70.

13. A small-screen controversial actor herself.

14. *The Times of India*, 16 June 2006.

15. 'This is the first time I have appeared in [c]ontroversy *properly so called*'; John Wesley, 'Preface', in *Principles of a Methodist*, London: R. Hawes, 1746, pp. 1–32. The currency becomes more contemporary in 1839; Thomas Keightley in his *History of England* talks about how something might put an end to religious controversy, and finally in 1875, Henry Manning in his *Mission of the Holy Ghost* speaks of 'This text has been the subject of endless controversy'. The last usages are significantly close to the sense in which we, and I in this book, use the term now.

16. Many highly sophisticated philosophical disagreements are also generally referred to as controversies. The same is the case with specialized debates and controversies in the fields of medicine, nuclear science or such others. Many of these are so special-knowledge-centred that non-specialists cannot, by definition, enter into the controversies. However, there may be larger implications for a society of the researches being carried out in certain highly specialized domains which might create controversies in the public sphere—contraceptives, nuclear fusion/fission, cloning, and so on. The 'Sokal controversy' is a very interesting case as the two warring parties, 'science wars' and 'culture wars' argued vehemently and along ideological axes, that they can be construed as two kinds of nations—the science nation and the culture nation. The essay by John Guillory (see John Guillory, 'The Sokal Affair and the History of Criticism', *Critical Inquiry*, vol. 28, no. 2, 2002, pp. 470–508) uses metaphors of warfare which corroborates my argument—war and fighting along axes.

17. Nancy Fraser, 'Rethinking the Public Sphere: A Contribution to the Critique of Actually Existing Democracy', *Social Text*, nos. 25–26, 1990, pp. 56–80. Also see, <http://www.jstor.org/stable/466240>, accessed 21 June 2014; Francesca Orsini, *The Hindi Public Sphere, 1920–1940: Language and Literature in Age of Nationalism*, New Delhi: OUP, 2002.

18. Orsini, *The Hindi Public Sphere*, pp. 10–11.
19. Raymond Williams, *Culture and Materialism*, London: Verso, 1988, p. 38; repr. 2005.
20. Jürgen Habermas, 'The Public Sphere', *New German Critique*, vol. 3, 1974, p. 49; quoted in Orsini, *The Hindi Public Sphere*, p. 11.
21. Sumit Sarkar, 'The Conditions and Nature of Subaltern Militancy: Bengal from Swadeshi to Non-Cooperation, *c.*1905–22', in *Subaltern Studies III*, ed. Ranajit Guha, New Delhi: OUP, 1994, pp. 271–320.
22. Ibid., p. 61.
23. Ashis Nandy, *The Illegitimacy of Nationalism: Rabindranath Tagore and the Politics of Self*, New Delhi: OUP, 1994, p. 86.
24. See Rabindranath Tagore's letter dated 29 March 1939; quoted in Prabodh Chandra Sen, *India's National Anthem*, Calcutta: Visva-Bharati, 1972, p. 7.
25. Sarkar, 'The Conditions and Nature of Subaltern Militancy', pp. 271–320.
26. Mrinalini Sinha, 'Rhetoric Agency and the Sarda Act', in *Gender, Sexuality and Colonial Modernities*, ed. Antoinette Burton, London and New York: Routledge, 1999, p. 210.
27. Clifford Geertz, *The Interpretation of Cultures: Selected Essays*, New York: Basic Books, 1973.
28. 'The idea of the modern nation-state entered Indian society in the second half of the 19th century, riding piggy-back on the western idea of nationalism'; Ashis Nandy, 'Preface', in *The Illegitimacy of Nationalism: Rabindranath Tagore and the Politics of Self*, New Delhi: OUP, 1994, p. xi. Ahmad also says, though in a different context, that '. . . far too many of us have come to believe in the very myth that we ourselves made and which was in its own time essentially of a functional nature. Too many of us are now unwilling to recall that the 'nation' is a modern construct, something that arose in the course of the anti-colonial movement itself'; Ahmad, *Lineages of the Present*, p. 145. This is where he also quotes Gramsci on the nation as an 'intellectual conceit'.
29. One might invoke here the model of Yeats's 'Dialogue between Self and Soul'. Unlike its medieval model where a compromise is sought and manufactured, here the self/body gains an upper hand. But the gyre is in a state of unstable equilibrium if I might prolong the metaphor.
30. T.S. Eliot was defining the term, 'classic', which I am replacing here by the term, 'controversy'. See, T.S. Eliot, *What is a Classic?*, Orlando: Mariner Books, 1975, p. 115.
31. D.D. Paige, ed., 'Letter to Homer Pound, 1913', in *The Selected Letters of Ezra Pound: 1907–1941*, London: Faber and Faber, 1950; repr. 1982, pp. 14–15.
32. Ibid.
33. M.K. Gandhi, *An Autobiography or the Story of My Experiments with Truth*, tr. Mahadev Desai, Ahmedabad: Navajivan Trust, 1927; repr.

1999. Almost around the same time when Gandhi writes about this experience in South Africa in his autobiography, Premchand invokes the question of taste and fashion by comparing the issue of 'mixed or hybrid Hindustani' with hybridized dress codes such as the combination of ackan and topi. He says, 'Some years ago, the English hat along with the Indian ackan [a knee-length kurta buttoned in front, for men] was considered outrageous and comic, but these days it is quite common'; Premchand, 'Urdu, Hindi aur Hindustani', in *Kuch Vichar: Sahitya aur Sambandhi Kuch Vichar*, New Delhi: Bharatiya Granth Niketan, 1990, p. 117.

34. John R. McLane, ed., *The Political Awakening in India*, New Jersey: Prentice Hall, 1970, p. 10.
35. Ibid.
36. Chatterjee, *The Partha Chatterjee Omnibus* (I), p. 26.
37. Ibid.
38. McLane, *The Political Awakening in India*, p. 11.
39. Chatterjee, *The Partha Chatterjee Omnibus* (II), pp. 159–60.
40. Ibid., p. 3. Ironically, in the aftermath of the recent JNU controversy, one can rephrase and repeat Partha Chatterjee's statement, 'Nationalism has once more appeared on the agenda of [Indian] affairs'.
41. Williams, *Culture and Materialism*, p. 38.
42. Chatterjee, *The Partha Chatterjee Omnibus* (I), p. 51.
43. Ibid., p. 40.
44. Ibid., p. 21.
45. Ibid., p. 30.
46. Chatterjee, *The Partha Chatterjee Omnibus* (II), pp. 126–7.
47. Ibid., p. 115.
48. Bipin Chandra Pal, *Memories of My Life and Times*, Calcutta: Modern Book Agency, 1932; repr. 2004.
49. Partha Chatterjee, 'Introduction', in *History in the Vernacular*, ed. Raziuddin Aquil and Partha Chatterjee, Ranikhet: Permanent Black, 2008, p. 18; especially quoting Bankimchandra Chattopadhyay, 'We must have our own history'. Also see, *The Partha Chatterjee Omnibus* (II).
50. Sarala Das's is the first translation of the complete *Mahabharata* by any single author in any language in South Asia.
51. Though Lisa Mitchell counters Sheldon Pollock's formulation, her arguments are rendered invalid in the context of Odisha, since both Sarala Das and Balaram Das seem to challenge the caste and gender hierarchies. See, Lisa Mitchell, *Language, Emotion, and Politics in South India: Making of a Mother Tongue*, Bloomington and Indianapolis: Indiana University Press, 2009, pp. 48–52.
52. Lisa Trivedi, *Clothing Gandhi's Nation: Homespun and Modern India*, Bloomington and Indianapolis: Indiana University Press, 2007, p. 26.

2

Meeting and Parting of Ways

Fakir Mohan Senapati, Premchand, and the Language Controversies in Late Colonial India

> But the boundaries of these states were not formed by rivers, or mountains, or any natural features of the terrain; they were, instead, walls of words. Language divided us.
>
> —SALMAN RUSHDIE

Lamenting the 'relative underdevelopment of the research genre of literary history in India', Aijaz Ahmad spoke of the frustrating experience of theorizing the category of Indian Literature.[1] He drew our attention to how 'histories of individual languages as discrete entities . . . tend to be misleading, since multilinguality and polyglot fluidity seem to have been chief characteristics which give "Indian Literature" its high degree of unification in the pre-modern phase'.[2] Ahmad was speaking more than two decades ago. Meanwhile, sustained research in the areas where gaps existed is increasingly making it possible to remedy the discreteness of individual literary histories.[3] It is now possible to recognize common concerns and shared histories of people across various Indian language literatures, and linguistic borders and barriers to try and break the 'walls of words' as Rushdie called it.[4] This in effect has consequences for the disciplinary rubric, Comparative Literature. I am not referring to Gayatri Chakravorty Spivak's highly sophisticated formulations on the death of the 'old' comparative literature, and her suggestions regarding the 'new' comparative literature.[5] I am merely suggesting how these recently ferreted archives might help comparatists study comparative literature more professionally.

To begin with, we must reiterate the twin banalities that (1) literature is made *in* language, and (2) the history of a literature cannot be separated from the history of the language it is in. Thus, to talk of the literature of a given language in a given period is to see it in terms of its embeddedness in history. Unfortunately, the high-profile Hindi-Urdu language controversy, the mother of all language controversies in India, has mostly been narrativized in terms of whether or not they constituted one or two languages with two scripts, but whether their polarization along communal lines was shaped by enthusiastic fundamentalists. In all this, major Hindi-Urdu-Hindustani figures such as Raja Bharatendu Harishchandra, Premchand, and Gandhi have been kept at the centre, if not the epicentre, of all discussions across seismic-cultural zones.[6] This line of enquiry, for all its richness and variety, seems to have run its course and it is time for scholarship to look beyond this rote-learnt teleology and explore questions of whether the other regions contributed to or were in any way affected by these controversies and to the eventual ascendancy and decline of Hindi and Urdu, respectively.[7] Also, many of the other language controversies such as the one in Odisha—among Bangla, Hindi, Telugu, and Odia—that finally led to the formation of one of the first two linguistically determined states (Odisha, the other one being Sindh) in 1936, cannot be seen in isolation. Similarly, the dialectization of older-than-Hindi languages like Maithili (to name just one), the jettisoning of, one after the other, Mithilakshar and Kaithi in favour of Devanagari for transcribing Maithili speech, were integral to the larger issue. In order to undertake any comparative study of writers of the time in any of the aforementioned linguistic clusters, it would be necessary to examine the imbrication of two or more sets by structuring their interpenetrating grids. In what follows, therefore, I propose to examine, with the help of the aforesaid emerging archives, the overlapping language/script controversies in and around the north-western region (Awadhi, Maithili, Hindi, Urdu), as well as that of Bangla, Odia in the east; and to examine the consequences of the attempt that both Fakir Mohan Senapati and Premchand made through their writing, to give Odia, Urdu, and Hindi distinct identities. Though the two were born thirty-seven years apart, when it comes to Fakir Mohan's prose fiction he was more or less Premchand's contemporary (their first short stories and novels were published a couple of years apart). It might be possible to see how the two contexts in which they worked, though distinct, were not entirely unrelated; and how a comparatist perspective on the two need not necessarily involve any mechanical juxtaposition of aspects of their work, but how by enlarging the two contexts to points of contact, and imbrications, we can examine their responses to these similar situations, and how their work-ethic and work-aesthetic responded to similar, if not the same, historical pressures.

Linguistic Utopia of the Past or Sectarian Nationalism of the Present?

Bipin Chandra Pal was one of the first to speak of the common heritage of Bengalis and Odias, especially in terms of language. Tracing the ideal world back to Chaitanya's time or before, he says:

When I first went to Orissa in 1879, my contact with Odia language and literature created the impression upon me that these represented only an ancient and archaic type of Bengalee language and literature itself. . . . [It] helped also to a closer racial and cultural fusion between Bengal and Orissa than was found between other neighbouring provincialities. This old process of interprovincial union or fusion was further advanced under British rule by the establishment of a common Administration over these two provinces. Bengalee promised to become the cultural language of Orissa when I first went there. Bengalee was in many places the second language in the Orissa schools, as in Bengal proper. There was as yet no jealousy of the Bengalee among the people of Orissa.[8]

These reminiscences, of course, have to be seen against the backdrop of the intense anti-Bengali movement across parts of Odisha under the then Bengal Presidency, from 1860s to 1900s—and Bipin Chandra was writing in the 1930s. If such local histories filled with nostalgia for a syncretic past (almost in pre-Babel terms) are not common, similar narratives of a common linguistic heritage in north India sound boringly familiar. One of the most recent examples of such a pining after an ideal past is Alok Rai's *Hindi Nationalism*—a book that hearkens back to an innocent past corrupted by modernity's 'poisonous politics'.[9] In Neeladri Bhattacharya's words, Alok Rai's narrative is marked by 'a deep sense of loss; lost moments, blocked potentials, lost ideals'.[10] There seems to be a consensus among historians that, in the pre-print era, a heteroglot lingua franca had emerged among neighbouring linguistic communities across the subcontinent for purposes of common intercourse.[11] With the coming of print, certain scripts (not languages) seemed to gain sacrosanctity over others, and the language associated with those particular scripts gradually acquired the status of languages of power.[12] This poisonous politics, it is often argued, resulted in division not only between Hindi and Urdu, but also more critically between Hindus and Muslims, and eventually led to the Partition in 1947. Rephrasing Eliot, one might say that we are yet to recover from these moments of an indigenous form of 'dissociation of [linguistic] sensibility', a quasi-mythological rupture, if I may call it, with its concomitant pining after the syncretic, if not 'organic', society. It might be necessary to try and redraw the map, and yet it might be pointless to seek and trace an originary moment of the polarization in question.

Antecedents and the Communalization of Language

The central issue of the communalization of Hindi-Sanskrit and Urdu-Persian has to be seen in the context of certain antecedents. That Sanskrit was traditionally associated with Hinduism can be seen in Macaulay's 'Minute on Education' (1835), wherein he challenges the Committee of Public Instruction by asserting that the Act of the British parliament did not mean by the phrase 'the revival and promotion of Literature', 'the revival and promotion of Sanskrit and Perso-Arabic', conflating all the time the languages and religious identities of the users ('Hindoo law is to be learned chiefly from Sanscrit books, and the Mahometan law from Arabic books').[13] Though Macaulay's understanding cannot be seen as the first of its kind, it is evident from his formulation that he associates governance with the control of knowledge—the binary being Western education and 'good' or desirable knowledge; and bad or undesirable knowledge contained in religious practices.

If we ignore Macaulay's views as misplaced, since he was an 'orientalist' outsider (not in the traditional, but in the Saidian sense), here is Gandhi's story: Gandhi's teacher, and later Gandhi himself, came to equate the two languages with the two communities (c.1870s). Gandhi tells us, in his autobiography, how his Sanskrit teacher was a hard taskmaster and the Persian teacher was lenient, because of which he, like his fellow students, had opted for Persian. His Sanskrit teacher, Krishnashankar Pandya, gently chided him by saying, 'How can you forget that you are the son of a Vaishnava father? Won't you learn *the language of your own religion?*' Around 1927, Gandhi writes, 'I deeply regret that I was not able to acquire a more thorough knowledge of the language, because I have since realized that every *Hindu boy and girl should possess sound Samskrit* [*sic*] *learning'* [emphasis mine].[14] Thus, the point I wish to make here is that whether or not there had always been a tradition of associating the two languages—Sanskrit and Persian—with the two communities of Hindus and Muslims, respectively, the linkages were certainly precipitated by the advent of European modernity with all its concomitants such as administrative convenience, print economy, pedagogic exigencies, or, to use one term—colonial governmentality.[15] The ground for division between Urdu and Hindi was already seeded in the long-standing perception regarding their parentage— Perso-Arabic and Sanskrit.[16]

The Language of Power and Print Capitalism

Rehearsing the well-known fact, we remind ourselves that after 1837, Persian ceased to be the higher-court language in any linguistic-territory of India with Urdu, Bangla, Odia, etc., taking its place at different points of time in the North-Western Provinces, Bengal, and Odisha (the dismembered territories of the last arbitrarily under the administrative jurisdiction of Bengal and Madras presidencies, and Central Provinces), to name a few. Though there had been some talk in different quarters about the various 'vernaculars', English effectively replaced Persian in the higher courts and the vernacular languages jettisoned Persian in the lower courts. The processes were expected to be smooth but the vernacular languages of power clashed and internecine debates in various pockets became the order of the day. The other issue following Macaulay's 'Minute' pertained to the medium of instruction in order to impart what was called (in Odia) 'Ingrāji Shikshā', that is, English (or Western) education. Since modern education in any language required an adequate number of textbooks, the fate of languages was also predicated on the availability of textbooks in that language. This added a new dimension to the language debates, fuel as it did a competition among users of diverse languages in setting up of printing presses, developing types, and production of textbooks. Educationists and administrators entered the fray as apologists or detractors of the media of instruction joining bandwagons of 'experts'.

As the number of languages vying for use in lower courts multiplied, and claims and counterclaims for linguistic mediums proliferated, colonial administrators were confronted by the prospect of incomprehensibility and unreadability of diverse Indian languages—both on the part of the receivers and givers of law. They were also forced to look into the immediate reality of claims and counterclaims while answering the question, 'in which language?' and as they did so, colonial administrators had to double up as philologists (or vice versa). At some point of time, the idea of using the universal Roman script was also mooted. However, given the fact that a large majority of the colonized population comprised the unlettered, if not uneducated or those who carried the baggage of mnemonic knowledge of scriptural texts, people were not concerned with the issue of script. Thus, the so-called communal divide across masses was more imagined than real, at least during these initial decades; and was at best confined to a small minority of educated class looking for jobs or wanting to partake of the petty crumbs of power.

Based on the trajectories along which the controversies flared up, they can be grouped under three broad categories. The first set of controversies, though arising out of exigencies of governance and administrative convenience, were conducted in the realm of jargon-ridden scholarship within the newly emerged disciplinary practices such as philology, pedagogy, and linguistics. I have in mind here the works of Robert Caldwell, John Beames, F.S. Growse, Rajendralal Mitra, George A. Grierson et al.[17] These scholar-administrators, using their newly forged analytical tools, would go into the history and evolution of languages and the respective language-community, for which, in turn, they would engage in or draw upon linguistic demographics, census data, and statistics. The stress on streamlining languages vis-à-vis native communities could have been impelled by similar developments back in Europe, where linguistic nationalism already held sway. The Indian scholars in this category, on the other hand, displaying scholarly interests also willy-nilly became complicit with and/or were indifferent towards the ideologies of empowerment or disempowerment of the respective linguistic communities. For example, it cannot be denied that post-1837, when Odisha was part of the Calcutta Presidency, the sub-imperialist perception among many Bengalis that Odias were inferior to them or, post-1857, the communal perception among many educated Hindus imbibed from the British officials that Muslims were jihadi anti-Christians, coloured their thinking around language issues.[18]

The second set of controversies comprised views of 'non-experts', who were not altogether 'lay', but were nonetheless affected by the issues in their respective professions—intellectuals, missionaries, educationists, and scholars engaged in discharging juridical-administrative responsibilities. These debates were often conducted at the level of common sense and were anchored on the first set of discourses that involved influential figures such as Rammohun Roy and Macaulay. Here I have in mind individuals like Saroda Prosad Sandel, the Attorney General; Sir Syed Ahmad Khan, the founder of the Aligarh movement; Babu Rangalal Bandyopadhyay, the Bengali poet-scholar-administrator; Bhudev Mukhopadhyay, the inspector of schools; Ayodhya Narayan Khattri, a court official; and last but not least, Lieutenant-Governor MacDonnell. They would often represent specific linguistic communities, and could sometimes be partisan, dogmatic, and judgemental. At times, they tended to align themselves with the powers-that-be. For example, Syed Ahmad Khan, who supported the East India Company in the aftermath of the mutiny, had a clear linguistic-communal (in the best sense of the term) agenda of guarding the interest of the Urdu-speaking Muslims—who he was trying to regroup under the umbrella of education. He even opposed the formation of the INC on the ground that it was going to be dominated by the Bengali Hindus.[19]

The authors (both literally and figuratively) of the controversies at the tertiary level comprised practitioners of literary writing such as Bankimchandra Chattopadhyay, Bharatendu, Fakir Mohan, Balmukund Gupta, Rangalal, and Premchand, to mention the best known, with intermediary figures like Madhusudan Das and Gandhi flitting in and out of such discourses. Many of these writers also held important administrative positions.

Of course, these three levels of discourse overlap. While drawing on or under the influence of the scholarly works of philologists and orientalists, these literary writers seldom went into any scholarly analysis of ideas that were already a 'whole climate of opinion', except at times when they wrote discursive pieces to explain their respective stance towards linguistic issues. Since their imaginative work often bore the marks of all these controversies, the historicity of these texts are well worth pondering in a comparatist framework.

The Primary Level:
The New Scientists of Language

In this section, I wish to underline the basic arguments on both sides that had a decisive impact on the debates. It took about two decades for scholars to be jolted into the realization that there was a need (following the 1857 turmoil) to develop and deploy tools of philological analysis to suggest, attack, or defend language and script choices. Major debates took place among orientalists and philologists around issues of 'The Application of the Roman Alphabet to Oriental Languages', 'On the Transliteration of Indian Alphabets', 'The Arabic Element in Official Hindustani', even an *English-Hindustani Law and Commercial Dictionary* by S.W. Fallon with an 'Introductory Dissertation', 'Some Objections to the Modern Style of Official Hindustani', and many others [emphasis mine].[20] These led to more localized debates about whether Hindi ought to be the court language of the North-Western Provinces and whether words of Perso-Arabic origin be used or purged in Bangla or Odia, and so on. The debates often conducted in consultation with 'Learned Natives' were taken up by the latter subsequently, so that questions as to whether Devanagari, Mithilakshar, Odia, Bengali, or any other script was to be used were debated among the natives themselves.

Before such scholars started their research and writing, a few administrators, historians, and commentators had already set the tone through their casual remarks in diverse territories run by colonials. As mentioned earlier, the question of imparting education in different languages prompted certain officials to treat one dominant language (dominant because of various factors such as well-developed print culture, availability of human resources, etc.) as a dialect of another, such as Bhojpuri, Magadhi, Maithili or Odia as offshoots of Hindvi/Hindi or Bangla, respectively and thus, propose the use of the latter as mediums of instruction across schools in the Mithila region or Odisha division of the Bengal Presidency. For instance, in 1859, Revd James Long expresses the view that 'the cultivation of the smaller dialects or "fractions of languages" in India promotes division and isolation, even natives when left to themselves prefer the cultivation of a more refined Indian language—thus in the Sonthal districts Hindi is being studied as also in Chhota Nagpur. . .'.[21]

A few leading lights from among the Indian experts toed these lines five years later. To begin with, the antiquarian, Rajendralal Mitra—in a paper read at Calcutta in 1864—underscored the importance of the Devanagari script as against Persian, which he said, was intrinsically inferior, and an attempt on the part of the colonial administration to impose the Roman script across all Indian languages. He said, 'As Sanskritic dialects the Hindvi and the Urdu have undoubted claims to the Nagari, for that alone can supply the necessary symbols properly to indicate their system of sounds. The Persian alphabet has no such symbols and therefore fails adequately to represent the phonology of the Hindvi, except by the aid of a cumbrous system of diacritical marks.'[22] Rajendralal Mitra goes on to supply instances, from Europe, of the consequences of introducing foreign languages and scripts in the occupied territories and argues against the removal of 'Deva Nagari'. He said:

One great cause of complaint in Poland, Hungary, Schleswig, Holstein and Austrian Italy is the attempt on the part of the conquerors to force their languages on the subject races, by introducing them *into* the courts of those countries, and a similar course in India, even if *confined* to the alphabet *alone, will, I* apprehend, prove a like source of discontent. The Hindus regard their alphabet *to be of* divine origin (Deva Nagari) and a gift from the Godhead. With it is associated their religion, their literature, and their ancient glory. To touch it is to meddle with their religion, their past greatness and their cherished recollections.[23]

We shall see how these arguments offered by Rajendralal Mitra are not only controverted by fellow philologists but are also reiterated four or five decades later by the protagonists of the Nagari movement. More to the point, one can see where Rajendralal Mitra's view was coming from. In the document already referred to, Long had recommended the introduction of Bangla as the medium of instruction in areas falling within the Bengal Presidency:[24]

Valuable as is the Uriya [Odia] language for imparting to the common people an *elementary* education, it is not likely to be much cultivated: the people of Orissa are too few to render it probable that the expenses of creating a literature can be borne by them or by Government, it will be much easier for Uriyas who wish to acquire knowledge to gain it through the Bengali, a kindred language which is rapidly developing itself.[25]

This must have been music to the ears of the hegemonistic Bengali elite. The extent of influence that Long's views must have cast—because they were expressed in the pages of a well-circulated and authoritative forum like that of the *Journal of Asiatic Society*— can be gauged by the reiteration of the same logic in subsequent years. Murmurings were heard in the corridors of power that 'Uriya' should be replaced by the Bengali script in school education. Rajendralal Mitra's paper was the weightiest and most forceful of these.

After Rajendralal Mitra gave his lecture in Calcutta, the selfsame advocate of Hindi and Nagari in the North-Western Provinces, strongly advised the Odias to reject their script in favour of Bangla. As Rajendralal Mitra himself was to recall in a paper in 1870, he

compared Uriya's attachment to this 'provincial patois' as injurious
to progress as a false sense of patriotism and an insensate love for
everything that was national. It is indeed significant how the
discussion of nation, good and bad nationalism, race and
development is being articulated so. For, we recall here Long's
observations nine years earlier regarding the rejection of the Nagari
script by the 'Uriyas', 'All the Sanskrit MS used in Orissa are written
in the Uriya [script] and not in the Nagari character, though the
latter is the *sacred character* of India and hence called the Deva
Nagari or divine character, but the Brahmanas will not accept an
universal character—*nationality* prevails over theory—and yet there
are men who dream of abolishing all the Indian alphabets and
substituting the English alphabet for them!'[26] Long's extract is
interesting also because of his misplaced observation that these were
the 'Brahmanas'. Fact is, it was across all social strata that Odia
(indeed all languages with their own script) was favoured in all
scriptures—the jettisoning of the Sanskrit *Mahabharata, Ramayana*
and *Bhagabata*, and several other sacred texts in favour of the
fifteenth- and sixteenth-century Odia translations. More importantly,
perhaps, one notes how Long superimposes the European script of
nationality and nationalism on the issue of language and script.

Meanwhile, in 1870, Kantichandra Bhattacharya, a certain
'Pandit' working in the government school of Balasore—where Fakir
Mohan too lived and worked—published a booklet in Bangla with
the title 'Uriya Ekta Swatantra Bhasa Noi' (Uriya is not an
Independent Language). Kantichandra Bhattacharya offered the
argument that Bengali should replace Odia. The Pandit's views
proved to be the proverbial last straw on the beleaguered Odias and
straw catches fire easily. In the case of Odias, it was virtually a
conflagration. But they found an ally in Beames.

Responding to the pamphlet, Beames wrote 'On the Relation of
the Uriya to the Other Modern Aryan Languages' and began by
saying:

A book has recently been published by Babu Kantichandra Bhattacharyya
[*sic*], a Pandit in the Government School at Balasore under the title, 'Uriya
is not an Independent language'. This little work, though profoundly
destitute of philological arguments, has created some stir among the
natives of the province, who are somewhat disgusted at finding their native
language treated as a mere corruption of Bengali.[27]

Rajendralal Mitra immediately responded by publishing a longer
piece in the same journal, arrogating the very logic that Beames had
employed to pronounce Bhojpuri as a dialect of Hindi:

In an excellent paper on the Bhojpuri dialect, Mr. Beames has shown that, notwithstanding much graver differences in glossology and grammar—in pronouns and the degrees of comparison—in adjectives and conjunctions—than what obtains in Uriya and Bengali, the Bhojpuri is a dialect of Hindi; and by a parity of reasoning, I expect he will admit the Uriya, in like manner, to be a daughter of Bengali.[28]

By now, the Odia public sphere had shaped adequately with the setting up of printing presses, debating societies, periodicals and newspapers in which the issue was deliberated and circulated. This was the genesis of the *'bhasa andolan'* that led to the setting up of the 'Utkal Sammelan' by Madhusudan Das in 1903. The details of the 'Save Odia' movement following the papers by Rajendralal Mitra, Kantichandra Bhattacharya, Beames et al. have engaged Odia scholars, and the sequence of events is too large a subject for discussion here.[29]

More to the context, two issues related to Rajendralal Mitra's paper deserve our attention here. First, he draws his readers' attention to the interrelatedness of language issues across several sets of Indian languages. Second, it is easy to see here how the same scholars (Beames and Rajendralal Mitra), using identical analytical tools, shape the basic tenets of the argument that catch on and influence the newly emerged native intelligentsia.

The Secondary Level:
The Context of Everyday Business

Views of individuals I deal with in this cluster of controversies are intertwined with those of scholars involved in the first set of debates. And these men of practical affairs started responding to the problems at hand in ways that clearly reflected their dilemma, even as they grappled for pragmatic solutions. In 1868,[30] Saroda Prasad (Accountant General) asks Syed Ahmad Khan (Judge, Small Cause Court, Benares) for advice on 'whether Hindi ought to be court language of the Upper court. By Hindi is meant, the present mixed language of these provinces written in Deva Nagari character'.[31] Syed Ahmad Khan responds by saying that these were two different issues—'the choice of the language' and 'selection of the character in which it must be written'. He goes on to say, 'the language of our courts in these provinces and Behar ought to be what you call Hindi . . . which I would choose to call Urdoo'. The question of script, Syed Ahmad Khan argues, can only be settled in the context of everyday business of the court. His answer is significant in that it shows how, gradually the polarization that appears to be moving along communal lines is actually along lines of linguistic identities. Consciously or unconsciously, Saroda Prasad struggles to avoid the potentially divisive terms, and is at pains to bring up this point. Around mid-nineteenth century, while Odias were trying to resist imposition of Bangla, these linguistic movements were far from being communal, for the common Odia people were wary of the usage of Bengali in legal documents such as land deeds as much as the non-Persian-Urdu-knowing people were wary of those who knew the language of court. Where the other linguistically hegemonized communities were fighting for their respective identity, it became difficult to keep their communal identities at bay. This is evident from the quote:

By the words 'Hindi language' I mean the language of the people of Hindoostan proper just as by the phrase 'Bengali language' is meant the language of the people of Bengal proper, and so of all other languages. If you say that, the language and Urdoo are one and the same, I must humbly differ from you, but so far only as there is a more copious sprinkling of the Persian in the latter. Hence the Persian language, which . . . was formerly the Court language all over India, has been superseded by Urdoo as being more intelligible to the people, so, it is true, that the latter should in its turn make room for Hindi, or the popular dialect, as still more so, to them, in the same manner, as the Bengalee and the Odia, superseded the Persian language in the courts of Bengal and Odisha. Besides, the measure is calculated to achieve another great object, viz., the improvement and purification of *the national language* [emphasis mine].[32]

Saroda Prasad disagrees with Syed Ahmad Khan's suggestion that Hindi and Urdu are merely two different names for the same mixed language as 'there is a more copious sprinkling of the Persian in the latter [Urdoo]'. With the twin objective to purify 'national language' and promote one that is more intelligible in 'Hindoostan proper', Saroda Prasad asserts that 'Urdoo must make room for Hindi, just as earlier Persian had made way for Urdoo'.[33] Apart from the crucial expression 'national language' (by far the earliest use of the term for Hindi), the letter is full of such key terms as 'indigenous' (for Devanagari) and 'exotic' (for Persian), 'character' and 'language', 'popular dialect', etc.

When Sir George Campbell, the then governor of Bihar, ordered the abolition of the Persian script from Bihar in 1873, it was supposed to be replaced by either Devanagari or Kaithi. Since the question of script remained open-ended, it led only to partial introduction of the Devanagari script in the Bihar province. Ashley

Eden, the then lieutenant governor, felt that the changes would never be completed until the Nagari script was used exclusively in all the official documents. To this effect, an order was issued forbidding Persian completely by 1 January 1881. Since, in the context of Mithila any administrative decision taken by the British Raj inevitably affected the Darbhanga Raj, the then Maharaja had already issued a similar order for his employees. For this reason, many hold the discriminatory policies of the Maharaja responsible for the replacement of Maithili by Hindi in Devanagari script from his court. In 1880, when Maharaja Lakshmeshwar ascended the throne, he issued an order dated 14 July 1880 to the effect that:

I have given orders for introduction of Hindi character and language in my office a very long time ago. This, however, cannot take place till our vernacular *amlas* get thoroughly to understand the character to read and write it fluently. However, I am sorry to say that none of our *amlas* knows how to do it. I have, therefore, been obliged to pass those orders. That all *amlas* should at once set to work to master the Hindi character and language. That I give them another three months to learn it. That is, in November they will have to master it thoroughly and to save me from the painful necessity of pensioning or dismissing old hands.[34]

This document holds the key to our understanding of the context in which Maithili and Mithilakshar were replaced by Hindi and the Devanagari script, respectively, in the Mithila region of Bihar. Grierson, who was then posted as deputy collector in the Munger district of Bihar, vigorously opposed this colonial decision. In his 'A Plea for the People's Tongue' (1880), he reasons that contrary to the assumption that usage of Hindi will make the official documents accessible to all, 'there never has been, is not, and never will be a Hindi such as is alluded to by the objector, and that Hindi, as meant by him, is not understood by ninety per cent of the people who are supposed to speak it'.[35]

On 18 April, Lieutenant Governor MacDonnell brought a resolution to recognize Hindi in Nagari script as the non-exclusive language of the court and the administration in the United Provinces.[36] However, in the neighbouring region of Bihar, a ban had already been imposed on the use of Urdu in official and educational spaces. Before coming to the North-Western Provinces, MacDonnell had worked in Bihar as a secretary to the lieutenant governor of Bengal and was instrumental in replacing Urdu with Hindi in the Nagari script. In 1871, Campbell prepared 'Lt. Governor's Minute on the Teaching of the Vernacular Language', which is a key document to understand the colonial decision to ban Urdu in Bihar. He remarked that flouting the official colonial policy of imparting primary education in the vernaculars, in the schools and official proceedings of Bihar, this

bastard language was not only flourishing in its fullest force in our official proceedings but that we were perpetuating by teaching it in our schools. I have heard during this visit a language more debased and artificial than I have ever heard before or deemed possible; and I found that in all our so called Vernacular schools this monstrous language, if it can be called a language, is being taught by Maulvies instead of the Vernacular. Unfortunately, too, a pretext has been given for this practice by the introduction of very important term Urdu.

Campbell suspects that the term was chiefly introduced by the Bengal education department and that it loosely refers to 'the court and camp language of the Delhi courtiers, not the vernaculars of the Country. I am determined to put a complete stop to the teaching of this language in our schools'.[37] Conspicuously, this happened without the intervention of the likes of Madan Mohan Malaviya and Shyam Sunder Das, as was the case in the United Provinces. However, even as Campbell rejects a Sanskritized Hindi on the one hand, and Urdu on the other, he does not have much use for the existing vernaculars of Bihar either and dismisses them as dialects.

Thus, MacDonnell can be seen as yet another instigator common to the diverse language controversies cutting across political jurisdiction. It was during his tenure as commissioner in Patna that the changeover had taken place from the Persian script to Nagari as early as 1872 in the Central Provinces, of which Sambalpur (then Koshal, and now a part of Odisha) was a district. The first indigenous and largest circulating Odia newspaper *Utkal Dipika*, reported the history of such experimentation, 'Urdu was introduced as the official language when the district first came under British occupation. When Urdu appeared as impracticable for official purpose owing to the people's ignorance of the language, Hindi was introduced. But the common people found it extremely difficult to acquire proficiency even in Hindi and after all those experiments, Odia was introduced.'[38] This again added fodder to Odia nationalist aspirations in areas that are now part of western Odisha, and the people of Sambalpur joined hands with those in Cuttack and Balasore to fight the battle against such 'foreign' impositions, euphemistically calling them 'Padoshi rajya' (ruling neighbours).

As a fallout of the controversies, resistance to Persian inflections in the vernacular languages—hitherto taken for granted—began to surface *c*.1865. On 19 May 1867, Rangalal chaired the session of Utkal Bhasha Uddipani Sabha at Cuttack. Speaking in Bangla, he lamented that Bangla had come under the sway of the foreign language since the *yavnas* (i.e. Muslims) arrived 750 years ago. But, he pointed out how, though Odia had retained much of its Sanskritic origin, 'the incidence of foreign words, i.e. Persian and Arabic, was more or less the same as those in Bangla, even though the "Mussalmans" had been in Odisha for only 300 years'. Rangalal goes on to supply examples of administrative categories in the idiom of the Muslim-ruled provinces, which continue till date and no Odia counterparts/synonyms have been adopted,

It is unfortunate indeed that so much of the Mussalman's language (Persian/Arabic) is incorporated in the Odia language even when there are Odia synonyms. . . . We do not oppose the use of foreign words as such; but we certainly feel it objectionable if, while writing Odia or Bangla, we use in two or three sentences, more than fifty per cent of words of foreign origin.

One of the recommendations that emerged from the Sabha was that, in order to develop the Odia language, an adequate number of books needed to be written and published, thus confirming for us the interconnectedness between print economy and textbook production. These moves also led to the gradual standardization of specific languages. The other stated reason for the recommendation was the endemic overabundance of foreign words in the school curricula of the Mughalbandi regions. However, the *gadajats* remained beyond the pale of Mughalbandi administration and continued to use *deshiya bhasa* (native or local language) for administrative purposes and in school curricula. It was also said that the steps would ensure that only those who knew Odia would get employment as clerks in government jobs, where Odia idioms and usage were to be corrected.

Rangalal could well be right in his assessment. In fact, in 1899, recalling the state of Odia in mid-nineteenth century, Fakir Mohan in 'Utkala Bhāshāra Bhūta Bhabishyata' (The Past and the Future of the Language of Utkala) was to echo the former's point, '[T]hose days to speak Odia infused with Persian vocabulary was considered a mark of sophistication and learning'.[39] Thus, the communal, *bideshiya* and *bijatiya* tags which were initially attached to Persian-Urdu, Nagari-Hindi, etc., came to haunt the non-Hindi, non-Urdu literary-cultural domain outside the North-Western Provinces region too, which we shall soon turn to.

The Tertiary Level: Authorial Interventions

It is indeed significant that Hindi, Urdu, Bangla, and Odia writers from the late-eighteenth century to the mid-nineteenth century or even beyond showed no anxiety or confusion about their choice of language in their literary endeavours and aspirations, as if no controversy was raging around them during those years. They wrote *kavyas*, as their predecessors had always written, with an intermixture of diverse linguistic inflections. A Dalit poet, Bhima Bhoi (1850–95), who was a contemporary of Fakir Mohan and Radhanath Ray, was yet untouched by modern education; and shows no signs of any impact of the contemporary linguistic discourses (on 'in which language?'). Poets such as Kavisurya Baladev Rath and Jadumani Mahapatra and others in Odia, and writers in Hindi/Urdu continued to write, totally unconcerned and oblivious of all the controversies raging around them. In the eighteenth century, the renowned Odia poet Brajanath Badajena had audaciously composed an entire long poem in Awadhi-Hindi, with numerous Perso-Arabic inflections. Between 1830 and 1850, Baladev Rath too used several words freely drawing on Perso-Arabic sources. A similar amalgamation of tongues, unconcerned with the politics of languages, characterizes the writings of Insha Allah Khan. Born in Murshidabad in 1756, he remained in the service of feudatory powers in Delhi and Lucknow. Between 1800 and 1808, he wrote 'Rani Ketaki ki Kahani' which is widely believed to be the first short story in Hindi. Referring to the genesis of his story, he avers 'it should neither lose its *Hindiness* nor should it be a dialect. All I wish to employ is an idiom that all good people use while communicating with each other; it should be represented as such, without the shadow of any language in particular. . . .'[40]

Even so, in the case of Hindi-Urdu, scholars tend to focus on Bharatendu and Balmukund (and later, Premchand) as examples of writers caught in the linguistic dilemma. The relative obscurity of the interventions of Ayodhya Narayan is an example of this tendency. He, who thought of himself as a philologist, and disagreed with Bharatendu by saying that the latter knew no philology, 'Bharatendu was no god, and that he knew nothing of philology. . .'.[41] Among the few who have highlighted Ayodhya Narayan's contribution, Alok Rai rightly points out that the former fancied himself as something of a linguist.[42] Thus, Ayodhya Narayan straddled all the three levels of discourse discussed.[43] In nineteenth-century Odisha too, literature flourished in imitation of pre-existing literary forms and idioms. A few began writing in Bengali while others translated from Bengali and English into an Odia idiom under Bengali influence. Besides poetry, histories, biographies, and other textbooks were produced too. Natabar traces the emergence of modern Odia literature through the contingency of textbook production.[44] Fakir Mohan and Premchand, the most prominent modern writers in Odia and Urdu/Hindi, respectively, were also educationists. Their concerns with language, textbooks, medium of instruction, and the belatedness of various language controversies—the concerns discussed at the secondary level—are reflected in their writings. Their cases, thus, might prove to be the most interesting manifestations of the language controversies making their way into the creative-literary concerns. Before taking up their cases, it might be necessary to showcase how the Hindi-Nagari issues had spread beyond the North-Western Provinces and how Odia writers were drawn into the issue of Hindi.

The Odia Advocate of Hindi

In 1899, a major Odia literary figure, Nandakishor Bal (1875–1928) gave a lecture on Jatiya Sahitya (National Literature) advocating Hindi as a national language.[45] In another essay published a year later called 'Bharatara Bhabishyat Bhasha' (Future Language of Bharat), Nandakishor made a similar assertion, 'We are not saying that the *pradeshika bhasa samasta* or the regional languages should perish. The first and the main reason [in favour of adopting Hindi as a national language] is the number of Hindi speakers and those from the other languages as per the census report of 1891 . . . Hindi is understood by people everywhere in Bharat.'[46] This seemingly was a suicidal assertion in the backdrop of widespread protests that had been staged when Odia-speaking people of Sambalpur district were forced to learn Hindi around this time. But perhaps, Nandakishor's motivation came from the general suspicion that Bengali might be raised to the status of a national language, as was allegedly proposed by some 'Bangiya writers'. But, almost immediately, Nandakishor attempts to allay the fears of those fellow Odias who were fighting hard for the official acceptance of Odia-speaking tracts. He also touches upon the inevitable subject of Hindi, Urdu and Hindu-Muslim unity long before Gandhi and Premchand came to focus on it. Nandakishor argues:

Since Urdu is mixed with Hindi, the currency of Hindi would strengthen the unity and understanding between the two arms of Bharat, the Hindus and Mussalmans to pave the way for the real development of Bharat. Hindi is both weighty and sweet; whereas Bangla lacks in the first. Perhaps for this reason, when Bengalis get angry they automatically switch over to Hindi. World famous Chanda Kavi and Tulsidas and such other *mahatmas* have sung their immortal compositions in this very language, Hindi. Thus, if only one language is to be used as a pan-Indian language, it has to be Hindi.[47]

In the lecture ('Jatiya Sahitya'), Nandakishor argues forcefully in favour of the introduction of Hindi. His main argument in favour of the introduction of a common language is that if India is to be a strong country, it must have the unity of language.[48] Nandakishor also touches on the subject of the Sanskritization of Odia and argues in favour of more languages opting for *tadbhava* and *tatsama* words so that their languages would be mutually comprehensible, particularly because most of these languages have one common root—Sanskrit. Thus, even while there would be a possibility of promoting a distinct *language* in each region, there would be a common 'National *Literature*'. Of course, there would still be the inevitable question of 'in which script?'. There could be two possibilities: Roman script and Devanagari, but Devanagari would be much easier to handle. More importantly, he argues that 'Urdu being a mixture of Hindi might bring about a unity among Hindus and Muslims. But then how practicable will this be?'

Purify the Dialect of the Tribe

It becomes clear as to how creative writers in diverse languages had begun drawing on the primary and secondary level of controversies to reflect on the question of language and idiom; usage in writing literary works, and the use of *sadhu bhasa* or chaste idiom *v. gharoi bhasa* (the spoken idiom). Long before the subject was discussed by Odia lexicographers such as Gopalachandra Praharaj, in Bengal, Bankimchandra Chattopadhyay wrote 'The Bengali Language: The Language of Books' on how in 'nearly all countries there is a difference between the spoken and the written language'. Finally, he concluded by saying that 'what there is to say should be said clearly, and you should say only that much which is to be said. For this, you may borrow the words that you need from any language—English, Persian, Arabic, Sanskrit, rustic or of the jungle—so long as it is not indecent.'[49]

What was not noticed was that there are times when these binaries become redundant; and what was seldom discussed and practised, or not practised, was how to handle conversations and dialogues between characters while presenting characters in short or long fiction. The two protagonists of Odia and Hindi nationalism, Fakir Mohan and Premchand, respectively, allowed their fiction to accommodate the then current discourses on various language as well as communal issues. Fakir Mohan's interventions in the context of language issue of the time were wide and astute at the macro level and discerning and nuanced at the micro level—often fusing practice and discourse in the same texts, be they stories, tales, or lectures. Not only did Fakir Mohan look at the issues of English education, the use of English for acquiring knowledge, the fight against linguistic hegemony, etc., but also theorized the connection between power and linguistic spread and looked into the Sanskritization of the local idiom through the influence of the so-called Mughalbandi. He had, in 1902, bemoaned the loss of regional flavour in the spoken Odia of the *gadajati* educated class. He begins by saying that the more dominant a *jati*, the more widespread is the propagation of its language. He gives the example of the historical period when the Chinese Empire was strong. The next, he says, is English. Due to the influence of the Mussalmans, the spread of Hindi (meaning Hindustani or Urdu) gained momentum and it became the largest spoken language. Of course, as is well-known, Fakir Mohan was a strong advocate of traditional education and was somewhat ambivalent towards the then new forms of English education. He constantly spoke of the 'mother tongue'; his target of the linguistic other being either English or Bangla. He himself used a Sanskritized style in his fiction only when the need arose in order to lend the context high seriousness, but was critical of the use of such artificial idioms among educated people in common conversation. He even goes to the extent of preparing a glossary of *gadajati* terms in order to 'museumise' them in an unfinished essay called, 'Alimalika'. He says, 'in our language [Odia], the number of *deshaja* words is reducing gradually, the number of Sansritic words is increasing. If you do not mind, the language of the educated class is turning into difficult-to-digest *khichudi*.' He says, with this, even our culture is losing its uniqueness; and, along with the preservation of *gadajati* terms, the age-old cultural practices, which are almost moribund, should also be museumized. Of course, this is sarcasm. Even as he advocated the cause of Odia, he also celebrated and championed the cause of diversity of the spoken Odia idiom as it was practised in different parts of what was then emerging as Odisha.

In a tale 'Mouna Mouni', he narrates the criminal practices of certain 'sadhus' (who were dacoits from neighbouring territories, and whose dialogues he cast in direct speech). As was his practice, the narrator suddenly intervenes, 'Just as French is a common language in Europe, Hindi is all pervasive in Bharatabarsha. Sadhus and sanyasis travel all over [B]haratabarsha; hence they have to speak Hindi. The language of our sadhu groups is an admixture of a low type of spoken Bangla idiom and Hindi with Bangla inflections.'[50] The idiom in the entire story is Sanskritized Odia or 'sadhu' *bhasa*, with the aim of giving the story a light-hearted treatment, at times sounding funny at the expense of the characters. Interspersed are dialogues by the Hindi-speaking 'asadhu' sadhus (dishonest holy men) too—'*deo ka māl, deo diyā. Deotākā sevā, tumhāre dharam*'.[51] Loosely translated, this staccato line would mean, 'these are the property of God, God has given these, service to God, your duty'.

For Odia writers, the motivation for producing a large number of study-worthy printed texts came from their anxiety over a real or imagined threat to their linguistic identity. With the advent of print technology, nineteenth-century Bengal was flooded with modern books in Bangla, a luxury that Odias did not enjoy. From 1866 onward, among others, Fakir Mohan and Gourishankar Ray[52] led from the front and with patronage from local satraps tried to ensure that there were good enough books for pedagogic as well as popular reading to stall the rising Bangla book business. Odia intellectuals also saw books in terms of pedagogic tools for nation-building purposes. All these factors are discernible in the '*Bhumika*' or Foreword to the first edition of the iconic Odia novel, *Chha Mana Atha Guntha* (*Six Acres and a Third*):

One often hears complaints of how there is a dearth of good reading material for entertainment in Odia. We have often hung our heads in shame on hearing such complaints. We know that these days, a new desire to write plays and novels has arisen in the minds of many; and a number of published and unpublished books in these genres have come our way. . . . The author of *Chha Mana Atha Guntha* is a well-established and accomplished servant of literature. . . . *It will at least partially fill the need of entertaining, good-read prose texts: it is in this hope that we came forward to publish the work.* We know that when the book was being serialized in the pages of *Utkal Sahitya* all the readers were highly appreciative of the work [translation and emphasis mine].[53]

Though this Foreword is not reproduced in any edition of the novel in any of the four major English translations, its significance in the context of late nineteenth and early twentieth century Odia book-history cannot be overestimated. It describes its author as well-established and suggests that the novel 'will at least partially fill the need of entertaining, *"pathanajogya"* or reader-friendly prose texts. . .'. Referring to the social inequality precipitated by the dominant position of English and Persian, the narrator of the novel concludes, 'It was Parsi first, and now it is English. . . . The fate of Devnagari is buried under the stone. The English educated say: "Sanskrit is a dead language." We clarify the matter further: Sanskrit is the language of a moribund people.'[54] This social decline is exacerbated by the remoteness of Persian script from the people, allowing the privileged few (the *Mian*) to 'become Zamindar merely by plying his pen backwards'. The Persian-Nagari dispute had its impact on Odisha (the parts under the Calcutta Presidency and Central Provinces, at any rate) as well. Before I take up the Odia-Bengali controversy, I would like to dwell on the less discussed Odia-Persian interface, where the suspicion was mutual. Here, it might be necessary to point out the shifting power equations in Bengal. At the peak of the Swadeshi movement in Bengal—in Sumit Sarkar's brilliant account of the flip-flop Hindu-Muslim relationship—it was the Muslims who appeared to be losing much ground. 'Where did the Hindu get his wealth from? He had nothing, he has stolen it from you and become wealthy. . . . Through the swajati movement we shall develop ourselves.'[55] The lines run as follows:

Shunare moslemgan haye ek man
Diyona hindur ghare aapnar dhan.
Moslem adham sei Moslem adham
Hindur sahite kare bande mataram.[56]

Translated, the lines mean, 'Listen, all moslems in unison/Don't give the Hindu your own paddy/The hapless Muslim will remain the hapless Muslim/and go on to sing, *Bande Mataram* with the Hindu.' Similarly, in Odisha, Fakir Mohan's portrayal of Dildar Mian shows the gradual decline of the Muslim zamindars [translation mine].

In a different context, Sudipta Kaviraj has pointed out how the landholding as well as business jargon under Bengal Presidency (of which Odisha was a part in Fakir Mohan's time) was all drawn from Persian.[57] The implication for us, therefore, is that it was possible for unscrupulous people to hoodwink even literate Odias into signing land deeds. Surely, Fakir Mohan was hinting at a similar practice when he put the following words in a character's mouth, 'some BA, MA qualified babu might complain, "Alas! Mian has become a

landlord by writing his name backward [an obvious allusion to the
Persian script], but we who are BA and MA, even after writing long
essays, plying the pen in the right direction, continue to starve!"'
Fakir Mohan was here expressing the common suspicion, even
complaint, that because most Odias did not have access to the
language of land transaction and loan, etc., they were swindled out
of their possession. He shared the anxiety of the Urdu-Hindi belt in
north-eastern India no less and also their anxiety over the exploitative
power of Urdu/Persian, as we have already seen. His short stories
and novels are replete with such subtexts. He would also draw
attention to the reversibility of truth and fiction in gazettes and story
books, epics and novels in a more elaborate manner by self-
reflexively linking two of his short stories, 'Mouna Mouni' and 'Ajaa
Naati Kathaa'.

Language and Community

Fakir Mohan's puzzlement over the complexities of India's past is
cast in the form of debates and arguments among imaginary and
historical characters. As Jatindra Kumar Nayak puts it, these debates
reveal 'Fakir Mohan's essentially humanist outlook on history and
[his] rejection of jingoistic or religious perspectives'.[58] Returning to
the subject of communalism in language politics, no example can
be better than Fakir Mohan's historical novel about the plight of
Odias during the reign of terror by the 'Marhattas'. In *Lachhama*,
Fakir Mohan distances himself from the anti-Muslim tirade that was
common in late nineteenth-century Bengal. According to the narrator,
the threat to Odisha's peace and happiness in the eighteenth century
was chiefly posed by the marauding Maratha Hindus and internecine
fights, rather than by the Muslims. Fakir Mohan puts words in the
mouth of one of the characters, 'As for the preservation of our
temples, a thousand Alibardi Khans or Aurangzebs cannot harm a
particle of the temples of Bhubaneswar or of Lord Jagannath. . . .
Even the infidel Muslim would shrink from committing such heinous
crimes [as the Marathas]'.[59] This is in sharp contrast to Bankimchandra
Chattopadhyay's somewhat monological historical vision, where
Muslims are blamed for all of Bharatabarsha's woes. As Kaviraj says,
'References to Islamic rule as foreign are quite widespread and can
be found in many Brahmo writings. . . . And hostility to Muslims in
the works of highly influential writers like Bankimchandra played a
significant role in this story.'[60] For Fakir Mohan, the same history
reads differently, and Odias of his generation generally felt that
Hindu-Maratha rule was so atrocious that Odias welcomed the

armies of the Company in 1803. In fact, one of the characters in
Lachhama praises the white men who were beginning to settle down
in Sutanuti.

Both Fakir Mohan and Premchand were sceptical about the
government's efforts to push English as the medium of instruction.
Their position on English is explicitly stated in their discursive
writings and lectures. In a clear case of interpellation, one can see
how their imaginative writing was not untouched by their views on
English and English education. In a lecture Fakir Mohan delivered
in 1914, he said, 'an utterly illiterate cowherd, abandoning his herd,
sits by a tree and sings a lore or two from *Bhagavata* or Upendra
Bhanja. You can well imagine how long it would take him to
memorize and sing verses of Shakespeare and Milton.'[61] When it
came to the question of English education, Fakir Mohan had his
own misgivings as reflected in his well-known story 'Dak Munshi'
(Postmaster). In this short story, the son of a poor postmaster
mistreats his father, upon acquiring English education and becoming
a *hakim*, and gives his father a couple of '*Ingreji ghussi*' (English
punches). In his last novel *Prayāschitta* (1914), the narrator says
that true knowledge cannot be acquired through a foreign language.
One of the characters harangues at a public meeting, 'The learned
linguist and Vice-Chancellor of Calcutta, Sir Asutosh Mukherjee
realized from his experience in life that true knowledge cannot be
acquired through foreign language; it is to be acquired through
one's mother tongue'.[62] His indictment of English education
reappears elsewhere too, 'nowadays much is being made of *ingrezi
siksha*. But it is very difficult for this impossible language to
percolate to the lower classes.'[63] These views of Fakir Mohan and
their redeployment in his fiction anticipate those of Premchand to a
significant extent. In a lecture the latter said:

I can't recall whether it was Madan Mohan Malavya or Sir Tejbahadur
Sapru who had said that even after breaking his head over English for fifty
years or so, he has doubts as to whether his use of English is correct or not
while speaking the language! We blind ourselves and break our backs and
burn our blood to learn and practice English, we try learning by rote its
idioms and phrases, but the works of the biggest stalwarts of India are not
seen to be fit even to feature in school text books. . . . Recently, two or
three days ago, the graduates of Panjab were found to be unable to express
their ideas in English and committing errors in spelling. This is the result
of taxing our eyes for twelve years.[64]

A suitable illustration of his views on the subject reappears in
'Bade Bhai Sahab' (Respected Elder Brother). In the story, the older

brother makes personal sacrifices to give his younger brother a Western education so that the latter may one day become a *hakim*. Worried about the younger sibling's blithe manners, he remonstrates, '*Is tarāh Angrezi padhoge to zindegi bhar padhte reh jāoge. Angrezi padhnā koi hansi khel nahin hai . . . yahan din rāt ankhen phādne padhni padti hai aur khoon jalānā padtā hai. . . .*'[65] which translates as, 'With your attitude to English, you will continue to struggle all through your whole life and yet fail to learn a letter. Learning English is not a joke . . . it demands steady concentration and blood'. Ironically, it is the older brother who, regardless of his discipline and rigor, fails repeatedly while his carefree younger brother moves up steadily. Premchand appears to underscore the sheer incongruity between the tradition of teaching and learning in India, and the demands of Western education which frustrates the diligent older brother. Nonetheless, the older brother has to persevere to succeed in life.

Urdu Will No Longer Do

Returning to the Hindi-Urdu controversy of the mid-nineteenth century, one can see how it continued to reverberate for decades to come, affecting national and personal interests. Premchand's response to it has been well documented.[66] On 1 September 1915, when Premchand was thirty-five years old, he wrote to Munshi Dayanarayan that he was 'now practicing to write in Hindi as well. Urdu will no longer do', further adding that 'like the late Balmukund Gupta, I'll also have to devote my life to writing in Hindi. Has any Hindu ever made a success of writing in Urdu that I will?'[67] By now, the estrangement between the two languages and communities had precipitated, and Amrit Rai's contention that 'modern' Urdu is not a language commonly shared by Hindus and Muslims in his *A House Divided* had already come to pass.[68] It is possible that Premchand's latter-day attempt to reconcile the two through Hindustani is a belated decision following Gandhi's political strategy to keep the anti-colonial stable safely bolted, although by that time, the horse of communal divide had already left the barn. But what exactly prompted Premchand to shift to Hindi, though well-considered, has itself been a subject of controversy.[69]

Harish Trivedi, among others, offers a most cogent argument on this—the commercial consideration. Urdu books did not sell and one of Premchand's novels in Urdu *Bazar-e-Husn* (The Brothel) could not find a publisher. It eventually appeared in Hindi under the title *Sevasadan* (1919). Communal factors too prevented a wider reception of Premchand's Urdu writings. His reference to Balmukund, who was among the first writers to switch from Urdu to Hindi in 1888, clearly suggests how the decision was based on the communal identity of the Hindi language. Moreover, as Harish Trivedi demonstrates, Urdu was perceived to be the language of the colonizer which placed certain communities in an unfairly advantageous position. Decades before Premchand, Bharatendu responded to this quandary through a questionnaire circulated by British Education Commission. Bharatendu said:

If Urdu ceases to be the court language the Mussalmans will not easily secure the numerous offices of Government of which they have at present a sort of monopoly. By the introduction of the Nagari character they would lose the opportunity of plundering the people by reading one word for another, and thereby misconstruing the real sense of the contents. . . . What wonders cannot be performed through their medium? Black can be changed into white and white into black. . .[70]

This, as we have already seen, is remarkably close to what the narrator in Fakir Mohan's *Chha Mana Atha Guntha* says in the case of Odisha. These, however, were by no means original insights either on Bharatendu's or Fakir Mohan's part. For, Fallon had suggested in his 'dissertation' that the binary between esteemed Arabic and the vulgar vernacular of ordinary people served 'to keep up that mystification which is the nefarious advantage of the few, and a wrongful injury to the many'.[71]

People's Writers

At a time when different kinds of linguistic nationalism were on the rise, it might be inaccurate to attribute motives such as the ideology of 'Hindi/Hindu Nationalism' to 'Hindiwallahs' without at the same time talking about Urdu nationalism (since historians already talk about Odia nationalism too non-pejoratively). In this context, Premchand's position on Hindi-Urdu, Nagari-Persian is too complex to generalize. His choice of Hindi as a medium was in part prompted by his realization that Urdu was too ornate, formal, and stylized for the common man.[72] Yet he never abandoned Urdu altogether. However, how does one explain such statements of Premchand as 'The number of Muslim population may be 8 crores; but the number of Urdu-speaking Mussalman is no more than one-fourth of that figure. Under these circumstances, and for the sake of nationalist considerations of the highest kind, is it not desirable that some necessary correctives and enlargement be introduced into Urdu in order to take it closer to Hindi? And, similarly, let Hindi be expanded to take it closer to Urdu . . . and, thus, whatever our writers write would not belong to one region but for the whole of Bharatvarsh.'[73] Stressing the need for a common script, he adds, 'If the whole country uses Nagari script. . . . Nationalist consciousness will not allow them to stay away from this for long.'[74]

During the Indore convention of Hindi Sahitya Sammelan, 1935, with Gandhi as chair, the Gujarati author Kanaiyalal Maneklal Munshi floated the idea of a Bharatiya Sahitya Sammelan to modify Hindi so as to make it more accessible in the non-Hindi regions and to start a journal to make available to the readers of Hindi the best of regional literature. Kanaiyalal expressed the hope that Hindi, thus modified, would eventually grow into a national script. In the editorial to the July issue of *Hans*, 1935, Premchand stresses the need to mobilize the triad of province, regional language, and literary awareness towards a national or pan-Indian literary culture. The model '*prant mein rashtriya sahitya*' or 'national literature in the province' would have bridged the gap between the region and the nation—a divide that Gandhi had sought to bridge ever since his arrival in India from South Africa. Citing absence of coordination or even mutual awareness between provincial/local literary societies, the editorial argues, 'familiarity with English literary and cultural landmarks far exceeds our knowledge of literature from a neighbouring province. . . . Whatever we know about Bangla literature is limited to the works of Dr. Rabindranath Tagore. Our knowledge of Gujarati literature is based upon the English translations of Mahatmaji's autobiography. . . . Those living north of Godavari know little about the new literature produced in Karnataka, Tamil Nadu, Andhra and Kerala.' The supra-regional/linguistic body, envisaged here, was conceived as an adhesive or a bridge that could hold India's diverse linguistic-cultural geography together. It was further proposed, on the authority of Gandhi, that Hindi should be the medium for inter-provincial exchange. 'In the Hindi Sahitya Sammelan convened last April with Gandhi as the chair, the proposal was accepted', the editorial announced. Further, the editorial expressed the hope that 'within a period of ten to twenty years' regional literatures will be integrated through Hindi. A letter by a certain Munshi Gulab Rai, published as an extension of 'Hansvani' (September 1935) spells out a plan of action for the proposed Rashtriya Sahitya Sabha. 'In every province' Gulab Rai writes, 'the Sabha must start a magazine that uses Hindi [Nagari] script, even if its language is regional'. Further, at various regional literary gatherings, 'for the benefit of the local participants, a discourse or two must be conducted in Hindi'. In October 1935, when *Hans* was re-launched as the mouthpiece of Bharatiya Sahitya Sangathan, under the joint editorship of Premchand and Kanaiyalal, it was supported by an editorial board in which all the Indian languages were represented with Gandhi as well others representing various linguistic areas—Maithili Sharan Gupt (Hindi), Sajjad Zaheer (Urdu), Nilakantha Das (Odia), C. Rajagopalachari (Tamil), K.M. Panikkar (Malayalam), and so on.

The Ideology of Nagari

All this seems to be a residual of what one might call the ideology of Nagari. At this point a longish digression may be in order before returning to Premchand. More than three decades earlier, in 1905, Justice Sarada Charan Mitra set up 'Ek Lipi Vistar Parishad' in order to promote the cause of Independence and present write-ups of various languages in a uniform script in 1905.[75] However, a momentous event in the history of the Indian languages movement across the subcontinent took place with the setting up of *Devnagar*. The subject, ironically enough, is taken up for serious discussion in *Odia*.

In 1908, *Utkal Sahitya* published an Odia piece, 'Devnagar: Introduction and Discussion' by a Bengali admirer of Radhanath Ray, Akhilchandra Palit.[76] The significance of the initiative in the form of the periodical and its discussion in the Odia public sphere can hardly be over-emphasized in the context of what I have discussed so far. Akhilchandra makes these points:

1. Diversity of language has divided people of one region from another.
2. English cannot eradicate this huge stumbling block in getting to know and understand one another.
3. Diversity of script rather than the diversity of language is more damaging to the unity.
4. All the languages in *Aryabrata* are derived from Sanskrit and Prakrit.
5. Though Bengalis can somehow understand the speech of Biharis, Hindustanis and Odias, but in their eyes the Bihari script and those of Urdu and Odia look strange.

6. Many feel that the Persian script is a great obstacle in learning Urdu.

Akhilchandra asserts that by looking at the issue of the magazine over a year, one could notice the way the complex problem of script-induced chaos has been sorted out easily and beautifully. He provides a detailed catalogue of the languages represented by the various issues of the magazine, and justifies that the whole country is indebted to those who have worked hard to bring it to such a level of success, including those who have sent essays from different corners of Bharat in Tamil, Bangla, Marhatta, Hindi, Gujarati, Telugu, Sindhi, Sanskrit, Pali, Malayalam, Odia, French, Kumaoni, Nepali, Panjabi, Urdu, Kurmachali, Japanese, and English—these twenty-one languages were in Devanagari script (except the essays in English). Then, of course, Akhilchandra makes the ambitious claim that 'readers will see how unfamiliar regional languages appear to be familiar. Marathi readers can understand about 75% of Bangla in Nagari script, and Bengali readers can understand almost all of Marathi essays. Hindi language is our Esperanto or lingua franca.' He further says, drawing on the primary level of discourses, 'Our teachers from the West have told us that Devnagari lipi was imported from Phoenician or such other sources; and we have believed them like obedient students. But, recently, the renowned scholar from Mysore, R. Shyam Shastri has conclusively proved that Devnagari is "swadeshi". By now [that is, post 1905], of course, everything can be made attractive by claiming it to be "swadeshi".'[77] The significance of the article, and the mono-script-multilingual periodical it is on, lies in the fact of their anticipation by more than three decades the effort of Gulab Rai et al.

Around these crucial years when Gandhi was beginning his journey throughout India to give Indian nationalist, anti-colonial struggle a new direction, Fakir Mohan was ending his life's journey, having fought his battle with hegemonic literary cultures. Also around this time, Gandhi's impact on local Odia identity politics took a decisive turn, with the Odia leadership accommodating his vision of Indian *Swaraj* within the framework of Odia identity politics. In 1921, after a brief period of power struggle between the two ideologues, the septuagenarian Madhusudan Das and the younger Gandhian, Gopabandhu Das,[78] *desha* no longer meant just Utkal desha, but both Utkal desha and Bharatabarsha. Until his death, Fakir Mohan pondered albeit playfully on the state of languages and the languages of the state—what was ideal or what was pragmatic for writers like him. He seems to have settled for the pragmatic option, and his use and views on language are as diverse as they are democratic. Yet, Odia and Odisha were his primary concerns, with occasional references to 'Bharatabarsha'. While he alluded often to the broader historical context, he nonetheless, was unconcerned with the world outside Odisha. For Premchand, 'Bharatabarsh' received top priority, and writing, his linguistic style, and characterization were all geared towards that priority.

More often than not, Fakir Mohan would put into the mouth of the characters in his fiction the idiom that they were most likely to use depending on their respective social class (poor/rich/feudal lord, etc.), community (Hindus/Muslims/white Europeans, etc.), or linguistic identity (Odia/Hindi/English, etc.). Though Odia was faced with a situation where its very survival was at stake, Fakir Mohan would often use the language of the dominant other[79] and engage with an entire range of issues. Rebati's story is not only about women's education but it is also about the learning of Odia language, where there is a reference to the historical reality of 'Madhusudan Rao's *Chhandamala*'—a language primer that the eponymous character reads from. Fakir Mohan was equally concerned with different possibilities, including the use of *'bisuddha gharei bhasa'*. In fact, when his very first novel was reviewed by the budding lexicographer, Gopalachandra, his language and idiom became the chief talking point. Even within the specificities of the Odia language, there were debates over *kathit bhasa* and *sadhu bhasa*. In 'Randipua Ananta' (Ananta the Widow's Son), and 'Punarmushikobhava', he fuses both kinds of idiom. I would like to further add the fact, with a view to counterpoising him against Premchand, that Fakir Mohan constantly spoke of the 'mother tongue'. In the same breath, he would bemoan the Sanskritization of the *gadajati bhasa*.[80] Though he would himself use a Sanskritized idiom in a narrative situation that would demand it, he said, 'in the language [Odia], the number of *deshaja* words is reducing gradually, and in their place the number of Sanskritic words is increasing'.[81]

In the case of Premchand, one notices on the other hand, how he gets engaged in the linguistic issues around the time Fakir Mohan dies in 1918, several decades after the questions of language were first debated seriously. In a way, a few issues had already been settled for good and were well-nigh irrevocable (or so it had seemed then). Premchand was to argue in a manner similar to that of Nandakishor of 1899 that 'if the advocates of these two languages (Urdu that is leaden with unfamiliar and obsolete Arabic and

Persian words, and a Hindi that is leaden with difficult Sanskritic words) stand before each other and speak using these literary idioms perhaps they would fail to communicate with each other'.[82] Unlike in the case of Odia, Hindi did not face the dire prospect of extinction, rather it was a question of consolidating the gains of his predecessors, building on the ground that had already been gained over Persian-Urdu. Premchand did not feel the need to displace or reject Urdu; but expected the two languages to coexist, maintaining their vaguely defined identity and difference. Though Premchand initially tried to ensure the identity of both Urdu and Hindi, not mixing them up while writing in either of the two languages to the extent possible, given their respective geneses. Finally, it was not a case of two scripts and one language, but a way of parting ways.

Making Possible an Inclusive Literary History of India

Thus, although the hectic and long-drawn linguistic controversies impacted the writings of Fakir Mohan and Premchand in different ways—depending on local peculiarities of circumstances—it is possible to identify common strands that connect the development and evolution of languages, the issue of language, and nationalism as it is dealt within the literatures across various Indian languages. I would like to reiterate the point I made at the beginning of the chapter about the need to expand and de-discretize the apparently disparate archives that constitute the rubric 'Indian Literary-Cultural History'. This will help us evolve a methodology different from the ones that are being employed currently. The existing and emerging body of new scholarship, best exemplified through the compendia put together by Pollock, Stuart Blackburn, and Vasudha Dalmia et al.,[83] have all broken new grounds and are absolutely indispensable and exemplary for future research. Yet, for all their brilliance, they are limited to making available to us an indiscriminate mass of mechanically juxtaposed discrete archives. Their immense contribution will remain unutilized if we do not engage in the more challenging task of interweaving the strands of individual linguistic-literary histories. Otherwise, conclusions drawn on one set of archives might be seen as anomalous when seen in conjunction with another. For example, the study of Hindi/Urdu linguistic divide along communal lines cannot be applied to study such other divides as Hindi/Maithili or Bangla/Odia (one a dominant and the other a marginal linguistic group); nor does the paradigm explain the partition of Bengal into East and West even when the language (Bangla) is common to both. The 1947 Partition saw the creation of East Pakistan; later in 1971, East Pakistan seceded from its communal brethren in favour of Bangla-speaking Bangladesh. Thus, the master-narrative of Hindi-Hindu/Urdu-Muslim division fails to explain other regional and linguistic divisions. Similarly, the after-lives of the two sets of controversies in India (Hindi-Urdu and Bengali-Odia) which had started on the basis of a master-slave paradigm, ended differently, with the peaceful and celebratory co-existence of Odia and Bangla, whereas the once dominant Urdu is now the linguistic other of Hindi.

I shall return briefly to Ahmad's pertinent observation that 'The vernaculars [of India] had to wage many of their cultural struggles against Sanskrit and against brahmanical classicism which is so large a part of the natural heritage associated with Sanskrit'. This is true from one perspective but does not explain the struggle of Odia, Maithili, etc., against the dominance of Persian or more recently Hindi. Not everyone will agree with Ahmad's assertion that 'India did not develop any indigenous vernacular language to replace Sanskrit as a language of rule'. For Ahmad will be the first one to admit that spoken Hindi poses a serious challenge to those assertions.[84]

Finally, I am proposing here a blueprint for writing a fuller and more comprehensive literary history of India by discussing the shared and intertwined histories of languages across the subcontinent. I have tried to demonstrate how the jigsaw puzzle comprising separate and discrete archives can be made to yield an integrative and recognizable pattern in which the different parts would more visibly relate to the whole. My discussion has also attempted to suggest how historians sometimes fall into a trap of their own making, by first settling for an emotive teleology, which becomes a pre-determining model for reading back a cultural past that answers to that teleology. An indication of this is the way two parallel (and interpenetrating) histories are read by liberal historians, one in the tragic, and the other in the celebratory vein. For, even while agonizing over the partition-inducing Hindi-Urdu controversy, we celebrate the other formations of language-based states—Odisha out of the Bengali-Odia controversy, among many others. While we decry one kind of nationalism as divisive, we celebrate the other as liberating and empowering.[85] On the evidence displayed above, much of the discourses of linguistic discord can be seen as 'derivative', defined as their frontiers were primarily by European scholars equipped with their newly acquired disciplinary tools, whether or not the nationalist discourse that accompanied them was derivative.[86] The implication of all this for students of comparative literature is rather profound. We can now see Fakir Mohan and Premchand as not working in isolated linguistic spaces, but as two writers who inherited and inhabited a shared discursive space and a history, even while responding to local ideological compulsions.

Notes

1. Aijaz Ahmad, *In Theory: Classes, Nations, Literatures,* Delhi: OUP, 1992, p. 245.
2. Ibid., p. 248.
3. Sheldon Pollock, *Forms of Knowledge in Early Modern Asia: Explorations in the Intellectual History of India and Tibet, 1500–1800,* Durham and London: Duke University Press, 2011; Shamsur Rahman Faruqi, 'A Long History of Urdu Literary Culture, Part I: Naming and Placing a Literary Culture', in *Literary Cultures in History: Reconstructions from South Asia,* ed. Sheldon Pollock, New Delhi: OUP, 2003, pp. 805–63; Sudipta Kaviraj, 'The Two Histories of Literary Culture in Bengal', in *Literary Cultures in History: Reconstructions from South Asia,* ed. Sheldon Pollock, New Delhi: OUP, 2003, pp. 503–66; and Stuart MacGregor, 'The Progress of Hindi, Part I: The Development of a Transregional Idiom', in *Literary Cultures in History: Reconstructions from South Asia,* ed. Sheldon Pollock, New Delhi: OUP, 2003, pp. 912–57.
4. 'But the boundaries of these states were not formed by rivers, or mountains, or any natural features of the terrain; they were, instead, walls of words. Language divided us'; Salman Rushdie, *Midnight's Children,* London: Vintage, 1981, pp. 261–2. But this was about the post-Independent reorganization. The language issues discussed here are late-colonial.
5. Gayatri Chakravorty Spivak, *Death of a Discipline,* Columbia: Columbia University Press, 2003.
6. Vasudha Dalmia, *The Nationalisation of Hindu Traditions: Bharatendu Harischandra and Nineteenth Century Banaras,* New Delhi: Permanent Black, 2010; Francesca Orsini, *The Hindi Public Sphere, 1920–1940: Language and Literature in Age of Nationalism,* New Delhi: OUP, 2002; Harish Trivedi, 'The Progress of Hindi, Part 2: Hindi and the Nation', in *Literary Cultures in History: Reconstructions from South Asia,* ed. Sheldon Pollock, New Delhi: OUP, 2003, pp. 958–1022; and MacGregor, 'The Progress of Hindi'.
7. Alok Rai discusses the way Bengalis supported the Nagari-Hindi movement, but does so en passant. See, Alok Rai, *Hindi Nationalism,* New Delhi: Permanent Black, 2000.

8. Bipin Chandra Pal, *Memories of My Life and Times*, Calcutta: Modern Book Agency, 1932; repr. 2004, p. 358.
9. Rai, *Hindi Nationalism*.
10. Ibid., p. viii.
11. Sudipta Kaviraj, 'Writing, Speaking, Being: Language and the Historical Formation of Identities in India', in *Language and Politics in India*, ed. Asha Sarangi, New Delhi: OUP, 2009, pp. 312–50.
12. Kaviraj, 'The Two Histories of Literary Culture in Bengal', p. 533.
13. See, <http://www.columbia.edu/itc/mealac/pritchett/00general links/macaulay/txt_minute_education_1835.html>, accessed on 27 September 2015.
14. M.K. Gandhi, *An Autobiography or The Story of My Experiment with Truth*, tr. Mahadev Desai, Ahmedabad: Navajivan Trust, 1927; repr. 1999.
15. Michel Foucault's term. Here, I am using it to suggest the way print economy becomes an all pervasive agent of the colonial government.
16. Nathaniel Brassey Halhed, *A Grammar of the Bengal Language*, Bengal: CUP, 1778. This first printed Bengali grammar book was the earliest attempt to associate the two languages with Hindus and Muslim. In this, one can already notice the process of cleansing Bengali of Persian words. Also see, Faruqi, 'A Long History of Urdu Literary Culture', p. 811.
17. Robert Caldwell, *A Comparative Grammar of the Dravidian or South Indian Family of Languages*, London: Williams and Norgate, 1856; and John Beames, *A Comparative Grammar of the Modern Aryan Languages of India*, London: Turner & Co., 1872.
18. Shan Muhammad, ed., 'Introduction', in *The Aligarh Movement: Basic Documents (1864–1898)*, Meerut: Meenakshi Prakashan, 1978, p. xii.
19. Ibid., p. xiv.
20. Several arguments in favour of and against Urdu/Hindustani were offered in books and journals. Lord Strangford's elaborate paper published in *Quarterly Review* (1865) was in response to 'Vamberley's Travels in Central Asia'. S.W. Fallon's paper was another. Beames quotes from Strangford to buttress his argument in favour of Hindustani, 'If Hindustani, adopted by us as the future general language of India, is to be a language and a jargon, it must become so by means of its alliance with Persian, the speech which all Indian Mahomedans have at their heart . . . for all their abstract thought, their politics, science, and poetry'; John Beames, 'On the Arabic Element in Official Hindustani, Part ii', *Journal of the Asiatic Society*, pt. I, no. 3, 1867, pp. 146–8. He also quotes the Hindi propagandists, 'Hindi is more native to the soil, and lies closer to the hearts of the people than Arabic or Persian, and its use is therefore preferable to that of the last named languages'. This is the *political* argument of the Hindi school. Fallon puts it thus, 'Hosts of Persian and Arabic words have been introduced *by natives of the country* who affect a foreign tongue, and make

transfers in the mass out of worthless books imperfectly understood'. See, S.W. Fallon, *English-Hindustani Law and Commercial Dictionary*, Introductory Dissertation, Banaras: Medical Hall Press, 1879, p. xviii, ad fin; as quoted in Beames, *A Comparative Grammar*, p. 147.

21. Revd James Long, 'Notes and Queries Suggested by a Visit to Orissa in January 1859', *Journal of the Asiatic Society of India*, vol. 28, no. 3, 1859, pp. 189–90. Even earlier, Amos Sutton had commented on the resemblance between Bangla and Odia, 'While, however the structure of the two languages, and a great proportion of the words employed, are the same, it is remarkable, that there should exist so great a difference in the pronunciation, a difference as great as that between English and French'; Amos Sutton, 'Preface', in *An Introductory Grammar of Oriya Language*, Calcutta: Baptist Mission Press, 1831, pp. ii–iv. Also see Gaganendranath Das, *Odia Bhasha Charchara Parampara*, Cuttack: Institute of Odia Studies, 1983, p. xii.

22. Rajendralal Mitra, 'On the Origin of the Hindavi Language and Its Relation to the Urdu Dialect', *Journal of the Asiatic Society*, no. V, 1864, p. 50.

23. Ibid.

24. In April–May 1861, at the request of author Dinabandhu Mitra, one of Long's former students at the Church Mission Society school, Long brought out a translation of *Neel Darpan*. The translation of the play was later attributed to Michael Madhusudan Dutt by Bankimchandra Chattopadhyay, even as Long remained silent on the identity of the translator. For commissioning the translation, he was tried and briefly jailed too.

25. Long, 'Notes and Queries', p. 190.

26. Ibid., p. 189. Noteworthy here is, as I have just mentioned, how the discourse of linguistic nationalism is gradually entering the Indian public sphere, which then circulates as 'social energy' although only among the intelligentsia—something that Dinabandhu Mitra was to harp on albeit critical of the valorization of nationalism, and distinguishing good and bad nationalism.

27. Taken from the *Proceedings of the Asiatic Society of Bengal*, no. 138, 1870, pp. 192–216; repr. in John Beames, *Essays on Orissan History and Literature*, ed. Kailash Pattanaik, Jagatsinghpur: Prafulla, 2004, p. 94.

28. The metaphor that Sitanshu Yashaschandra uses in the first context is equally applicable to Dinabandhu Mitra's argument, 'Calling Maithili and Bhoajpuri etc. "dialects" of Hindi is as absurd as calling a 60 year-old woman the daughter of a 30 year old woman'. See, Sitanshu Yashaschandra, 'From Hemacandra to *Hind Svaraj*: Region and Power in Gujarati Literary Culture', in *Literary Cultures in History*, pp. 567–611.

29. Bansidhar Mohanty, *Odiā Bhāshā Āndolana*, 2nd edn., Cuttack: Sāhitya Sangraha Prakāshana, 2001; Gaganendranath Das,

'*Jagannātha* and Oriya Nationalism', in *The Cult of Jagannath and the Regional Tradition of Orissa,* ed. Anncharlott Eschmann, Hermann Kulke and Gaya Charan Tripathi, Delhi: Manohar, 1978, pp. 359–74; and Nivedita Mohanty, *Oriya Nationalism: Quest for a United Orissa, 1866–1956,* revised and enlarged edn., Jagatsinghpur: Prafulla, 2005.

30. It is not insignificant to note here that around the time that Odias are trying to fight their battle against the imposition of Bangla, these linguistic movements are far from being 'communal' in the beginning. For, the common Odia people were wary of the dominance of Bengalis as much as the non-Persian-Urdu-knowing people were wary of those who knew the language of court. The Odias did not want to deal with the Bengalis who wanted to use their language to sideline the Odias on the job front as well as the land deeds.

31. Shan Muhammad, Letter dated 31 October 1868, *Aligarh Movement: Basic Documents (1864–1898),* Meerut: Meenakshi Prakashan, p. 326.

32. Ibid., p. 325.

33. Ibid.

34. Jata Shankar Jha, *Beginning of Modern Education in Mithila: Selections from Educational Records, Darbhanga Raj, 1860–1930,* Patna: K.P. Jayaswal Research Institute, 1972, p. 69.

35. George A. Grierson, 'A Plea for the People's Tongue', *The Calcutta Review,* vol. LXXVI, 1880, pp. 151–68.

36. Rai, in *Hindi Nationalism,* calls it 'the most fateful decision in the evolution of modern Hindi', and perceives it as one of the factors which eventually led to the Partition of India. But as we have seen the decision was seeded much earlier in the 1860s, administrators were merely implementing what was 'scientifically' and statistically proved.

37. Quoted in Jha, *Beginning of Modern Education.*

38. *Utkal Dipika,* 6 June 1894. The relative level of difficulty in learning these languages is captured by a still extant proverb in Bihar, '*Ārabi nikāle charbi, Phārsi nikāle tel, Urdu hai kuchh kuchh Hindi hai khel*' [Trying to learn Arabic will draw out your fat; Persian will extract your oil; Urdu is somewhat tough; but Hindi is child's play (translation mine)].

39. *Utkal Sahitya,* vol. 3, no. 12, 1899, p. 273.

40. Bachchan Singh, *Hindi Sahitya ka Doosra Itihas,* Delhi: Radhakrishna Prakashan, 2014, p. 289; Quote translated by Gautam Choubey.

41. Rai, *Hindi Nationalism,* p. 87.

42. Ibid.

43. Ibid.

44. Natabar Samantaray, *Odia Sahityara Itihasa (1803–1920),* Bhubaneswar: Bani Bhavan, 1964; 2nd edn. 1983, pp. 95–200.

45. Nandakishor Bal, '2nd Khanda [Part II] Chhāndamālā', *Utkal Sahitya,* vol. 3, no. 10, 1899, pp. 220–9.

46. Bhāratara Bhabisyata Bhāshā', *Utkal Sahitya,* vol. 4, no. 1, 1307 (AD 1900), pp. 17–20.

47. Fakir Mohan Senapati, *Granthabali, Trutiya Khanda* or *Complete Works of Fakir Mohan Senapati*, vol. 3, ed. Debendra Dash, Cuttack: Grantha Mandir, 2008.

48. Bal, '2nd Khanda Chhāndamālā'.

49. Bankimchandra Chattopadhyay, 'The Bengali Language: The Language of Writing', tr. Gautam Chakravarty, *Indian Literature*, vol. LVII, no. 3, May/June 2014, pp. 26–33; originally published in *Bangadarshan*, 1285 Jaishta (May 1879).

50. Fakir Mohan, *Granthabali*, p. 137.

51. Ibid., p. 136.

52. Gourishankar Ray (1838–1917) played a key role in the Odia public sphere, especially as editor of the influential newspaper *Utkal Dipika*.

53. Fakir Mohan Senapati, 'Foreword', in *Chha Mana Atha Guntha (Six Acres and a Third)*, 1902; repr. in Fakir Mohan, *Granthabali*, p. 2.

54. Ibid., p. 24.

55. Sumit Sarkar, *The Swadeshi Movement in Bengal: 1903-1908*, tr. Sumit Sarkar, New Delhi: People's Publishing House, 1973, p. 457.

56. Ibid.

57. Kaviraj, 'The Two Histories of Literary Culture in Bengal', p. 530.

58. Jatindra Kumar Nayak, *The Historical Novel in Oriya*, Cuttack: Cuttack Students' Store, 1982, p. 81.

59. Fakir Mohan Senapati, *Lachhama*, tr. Chandan Das, New Delhi: Three Rivers Publishers, 2013, pp. 28–9.

60. Kaviraj, 'The Two Histories of Literary Culture in Bengal', p. 541.

61. Fakir Mohan Senapati, '*Sabhapati Abhibhasan*', 1914; repr. in Fakir Mohan, *Granthabali*, p. 423.

62. Fakir Mohan, *Granthabali*, p. 281.

63. Ibid., p. 416.

64. Premchand, *Kuch Vichar: Sahitya aur Sambandhi Kuch Vichar*, New Delhi: Bharatiya Granth Niketan, 1990, p. 123.

65. Premchand, see, <http://www.scribd.com/doc/6691922/Bade-Bhai-Sahab>, accessed 9 July 2015.

66. Dalmia, *The Nationalisation of Hindu Traditions*; Zafar Raza, *Premchand, Urdu-Hindi Kathākār*, Allahabad: Lokbharti Prakashan, 1993; and Kamal Kishore Goyanka, ed., *Premchand ki Hindi-Urdu Kāhāniyan*, New Delhi: Bharatiya Jnanpith, 1990.

67. Amrit Rai, *Premchand: A Life*, tr. Harish Trivedi, New Delhi: People's Publishing House, 1982, p. 104. Also see, Balmukund Gupta, 'Hindī mein bindī (1900)', <http://www.columbia.edu/itc/mealac/pritchett/00urduhindilinks/shacklesnell/308gupta.pdf>, accessed 12 August 2015.

68. Amrit Rai, *A House Divided: The Origin and Development of Hindi/Hindavi*, Delhi: OUP, 1984, p. 28. Also see Ahmad's surprise at his contention in Aijaz Ahmad, *Lineages of the Present*, London: Verso, 2000, p. 338.

69. Krupa Shandilya, 'The Widow, the Wife and the Courtesan: A Comparative Study of Social Reform in Premchand's *Sevasadan* and the Late-Nineteenth Century Bengali and Urdu Novel', *Comparative Literature Studies*, vol. 53, no. 2, 2016, pp. 272–88 (for a more detailed discussion of the issue).
70. Trivedi, 'The Progress of Hindi', p. 964.
71. Fallon, '*English-Hindustani Law and Commercial Dictionary*', pp. xii–xiii; quoted in Beames, 'On the Arabic Element in Official Hindustani'.
72. Harish Trivedi brilliantly showcases the difference in 'The Progress of Hindi' and I use his examples of the translations to bring out this point.
73. Premchand, 'Urdu, Hindi and Hindustani', p. 114.
74. Premchand, 'Rastrabhasa Hindi aur Uske Samasyaen', in *Kuch Vichar: Sahitya aur Sambandhi Kuch Vichar*, New Delhi: Bharatiya Granth Niketan, 1990, p. 138.
75. Krishna Bihari Mishra, *The Origin and Growth of Hindi Journalism in Kolkata*, Kolkata: Press Club, 2005.
76. *Utkal Sahitya*, 1908, pp. 96–103. It is said that Akhilchandra Palit had learnt Odia in order to be able to read Radhanath Ray's Odia poetry. The *Radhanath Jibani* carried numerous letters from Akhilchandra to Radhanath Ray in Bangla. See Durgacharan Ray, *Radhanath Jibani (1941)*, Cuttack: Friends Publishers, pp. 416–40.
77. Ibid.
78. Gopabandhu Das (1877–1928) was the pre-eminent Mahatma Gandhian leader of Odisha. He was also close to the other nationalists including Subhas Chandra Bose, and was a leading nationalist poet. He founded two major institutions, the Satyabadi Bana Vidyalaya in 1909 and the newspaper *Samaj* (1919).
79. It is intriguing to note the near-total absence of Bangla words, phrases and even characters. In the absence of evidence, one can only offer conjectural reasons for such a conspicuous omission. It may have been because many *pravashi* Bengalis happened to be his close friends, who worked alongside 'pure Odias' in the interest of Odias.
80. Fakir Mohan, *Granthabali*, p. 334.
81. Ibid.
82. Premchand, *Kuch Vichar*, p. 108.
83. Sheldon Pollock, *Literary Cultures in History: Reconstructions from South Asia*, New Delhi: OUP, 2003; Stuart Blackburn and Vasudha Dalmia, *India's Literary History: Essays On the Nineteenth Century*, Delhi and Ranikhet: Permanent Black, 2004.
84. Ahmad, *Lineages of the Present*, p. 131. What I have in mind here is the increasing use of *tadbhava* and *tatsama* words in Hindi, its pan-Indian oral currency helped by the electronic media and government patronage.
85. Of course, nationalist historians do otherwise. They celebrate both Hindi and Urdu as two 'national' languages—one in India the other

in Pakistan. For such liberal and not so liberal histories, see Dalmia, *The Nationalisation of Hindu Traditions*; Rai, *Hindi Nationalism*; Goyanka, ed., *Premchand ki Hindi-Urdu Kāhāniyan*; Raza, *Premchand, Urdu-Hindi Kathākār*; Faruqi, 'A Long History of Urdu Literary Culture'; Das, *Odia Bhasha Charchara Parampara*; Mohanty, *Oriya Nationalism*; and Bishnu Mohapatra, 'Ways of Belonging: The Kanchi Kaveri Legend and the Construction of Oriya Identity', *Studies in History*, vol. 12, no. 2, 1996, pp. 203–21.

86. Partha Chatterjee, 'Nationalist Thought and the Colonial World: A Derivative Discourse?', in *The Partha Chatterjee Omnibus: Comprising Nationalist Thought and the Colonial World, The Nation and its Fragments, and A Possible India* (II), New Delhi: OUP, 1999. What I have in mind here is the following: prior to the 'linguistic moment' in Indian cultural history that was heralded by the European scholars, there was an alternative, albeit under-theorized view of the *desha* or jati before the superimposition of the concept of the modern nation state took place.

3

Milton, Macaulay, and the Learned Natives

Radhanath Ray's *Mahayatra* Interrupted

John Milton's afterlife has been nothing short of spectacular. No other English poet, barring William Shakespeare, has exerted the kind of decisive influence that he cast on the colonial literary culture of India. Both of them were among those who could fill the European bookshelves, even one of which 'was worth the whole native literature of India and Arabia' (thus spake Macaulay, vaunting aloud).[1] In a less talked about section in the same 'Minute', he refers to the Oriental system of education following the Charter Act of 1813, and speaks of how 'the gentlemen who compose the Committee of Public Instruction ... [and who] have hitherto pursued the course have made it appear as if it was strictly prescribed by the British Parliament in 1813'. Challenging those gentlemen, he says:

It [the Charter document] contains nothing about the particular languages or sciences which are to be studied. A sum is set apart 'for the revival and promotion of literature and the encouragement of *the learned natives of India*, and for the introduction and promotion of a knowledge of the sciences among the inhabitants of the British territories'. It is argued, or rather taken for granted, that by literature, the Parliament can have meant only Arabic and Sanscrit literature, that they never would have given the honorable appellation of 'a learned native' to a native who was familiar with the poetry of Milton, the Metaphysics of Locke, and the Physics of Newton; but that they meant to designate by that name only such persons as might have studied in the sacred books of the Hindoos all the uses of *cusa-grass*, and all the mysteries of absorption into the Deity. This does not appear to be a very satisfactory interpretation [emphasis mine].[2]

It is interesting to note here the collocation in a document pertaining to Indian education of three different disciplines of knowledge represented by the three figures—Milton, John Locke and Isaac Newton. These three, between them, and in a way, are early prefigurations of the Enlightenment project and contribute to the ushering in of European modernity. Also interesting and ironic is the manner in which Macaulay presses into service someone like Milton, for the acquisition of 'true' knowledge of science and history, but whose Raphael admonishes Adam to be mindful of the limits of knowledge set by an interdictive God. Notwithstanding Milton's kind allusion to Galileo, Macaulay's collocation of Milton and Newton remains intriguing, if only because of the symbolic value of the apple being contrastively viewed by each. But Macaulay presses both of them into service to supplant the *cusa*-grass, a trope for a knowledge system propelled by centuries of religious practice. In their vernacular knowledge system, Macaulay alleges that the 'Hindoos' learnt all the false things, 'We are to teach *false History*, *false Astronomy*, *false Medicine*, because we find them in company with a false religion' [emphasis mine].[3]

By the end of the nineteenth century, the number of English-educated Indians who had internalized not only Macaulay's argument, but also such European classics as Homer, Virgil, and Sophocles, as well as Shakespeare and Milton was not insignificant. Even so, many of the English-educated 'learned native' elites had not unlearnt the Indian classics. That the latter was partly possible through the Orientalists cannot be gainsaid. Biographies of these nineteenth-century elite class of Indian writers never fail to highlight the inextricable and intricate confluence of the two traditions—one colonial, the other indigenous.

Do these learned natives take to Milton and the others the way Macaulay had envisaged? If yes, what were the consequences? The first part of this chapter enquires into the nature of the impact of Macaulay's agenda on 'the learned native' by studying the use to which they put their knowledge of Milton, who Macaulay singles out from among the English bards as an indispensable model. But the story of Milton's impact on any slice of Indian literary culture is complicated and locally underdetermined. Both Michael Madhusudan Dutt (1824–73) and Radhanath Ray (1848–1908), who played pioneering roles in modernizing their respective literary cultures, are best known and discussed, from among their several other works, for their respective Miltonic masterpieces—*Meghnadbadh Kavya* and *Mahayatra*. I shall also highlight Radhanath Ray's strategies in hybridizing certain stylistic and structural aspects of the indigenous epic-traditions with the European, especially the Miltonic modes. In the second part, I look into the reception of *Mahayatra* and the controversies that ensued. In the third part, I shall try to situate the specific controversies in the larger context of late nineteenth-century Odisha.

I

Though two of the most obvious candidates for the appellation 'learned natives' are Michael Madhusudan Dutt and Radhanath Ray, this chapter will focus primarily on the latter. But, first, are there any grounds for comparison? What might justify my diachronic juxtaposition of Milton's *Paradise Lost*, Michael Madhusudan Dutt's *Meghnadbadh Kavya*, and Radhanath Ray's *Mahayatra*? Is there a prima facie case for such comparatist juxtaposition here? The answer is yes, beginning with certain obvious formal aspects.

Initiation Rites

To begin with, we can look at the intellectual growth of the two 'learned natives'. In a recent discussion of Michael Madhusudan Dutt, a critic refers to his early training in Bangla, some Sanskrit and Persian, and arithmetic. At the age of seven, he also attended afternoon sessions at a *maulvi*'s school, where he acquired facility in Persian. '. . . Dutt attended a grammar school near the courthouse, learning English, Latin, and Hebrew, and in 1837, he joined Hindu College, where he excelled in English and mathematics.'[4] Similarly, a biographer of Radhanath Ray speaks of how the latter had learnt Sanskrit by 1856, thanks to the efforts of Pandit Sadashiv Nanda. By 1862, his knowledge of English received commendation from the district magistrate of Balasore, and by 1868, 'fair progress in English literature' was reported.[5]

More substantively, both use the 'invocation'—so much part of the Indian *kavya* tradition no doubt—but hybridize the form by using the Miltonic version of the device. For example, unlike in the case of the Hindu/Bangla/Odia epic-tradition where many gods are invoked for many brief invocations, and *stabas* and *vandanas* are offered to these gods, Madhusudan Dutt and Radhanath use invocatory passages only in specific books. To *Paradise Lost*'s four invocations we have two in *Meghnadbadh* and one in *Mahayatra*. Each begins with an invocation in Book I—Michael Madhusudan Dutt invoking Bharati first and then, in Book IV, Valmiki. In Radhanath Ray, the first invocation is to Pankajabasini, which quickly shifts to Utkal Bharati, Sarala (Saraswati of Utkal) in the same Book, and then in Books V and VI, he invokes the two Rajas of Mayurbhanj and Bamanda for reasons of patronage in what appears to be a shift from the sublime to the ridiculous. It is interesting to note Radhanath Ray's use of local deities and kings (Is it possible that he had the *Faerie Queene*'s allegorical structure too in mind while invoking the local kings?). Apart from *Mahayatra*, he is not known to have used any invocatory passages in any other poem of his. As Natabar Samantaray says, it was 'Radhanath's intention [in invoking this quintessentially Odia deity] to create a firm belief in the mind of the reader right at the outset of the epic that *Mahayatra* was the result of using as model Sarala Das's Mahabharata which in turn was the product of the inspiration of the renowned deity from village Jhankada'.[6] This shows Radhanath Ray's anxiety to try and belong to the literary tradition of Odisha.

The theme in each case, *Meghnadbadh Kavya* as well as *Mahayatra*, is introduced as part of the invocatory passages, comprising and combining the invocation and the principium, stating the scope of the action, beginning in the form of questions, as they use the interrogative mode to ask their respective muses to help the epic poet with the task, exactly the way Milton did the argument stating in *Paradise Lost*, 'In the beginning how the heavens and earth/Rose out of chaos . . . what cause . . .?' and so on. Michael Madhusudan Dutt, '*kaun birabare bari senapati pade*' (which brave-heart, taking on the role of Senapati etc.?) moving to '*ki kausale rakshasa bharasa Indrajit Meghnade, Indreyni shankile?*' (Using what strategy did the trusted of the rakshasas . . ., etc.). Radhanath too follows the same pattern, 'Say what did Kuruchudamani do/when he heard from the brave messenger. . .' and then 'How did he receive such dire message?'.[7] In both the cases, Milton's highly Latinate English is replicated in Sanskritized and ornate Bangla and Odia, with Radhanath Ray often simulating the Miltonic inversions. Further, what must have sounded music to the ears of the natives trained in *alankaric* and *rasa* traditions, was the familiar *veera rasa* they discover in Milton's declamatory passages given to Satan, which, in turn, must have encouraged both Michael Madhusudan Dutt and Radhanath Ray to select their respective themes, as is apparent from their letters and prose writings, and the generous use of similar passages in their respective narratives. Radhanath Ray's elevated, ornate, and highly Sanskritized style and syntax seems to have been consciously modelled on the Latinate style of Milton. Similarly, though I have not attempted to trace epic similes in Madhusudan Dutt, Radhanath Ray puts the

Miltonic-epic device to good use, and a few echoes can be heard in such Miltonic similes as the elaborate, 'as when at the marriage altar a spark of fire bursts into flame, dispelling darkness, and startles the onlookers suddenly . . . or as the sudden sun-rise in the eastern sky dazzles the eyes of a mariner of a skiff in the night-engulfed-ocean . . ., etc.' (translation mine). The last image, *naisha-sindhu-bahi-nabika*[8]—an unusual and highly Sanskritized Odia compound word—is a masterful translation of Milton's simile in Book I, as anyone can recognize, 'pilot of some small night-foundered skiff'.[9] Similarly, Radhanath Ray's use of the unusual Odia phrase, '*vivek-prahari*' for Milton's 'Umpire Conscience' in Book III is a clear indicator of his debt to Milton.

As is well-known, Milton had seriously thought of taking up one of the national themes, the Arthurian legend, but that was before the Civil War. Though he discarded the historical subject in favour of a theological one—and the elect nation yielded place to an emphasis on the salvation of individuals—the latter gets redefined and reinvented in historical and political terms. Tragedy was transformed to epic, but elements of tragedy remained. It has been said that the 'Fall' is a more democratic subject than the Arthurian legend. It is possible that his decision to shift to the more democratic subject of the 'Fall of Man' was determined by his view of the political and social well-being of a nation which had just begun to dominate and colonize the New World, and the rest of the pagan world, but was threatened by a misguided and corrupt Church and monarchic government that had begun to falter and ran the risk of losing that chance. But the 'Fall of Man' was as much a theological as it was a political concern in need of timely intervention. Thus, one can see how the vision of the expanding colonies that comes flooding in cataloged form in Book XI is a vision of the extent of the risk involved in Church misgovernment. Certainly, the form of the jeremiad that *Paradise Lost* often takes is a political exhortation, a form of surrogate patriotism that Radhanath tries to use as a model. In fact, he almost wholly models his epic along the lines that *Paradise Lost* would have suggested to him. One does not expect him to appreciate Milton's borrowings from the radical underground, but surely in broad terms his theodicy is as conformist as Milton's was to the broad tenets of Puritanism.

In this sense, Madhusudan Dutt's use of the Miltonic model is problematic. His chief aesthetic concerns are personal rather than 'national' or 'public'. It is his sense of the personal, romantic, and egoistic rebellion that provides the telos of his epic grandeur, rather than a rebellion for power as it unfolds in Milton's epic. The use of

Satan as a metaphor for a romantic rebel of this kind is, of course, a post-Blakean invention. In keeping with the discourse of freedom against servitude, Milton uses the unrhymed verse as he unambiguously spells out in his prefatory note under the caption 'The Verse'. Madhusudan Dutt's use of *amitrakshar chhanda* (unrhymed) is predicated on his attempt to match Satan's rhetoric on freedom. That this rhetoric was shown to be fallacious by Milton was of course not apparent to Madhusudan Dutt, drunk on the Byronic punch. Thus, two of his main borrowings are based on unconscious misreading—the unrhymed heroic verse and the character of the chief antagonist cast as a hero.

Progress, not so Fair

Radhanath was excited by the new form that Madhusudan Dutt made available to him. Having been familiar with the debate about the use of the new meter in Bangla, he not only used the meter for his Odia *kavya*, but because of his familiarity with Milton's epic, he used many aspects of *Paradise Lost* that Madhusudan Dutt had not. Anticipating the controversy that the use of the unconventional meter might cause in Odisha literary circles once the unfinished epic appeared in book form, he requested Madhusudan Rao, a highly respected Odia intellectual of his generation (himself of Marhatta descent, and a major Brahmo adherent and proponent in Odisha) to write a prefatory note as a shield against likely criticism. Radhanath Ray, by now beleaguered from several controversies, one of them being around his kind of poetry *v.* Upendra Bahuja's poetry, was in no mood to face another. We may need to digress a bit and dwell on Madhusudan Rao's note.

In his prefatory note, Rao praises the high-seriousness of the theme, greets *Mahayatra* as the first epic of *Utkal Sahitya*, and draws a parallel between the European and Sanskrit epic-traditions. He commends the epic for its unity of action, the sublimity of its theme around the action of a godly man, and the nobility of his character, thus establishing the befitting role of the hero Yudhishthira. He goes on to say quite understandably, 'Some of the descriptions of the action in the epic are not befitting the epic mode, especially of Milton's, and some are against modern scientific beliefs. Some of the descriptions may not be in keeping with modern liberal belief.'[10] He is reluctant to give any credit to Radhanath Ray for his use of the *amitrakshar chhanda* for it is the meter pioneered by Michael Madhusudan Dutt. However, he points out how no other Odia poet has succeeded in using the same. In one of his remarks about the controversial verse form, Radhanath would say, 'Some say that unrhymed verse is essential for expressing sublimity. They give the example of Milton to reinforce their argument. I do not understand the validity of this argument. Dante is greater than Milton, whereas Dante had composed his epic in rhymed meter. My humble submission is that greatness is determined by ability not meter.'[11] These comments show the extent to which the Odia poet was conscious of his indebtedness to Milton.

Beyond the few formal and surface parallels between the two epics, as one goes along, one notices the ever-increasing gap between the substantive uses to which Madhusudan Dutt and Radhanath put Milton, begins to widen.[12] The borrowings can be seen to have been undertaken under dissimilar ideological motivations. The extent of the controversy that arose around *Meghnadbadh* cannot be underestimated, though only the use of unrhymed verse is what is often taken as the chief irritant, it is the irreverence shown to the Hindu icons such as Rama and Lakshmana that drew the ire of the epic's immediate audience. Michael Madhusudan Dutt's chief motive was not only to justify his hasty decision to convert by showing the Hindu theodicy in as poor light as someone like Macaulay would have him, but also to follow the dominant romantic ideology of freedom and nonconformist rebellion. In Odisha, the reverberations continued to be heard.

As late as 1905, Fakir Mohan published a long piece on the subject in the Odia periodical *Utkal Sahitya*.[13] While recognizing the greatness of the Bengali poet, Fakir Mohan is critical of the travesty that Madhusudan Dutt had made of the great Hindu epic, and thereby hurting the cause of the Indians:

But the epic which we venerate as our scripture, and consider depiction of episodes therein as incontrovertible truth; and the portraits of which are inscribed on the Hindu heart as if engraved in stone, if those descriptions and portraitures are twisted and caricatured, the Hindu heart is justified in feeling hurt. If the Hindu has anything to feel proud of, they are the *Vedas*, *Mahabharata* and *Ramayana*. Through civil wars and diverse atrocities the Hindu has lost all; but no one can touch the Hindu's proudest monuments. The foundation of this pride lies in the Hindu heart. Any attempt to distort these icons will naturally hurt the Hindu heart. That is why we have said all these things about *Meghnadbadhbadh*.[14]

Fakir Mohan's views may have been shared by other Odia writers, for none of them attempted to cast the well-known antagonists from Hindu mythologies into tragic figures; but nonetheless Madhusudan Dutt's idea of rewriting existing Hindu texts appealed to many Odia poets, including Radhanath Ray himself, Gangadhar Meher and Chintamani Mohanty—their titles echoing that of *Meghnadbadh*.[15] It is possible that the Romantic poet-critics from Blake onward took possession of most of the writers of Madhusudan Dutt's generation, and especially their admiration of Milton's portrayal of Satan. Unsurprisingly, it is not merely the freedom of the unrhymed blank verse of iambic pentameter that Milton taught Madhusudan Dutt, but mediated by the Romantics, Satan was turned into an unambiguous heroic character. Even the figure of the Byronic hero now appealed to the imagination of the English educated Bengali. 'I am reading Tom Moore's Life of my favourite Byron. . . .' Also, he boasts, 'I must tell you, my dear fellow, that though, as a jolly Christian youth, I don't care a pin's head for Hinduism, I love the grand mythology of our ancestors . . .' or 'It is my ambition to engraft the exquisite graces of the Greek mythology on our own . . . I mean to give free scope to my inventing powers . . . and borrow as little as I can from Valmiki. . .' or 'the subject is truly heroic: only the Monkeys spoil the joke—but I shall look to them'.[16]

As against this, Radhanath Ray's erudition is less obviously anglophilic, if at all, and his claims more modest. It is true, though, that he began by recasting many of the Greek and Latin myths on to Odisha's cultural ethos. Bhudev, whom Chatterjee calls 'the most brilliant rationalist defender of "orthodox" tradition',[17] had come to know Radhanath during his visits to Odisha in his official capacity as the inspector of schools. During these years Bhudev commended Radhanath's learning more than once, He 'rejoiced to find that [Radhanath] was as well a Sanskrit as an English scholar. . .'.[18] In 1882, Bhudev, who was a childhood friend of Madhusudan Dutt, wrote to Radhanath, '. . . it does not seem to me that your reading of the "Gita" and the "Bhagabat" have as yet succeeded in bringing you out of the slough and Jewish thoughts imbibed through your English readings. . .'.[19] One does not know what in Radhanath Ray's letter had provoked such an extreme remark from Bhudev. What is obvious is the contempt with which Bhudev viewed the ideological underpinning of English education nearly half a century after Macaulay's 'Minute', a supreme example of intellectual independence that many were striving to achieve in mid-nineteenth century colonial India. The reference to 'Jewish thoughts' could be more in the nature of a metaphor or euphemism for non-indigenous thought than a racist sneer.

Radhanath was also friendly with many other Bengali intellectuals of his time, and his biographer has reproduced his correspondence with, apart from Bhudev, R.C. Dutt, Nabinchandra Sen, Chandranath Basu, and Akhilchandra Pal, to name a few.[20]

Writing History and Righting History

I shall now go on to discuss certain ideological issues around indigenous and imbibed modernity, especially questions of vernacular or metropolitan historiography. I would also like to examine how writers of vernacular history unconsciously negotiated Macaulay's anxiety about inculcating false history in the learned natives. It is time to return now to Macaulay. In the same document I have already referred to, his Minute on India, Macaulay derides existing traditional practices of history writing thus:

and whether, when we can patronise sound Philosophy and true History, we shall countenance, at the public expense, medical doctrines, which would disgrace an English farrier,—Astronomy, which would move laughter in girls at an English boarding school—*History, abounding with kings thirty feet high, and reigns thirty thousand years long*—and Geography, made up of seas of treacle and seas of butter.[21]

Obviously, these absurd tall tales that Macaulay so scornfully alludes to are part of *Puranic* histories (to be called *Pauranic Mithya* or *Bhaktik Mithya* by Nilakantha Das in the 1950s).[22] In fact, they are part of any pre-modern cultural history, and are not necessarily typical of Hindu mythology. One wonders whether Macaulay, in his hurry to denounce that practice as he may well have seen in Mrityunjay Vidyalankar's *Rajabali*, written under the aegis of Fort William College as part of the 1813 project, had forgotten that even Christian mythological histories are not free from such exaggerations, a tradition that Milton himself follows.

Radhanath Ray, who had been following the *Navyasavya* Bengali writings regularly through the Bengali periodical press and books, may have been familiar with many of these discursive histories. 'We Must Have a History' is the clarion call that Bankimchandra Chattopadhyay had given to fellow Bengali intellectuals.[23] Radhanath joins the race in a novel way which is not so novel if one thinks of his model, Milton.[24] The Miltonic technique he follows is one of prolepsis that involved the introduction of a situation where a less gifted person is shown the future by a celestial being through a magical device. In *Paradise Lost*, Book XI, Michael commands Adam:

Ascend
This hill . . .
So both ascend
In the visions of god: it was a hill
Of Paradise the highest, from whose top
The hemisphere of earth in clearest ken
Stretched out to amplest reach of prospect lay . . .[25]

Instead of immediately revealing to Adam the mythical future, Milton's narratorial voice intervenes and reminds the reader of the future history of Mankind that the Tempter had shown to the 'Second Adam' from another but not dissimilar hill as it is described in Matthew 4 : 8 that in Milton appears thus in Book XI:

Whereon for different cause the tempter set
Our second Adam in the wilderness,
To show him all earth's kingdoms and their glory. . . .

In a long passage that Milton casts in the form of what one might call a prolepsis of the undesirable, he outlines the ignoble sights, 'the earth's kingdoms and their glory./. . .City of old or modern fame, the seat/ Of mightiest empire, from the destined walls/ Of Cambalu . . .,', '. . . and thence/ To Agra and Lahore of great mogul. . .'. Of course, Milton's proleptic history is through mere catalogues of people, places, and empires, and is the synoptic history of the world up to the seventeenth century, with brief descriptions such as 'rich Mexico . . .; yet unspoiled Guiana,' and so on. This is unsurprising. After all, it was during Milton's lifetime that the Company strengthened its hold on India, both before and after the Restoration, even during Oliver Cromwell's time, maybe when Milton was a part of the Commonwealth. In 1657, Cromwell renewed the charter of 1609, and brought about minor changes in the holding of the Company. Around the time that *Paradise Lost* was published, the status of the Company was further enhanced by the restoration of monarchy in England. By a series of acts *c.*1670, Charles II provisioned it with the rights to autonomous territorial acquisitions to mint money, to command fortresses and troops and form alliances, to make war and peace, and to exercise both civil and criminal jurisdiction over the acquired areas. Later, the Company established a trading post in Canton (Guangzhou), China, to trade tea for silver. But that was after Milton's time. Soon after the vision of empires, Michael subjected Adam to another kind of sight, the mythographic history—by removing the divine film: this time it revealed the slaying of Abel by Cain; the coming of death to Mankind, the Flood and finally the Coming of Christ.

This kind of proleptic vision must have inspired Radhanath while he composed *Mahayatra*, as may be seen in the following description in the unfinished epic. After conducting the Pandavas and their wife Draupadi along with *swana-rupi* (dog-incarnate) Dharma on a tour of the flora and fauna of Utkal, Radhanath Ray's Agni asks:

> If you so wish, come with me Kurumani
> you will see with amusement from this hill-top
> the Kali-avatar with the help of my divine vision
> . . . only your eyes can withstand
> such a divine effulgence, come in haste.[26]

Counterfactual History

This narrative manoeuvre in a way also helped Radhanath execute Bhudev's advice. For, in his memoir, he speaks of the many visits of Bhudev to Odisha, and how Radhanath Ray would usually be asked by him to accompany him and engage in discussion and debate about several literary and intellectual issues. It is possible that they also discussed history. The incident that is especially relevant here is that of the journey they undertook together to Balasore from Cuttack in 1879. Radhanath had given Bhudev a *kavya* composed in Bangla by him, an imitation of Madhusudan Dutt's 'Birangana'. After going through it carefully, Bhudev commented, 'I am pleased to read your work, and I shall get it published in *Education Gazette*; but I hope you will write of new things. You have tried to portray Subhadra's character. But you will not be able to surpass Vyasa's portrayal even if you try hundreds of times. You must attempt new things.'[27] Radhanath expressed his inability to do so because he believed, he did not have the talent for it. But of course he heeded Bhudev's advice about using the beautiful landscape of Odisha.

More to the point is what followed this conversation. The two were passing by a certain territory known as Drapana Rajya, the Raja of which served the emperor of the ancient lineage of a Ganga Emperor of Utkal, and about which legends thrived. Bhudev asked Radhanath about the significance of the name, Drapana Rajya. On hearing the legend about the disappearance of a child in a real lake (of a certain traveller passing by), Bhudev immediately retold the story giving it a twist of his own. Radhanath later admitted that he learnt his lesson from this about inventing his own tales without repeating the story as it was handed down to him. This, coming as it does from the author of *Swapnalabdha Bharatvarsher Itihasa*, gives some idea of Bhudev's much derided historiographical methods. P.K. Datta, in a more sympathetic essay, calls this mode of history-writing 'a counterfactual history'.[28]

Let us take a closer look at Radhanath Ray's construction, reconstruction, and fusion of the mythical and real histories in his Miltonic epic. He begins by outlining the coming of *Kali*, where he follows the morality tradition, especially mediated by Milton, personifying Hindu virtues and vices almost along the lines that Milton does—*dharma, satya, nyaya,* as well as *kama, krodha, lobha, moha,* and so on. These personifications of good and evil forces show the puritanical strain in Radhanath which he had imbibed through contacts with reformist zealot Brahmos, and he tries to represent the personified versions of the abstract qualities through befitting body language. He seems to be trying and matching here Milton's puritanical concerns as can be seen through Milton's roll call of the fallen angels, the would-be pagan gods—Sin and Death— not to speak of Moloch, Mammon, Belial and others. Radhanath did not have to adjust and invent too much as he moved from Milton's model of the 'Fall of Man' to his theme of the 'Fall of the Arya descendants of Yudhishthira'.[29] He follows up the detailed chronicling of the arrival of *Kaliyuga* on Bharatabarsha with the portrayal of Buddhism as a version of *dharma*, since brahmans were corrupted by *Kali*, reversing the views of Tarinicharan Chattopadhyay's version about Buddha being the great enemy of Hinduism. Finally, Radhanath devotes two whole *sarga*s or Books to the pet subject of most vernacular histories—the perceived turning point in Indian history, the last Hindu ruler and the advent of foreign rule. However, here Radhanath follows Tarinicharan Chattopadhyay's rather than Mrityunjay Vidyalankar's portrayal of Prithviraj Chauhan as a real hero, with traces of Aryan virtues. As Kaviraj argues, Rajput history is appropriated for Bengal/Bharatabarsha.[30] His exhortation of his diffident army smacks of the rabble-rousing war cry that Satan had used to rouse his army.

Like Bankimchandra Chattopadhyay before him, Radhanath had his quarrel with British writing on India.[31] Like him, both Radhanath and Fakir Mohan suddenly began to project the glorious history of Rajputs as if it was their own. Unlike in the case of Bankimchandra Chattopadhyay's narratives and the discursive writing of his contemporary Tarinicharan Chattopadhyay—located in contemporary

Bengal—it is not very difficult for Radhanath Ray to establish a kinship with the distant Rajputs in his imaginative history. His self-identification with the Aryas does the trick. Both Buddha and Prithviraj Chauhan are the *aryasutas* (descendants), the progeny of Dharmaraj Yudhishthira.

Unsurprisingly, Radhanath also reveals his dual identity, sometimes identifying his subject as 'Odia' and at other times as 'Indian' (*bharatavasi*), similar to what is said about Bankimchandra Chattopadhyay's ambivalent nationalism, Bengali, and *bharata-varshya*. In either capacity, both Bankimchandra Chattopadhyay and Radhanath—like perhaps many others of their generation—name the foreign ruler and aggressor as the *yavan*. This took the form of controversies, in the case of Radhanath, following his publication of *Mahayatra*.

Like Milton's stance on regicide, which almost cost him his freedom, had Andrew Marvell not intervened, and just as Bankimchandra Chattopadhyay's writing had been perceived to be anti-British, and he had to revise his lines in *Anandamath* when it appeared in book form (it had still resulted in a transfer for him), Radhanath Ray ran the risk of losing his job because he had used the term *yavan* to criticize 'foreign' invaders of India. This was reported to the British officials by a former friend and ally, now estranged. Radhanath destroyed his manuscripts. But there is much speculation and less evidence in these claims. Radhanath Ray faced another problem though, in that most Odia elites considered themselves doubly colonized, both by the British and Bengalis. His plight can be guessed from the fact that he first wrote his poems in Bangla before switching over to Odia. After he gained some prominence and official position of power, Radhanath was often accused of aligning with Bengalis and working in their interests. He was not helped by Balasore's proximity to Bengali-speaking territories. He had to prove his allegiance to Odisha and craved for recognition among the Bengali elite, but could not go against the British for fear of losing his job. His entire oeuvre has to be seen in this context. This certainly explains Radhanath Ray's overabundant use of Odisha's topography. As advised by Bhudev, he frequently used similes drawn from Odisha's flora and fauna. The use of geography and topography can also be seen as a strategy for identity construction, like history. But for Radhanath it was also the case of having to prove his loyalty to Odisha. Thus, it is not merely Bhudev's visionary history that Radhanath finds useful, but also his advice to use the rich landscape of Odisha for the setting of his plots.

In many ways he uses Bhudev's methods, fusing them as he does in his Miltonic, and partly magical *mahakavya*, *Mahayatra* with Mrityunjay Vidyalankar's *Rajabali*. At least the broad temporal schema in *Mahayatra* resembles that of his minus the intricate details, e.g. the cycle of *yugas*, 'For the first 3,044 years of *Kaliyuga*, the prevailing era (*saka*) was that of King Yudhistira. The next 135 years comprised the era of King Vikramaditya. These two eras are now past'.[32] *Treta* is followed by *Dwapara*, which in turn is followed by *Kali*. Radhanath Ray's Agni refers to *Treta* (*sarga* I). He draws his theory from Mrityunjay Vidyalankar that it was because of the failing of the brahmans that the Indian kings strayed from the path of dharma and, thus, lost the blessing of god. Since the brahmans had failed in their duty to guide their kings along the right path of dharma, they brought about the divine wrath which ended the rule of the Hindu kings and established the rule of the *yavans*. Radhanath did not waste any time in seeing this as being similar to the 'Fall of Man'. Though in later histories the role of divine intervention in history became less credible, the story of the 'Fall' acquires in the modern writings, the form of a general decay of society and polity.[33] But Radhanath Ray, while using the latter version in his *Mahayatra*, retains the former as well.

Vernacular History

Much has been written about the role played by the colonial forms of history-writing in the shaping and modernization of indigenous traditions. Whereas various kinds of vernacular history writing have been finely differentiated and seen in nuanced ways, European history-writing is homogenized under the rubric 'modern academic practice of Western historiography',[34] marked by evidence and reasoning, exactly as Macaulay would have us believe in contradistinction to the tradition of the tall or Puranic tales masquerading as history. That even Europe had traditions of non-discursive forms of historiography—the magical-mythical—and that not an insignificant part of European history is constructed from epics, plays, and myths, has not been taken into account in many of the recent studies in historiography.[35] Whether or not such histories have been taken seriously by European historians is debatable. But their reception at the hands of the Indian intelligentsia has been far from whole-hearted. Even while bemoaning the absence of the tradition of history-writing in India, the European histories of India were thought to be suspect by the native intellectuals and held in deep distrust which is one reason why Bankimchandra Chattopadhyay called British writing on India, '*mahapap*'.[36] It is said that W.W. Hunter's history of Odisha was constructed out of stray conversations with people using local, oral narratives, a method that fellow Englishman, Beames was highly critical of. About Hunter's methodology, John Beames said that:

About this time we received a visit from that vivacious but not very accurate writer, Dr. WW Hunter . . . He was then a small, lean, hatchet-faced man with a newspaper-correspondent's gift of facile, flashy writing, and a passion for collecting facts and figures of which he made fearful and wonderful use afterwards. The light-hearted subalterns of the regiment at Cuttack had amused themselves by inventing for his benefit wonderful yearns, all of which he duly entered in his note-book and reproduced in his book on Odisha. . . . Hunter's Odisha in two volumes was the result of his visit. It . . . [contained] many inaccuracies.[37]

No wonder, Odia intellectuals too made fun of such history-writing. In his *Mahayatra*, if not through his discursive writing, Radhanath imaginatively critiques Western forms of writing history, as can be seen in his depiction of what '*mithya*' in *Kaliyuga* will do to the fallen Bharatabarsha. 'Some traveller from a distant land would/describe how he had seen a bird diving from above to pick up three from a herd of hippopotamus in Manosorovar.'[38] The most significant of all these lies that Radhanath enumerates is the one about someone claiming to have seen 'in Kashmir men with huge ears so huge that they would sleep on one ear and use the other to wrap themselves up'. Anyone familiar with Hunter's work would recognize this piece to be from his *Odisha*, where he describes the reason behind the Raja of Parikud's reluctance to fight for the British army against the Maratha warriors. Hunter's could well be the tall tale made up by the subalterns from the Cuttack garrison, which he reproduces as a fact. No wonder, Fakir Mohan was equally suspicious of British writing on India. Among several broadsides on British historians in his novels and discursive writing, one finds the following observation while the narratorial voice reports what he had purportedly heard by way of the 'history' of the famous pond Asuradighi in *Chha Mana Atha Guntha*. This fantastic story was told to him by the ninety-five year old weaver Ekadushia about the *rakshasas* who had dug the pond. Suddenly, Fakir Mohan burst into a diatribe against British historiography, when the narrator says, 'Beware English-educated babus! Do not laugh at the history of our Ekadushia, the weaver! Else, half of your knowledge derived from the writings of Todd and Marshman will evaporate!'[39] More to our context, Milton's fragmentary construction of colonial history in his poetry has been critiqued by scholars like B. Rajan.[40] In any case, as we have seen, Milton provides Radhanath Ray a form of history-writing that fitted into the narrative economy of indigenous practices. Speaking of these vernacular histories, Chatterjee writes: 'By indulging in the fabulous and the enchanted, they mock the scientific rationality that is the ideology of the academic historian. They are often given voice to identities and aspirations that find no place within the institutional structures of professional history writing' (which he characterizes as European). While one easily agrees with the first part of Chatterjee's formulation, the point he makes about 'structures of professional history writing', requires a more nuanced formulation.[41] The way Radhanath appropriates Milton, and the way he—along with the other 'learned natives'—critiques the history written by the Europeans as has already been seen in the foregoing discussion, serves a warning to the strict binary between the European-modern and Indian-*Puranic* forms of history-writing. At least in the case of learned natives like Bhudev, Radhanath and Fakir Mohan, history writing was more of the kind Milton had foreshadowed through his epic rather than those of his nineteenth-century advocate Macaulay had anticipated through his colonial vision. Thus, just as Macaulay was suspicious of 'History, abounding with kings thirty feet high, and reigns thirty thousand years long—and Geography, made up of seas of treacle and seas of butter', so the learned natives were suspicious of their Todds, Marshmans, and Hunters. The great irony in Radhanath Ray's enterprise is revealed through the consequences of his version of the history of the Aryas and Bharat. For, it is one thing to be writing a vernacular history as a counter discourse and critiquing metropolitan history and quite another to offer a perspective that would be equally acceptable to the 'home' audience. A 'writing back' to the metropolitan other is also a 'writing to' a home audience, and the 'learned natives' among whom are a heterogeneous category with internal differences of opinion. For example, the Brahmos who were generally against the Hindu caste-system were already a divided lot with internecine squabbles.[42] At this point, the trajectory of my argument swerves radically in order to be able to address the backlash of Radhanath Ray's experiment in rewriting 'Arya history', a rewriting involving diverse caste and communal issues that ruffle the feathers of orthodox Hindus, especially brahmans. In the following section, I shall discuss the repercussions of Radhanath Ray's experiment.

II

Radhanath Ray's Great Rite of Passage and the Big Debate

That his literary and professional careers (he was inspector of schools besides being a poet) not only crisscrossed, but the controversies in the two spheres too overlapped and influenced his reputation both as administrator and poet, are well-known facts of Odia literary-cultural history. Not all these controversies were caused by his literary publications and not all had to do with his public life as an inspector of schools. Some arose out of seemingly small minded personal quarrels over petty matters in cultural politics, and some others, as Natabar Samantaray has shown,[43] sprang from his alleged manipulation of textbook publication and prescription in syllabi leading to profits from the burgeoning print capitalism. All these impacted his reputation as a poet too. The spurt in readership is a noticeable feature of the late nineteenth-century literary culture of Odisha, when the circulation figures of periodicals and newspapers were astoundingly high. Students familiar with English literary history might recall a parallel eighteenth-century London, during which scurrilous writing, satires and invectives had a field day. The infamous controversy over the seventeenth century iconic poet Upendra Bhanja, between the two little magazines, *Indradhanu* (a pro-Upendra Bhanja organ, which attacked Radhanath Ray) and *Bijuli* (which attacked Upendra Bhanja; allegedly with the tacit support of Radhanath), is a case in point.[44] Since Radhanath was already a well-known literary and public figure, many of these petty controversies spilled over to the 'literary' arena too. A few other controversies remained confined to personal attacks on Radhanath Ray's stinginess and his Bengali (non-Odia) identity. The replication of the eighteenth-century English literary culture can be seen in invective-laden pieces like 'Bakacharita' and 'Odisha's Grief'.[45]

There were a few other private and public quarrels related to the patronage of the Maharaja of Mayurbhanj that led to 'literary' controversies involving Radhanath. The obvious example is the state patronage of *Utkalprabha* leading to accusation of Radhanath Ray's indirect role in the articles and poetry that appeared in it.[46] In fact, even during the time that the *sargas* of *Mahayatra* were being serialized in *Utkalprabha* (1892–3), readers objected to many of these aspects. One of the first ones took off from the then current image of Radhanath as a self-serving, exploitative official who was warming up to his patrons or the powers that be. So, on 25 May 1893, an anonymous writer, signing as 'An Odia' complained in *Baleswar Sambad Bahika* that *Mahayatra*, while being serialized in *Utkalprabha* was monopolized by Radhanath's epic, that the surge of the work continued unabated and had displaced all other writers' works. These were countered by a few Radhanath supporters in *Sambalpur Hiteisini*. But not all of this was the result of Radhanath's personal predilections. Maybe they were, but these seem to have acted merely as a tinder that ignited when it was caught in the middle of several inflammatory sociological circumstances as we shall examine below.

Radhanath's Agni Pariksha

In the context already, it is not surprising that when his ambitious but unfinished epic *Mahayatra* was serialized in *Utkalprabha* in the early 1890s and eventually published in book form in 1896 under the patronage of the Rani of Kanika, it created quite a stir among its readers. Against the backdrop of the endless bickering, when *Mahayatra* was published, the reception was equally divided with the anti-Radhanath's lobby baying for his blood. The author, undoubtedly, was apprehensive of the response of his many detractor-readers, and was not entirely unwary of the possibility that questions would be raised regarding the novelty of his subject, and the epic's meter and style. Accordingly, he had tried to preempt further objections by readers of the epic by not only supplying footnotes, but also as has already been mentioned by obtaining a prefatory defence and explanatory note from the then intellectual heavyweight, Madhusudan Rao.[47] Several laudatory reviews and announcements were also stage-managed. In spite of all precautions, no sooner had the book appeared than attempts to undermine the achievement of the work got underway. In spite of Madhusudan Rao's apologia on Radhanath's use of the unorthodox meter, when the controversy broke out post-1896, the subject was discussed threadbare by a few critics; an important one being the pseudonymous 'Sri Go', who carried on with the old feud. In the first issue of the second phase of *Indradhanu*, in 1897, he critiques Radhanath's use of the Miltonic meter that the latter had borrowed from Michael Madhusudan Dutt's experiment. In doing so, Sri Go goes to great lengths in order to foreground Milton's unparalleled stature as a poet (almost vindicating Macaulay's esteem of the English poet). He also expends a lot of critical energy in justifying the use of the meter to add poetic value and effect of the sublime. Thus, though Radhanath Ray's fears were not entirely unfounded, he must have been taken aback by the vehemence of the controversy that followed the publication of his unfinished epic. Perhaps, he had not quite anticipated the extreme hostility in the responses in respect of the issue of caste and religion.

In Bengal, too, not everyone gave Michael Madhusudan Dutt's *Meghnadbadh Kavya* unqualified praise. Though generally favourable, there were a few significant murmurings in the Bangla periodical press. A couple of voices of disapproval were to come decades later. The young Tagore (1861–1941), born the very year in which *Meghnadbadh Kavya* appeared, thought that the work failed, that it was no epic at all. In *mahakavyas*, he wrote, 'we want to see a grand personage; we want to see grand feats accomplished by that grand personage'. There was nothing superhuman about the characters, not even in the protagonist Meghnad himself; certainly not in Ravana, Rama or Lakshmana. 'Which of the characters created by [Michael Madhusudan] Dutt who inhabits the world of our imagination?'[48] The answer Tagore gives to his own rhetorical question is 'none. . . . I have not analysed *The Slaying of Meghanad* bit by bit. . . . I found it had no breath of life. I found it was no mahakavya at all.' Of course, working in the same tradition, Tagore was to rewrite characters from the great Indian epics. His radical representation of Chitrangada in his *gitinatya* and *nrityanatika*, *Chitra* and *Chitrangada* is subversive without being aggressively so, as we shall see in a subsequent chapter. The next significant criticism comes from Pramatha Chaudhuri (1868–1946), editor of *Sabuja Patra*, who was critical of *Meghnadbadh Kavya* for being 'foreign, too foreign'. 'It was not of this land . . . and therefore does not smell right—doesn't smell at all. . . .'[49] However, the question of not treating poetry as history was discussed at length as part of an enormous controversy that arose following the publication of Nabinchandra Sen's epic poem *Palasir Yuddhya* (1875). Tagore too commented on the history version of *Sirajaddoula* by Akshaykumar Maitreya (1897).[50]

Though Radhanath was no iconoclast of Michael Madhusudan Dutt's kind, his attack on orthodox Brahminism was enough to ruffle the feathers of conservative Odia readers. Bengali readers were by and large no stranger to the attacks on Hinduism since the time of Rammohun Roy. The objectionable part to which a section in the Odia reading public took strong exception occurred in the fifth *sarga* (as has been mentioned while discussing Radhanath Ray's borrowings from Milton, especially the ventriloquizing through Agni his own version of the history of the Aryas). After Agni's eloquent introduction to the arrival of *Kali*, Yudhishthira gets curious, and asks the Fire God, 'Since you are the witness to past, present and future, tell me how will such calamity befall Bharat? Will the progeny of the Arya race surrender to the foreigner all the natural wealth of this ['*sujala, suphala, shashya shyama*'] land? How will this come about?'. Here, Radhanath Ray's use of the phrase, '*sujala, suphala, shashya shyamala*' from Bankimchandra Chattopadhyay shows not only the popularity of the slogan well before the Swadeshi movement, but also how the learned natives had imbibed the European nationalist discourse, turning the epic into a contemporary national allegory. Agni responds by drawing Yudhishthira's attention to the way the brahmans will take over the future of the Aryas, and bring in for self-aggrandizement a hierarchy in the form of exploitative and divisive caste system. These brahmans will break the Arya unity by creating hundreds of castes and subcastes. Agni replies to Yudhishthira's query by squarely blaming the brahmans, who will then give up their celibacy and fall in the trap of greed-avarice—they will serve ignorance. The Twice-Born will fall into slothfulness and indulge in *shath karma* and *shastha karma*. They will avoid principles of meditation, self-control and in order to maintain their dominance and power, they will break the unity of the Arya race, and hundreds of subcastes. 'Thus creating dissention among men . . . they will introduce pollution by touch. Thus creating civil discord, the Arya race will disintegrate. . . .'[51] This protracted diatribe against brahmans continues for over a hundred lines of resonant blank verse.

After Agni's detailed dystopic portrayal of the 'misdeeds' of the brahmans which result in the decline of the Arya race, Yudhishthira asks, 'Will no one come to the rescue of the Aryas from such misdeeds of the Brahmans?', Agni presents a glorious future. As we have seen, the proleptic historical part dealt with the theme of the arrival of the Buddha to dispel the 'darkness of Kali' and the subsequent dying out of the light of dharma due to the arrival of the blindly selfish *dwija* (i.e. the brahmans). Loosely translated, these lines might read as follows:

Then said Agni, 'this land would
Give birth only to charcoal
Many centuries afterwards
from the same mine will emerge
a priceless gem of diamond
whose rays will brighten . . .

But, this effulgence would be short-lived as Kali will act through the brahmanical dispensation and usher in an era where Kali-induced vices will result in slothfulness and depravation to the extent that the Aryas would invite the *yavans* to destroy temples and rule over Bharatabarsha.

The Backlash

One of the first letters to the editor on the subject appeared in *Sambalpur Hiteisini*, and the author of the critical piece was one Madhusudan Mishra. Though he complained of several other issues, the main target in his polemic were the inaccuracies in the history that Radhanath had dealt with. Madhusudan Mishra, commenting on the relevant passages, says, 'On hearing from Agni these words of praise about the emergence of Buddhism, did the expression on Yudhistir's visage not turn sour recalling [Yudhishthira's] own role in the history?'[52] Obviously, the critic confuses between the historical section of a work of literature and history. His comments here show how the 'residual' ideology of traditional belief-system that treated the scriptures as historically true was still evident in the 1890s, in spite of the advent of modernity. The writer further complains that the 'elements of words, versification, aesthetic beauty, surpass our expectations. But certain portions are extremely polluted because of which we are forced to deny any poetic value to *Mahayatra*.' Another reader complained of the way 'the poet's anger is directed towards the decadent modern Brahmans'.[53]

After quoting several examples from Radhanath Ray's poem, one 'Ni/Shri' (an obvious pseudonym) in *Utkal Dipika* said, 'like these, one comes across many other instances of hostility towards Hinduism and anti-Brahminical tirades at many places in the poem'. Then he questions the veracity of Agni's words, 'Did Agni actually say this? It does not look like being true since our hoary sages have said in the *Purana* and *Samhita* etc. that Agni is a lover of Brahmans and the *Vedas*.'[54] He also questions, 'whether sages such as Harith and Yajnnabalka who spoke of castes came after the Buddha. Also there is ample evidence of the Varnashrama in *puranas* such as the *Mahabharata*; did these not precede the Buddha?' It is surprising that the proleptic vision presented by Radhanath Ray appeared to be an invention on the part of the poet even to the 'pandits'. The sources of Radhanath were from the revered pantheon of the *Panchasakha*.[55]

The barrage of attacks continued and though a few defences appeared in the same periodical, *Hiteisini*, their numbers were far less than the number of hostile responses. What the poet may not have anticipated was the caste-angle in the controversy that ensued. Subsequently, the intensity of this controversy waned but never 'died down'. When Radhanath Ray's son-in-law Durgacharan Ray wrote the biography *Radhanath Jibani* in 1941, he made it a point to highlight instances of the former's positive attitude towards brahmans in his personal life.[56] However, controversies continued to dog Radhanath even in his afterlife, if anything, more vigorously in scholarly circles of Odisha almost a century later. By then, the frames of reference had shifted from caste and religion-based questions to why Radhanath either refused to complete the epic, or why and whether he destroyed the unpublished manuscripts of the epic, and also whether the published portions had already created problems with the then censorious British administration. And further, if he was implicitly against the British or against the Muslims or Moghuls while attacking the *yavans*.[57] I am not concerned immediately with this latter-day controversy; and shall continue to focus on the controversies during Radhanath Ray's own time, beginning with the immediate aftermath of its phase-wise publication in 1892. The arguments then revolved around the 'historical' inaccuracies in the long poem, when the contentious issues revolved either on caste-related questions, or on the taking over of the Buddha into the Hindu-Arya fold in the context of the *Mahabharata*. Why does a poem, purportedly a modern reinvention of the *Mahabharata* and that is apparently and self-consciously experimenting in a new form, get mired in controversies and issues of caste and religion?

In what follows, I shall venture to offer reasons as to why and how the poem was caught in the crossfire of certain debates and what were their contexts. A close analysis of the first wave of the controversy with a dominant hostile reception will indicate that a few issues had got mixed up. The question of caste is certainly one of them, with the brahman scholars, especially from Puri, taking offence. The second issue affected orthodox Hindus on account of the dubious appropriation of Buddha into the fold of Arya Hinduism. But both indubitably emanate from the by now fashionable trend of history-writing, archiving the past.

III

The Context of Reception

The portions that offended a large section of the reading public had already been serialized in two periodicals as noted earlier. Biswanath Kar had even quoted some of these brahman-baiting lines earlier. But very few seem to have then questioned Radhanath Ray's depiction of depraved Brahmanism. But all hell broke loose when the same portions appeared in the unfinished book form.

Reformation Movements and the Question of Caste in Odisha

As already discussed, the strong reforms carried out in Bengal from the time of Rammohun Roy were accompanied by and perhaps the consequence of intense Christian missionary activity in Odisha. Each time there was a major conversion, a strong public reaction would erupt. Natabar Samantaray, in his *History of Modern Odia Literature*, has discussed this in some detail with documentary evidence.[58] He has shown how, though the missionary activities started in the first three decades of British occupation of Odisha, the real impact was felt only towards the end of the century. Of the two sets, the Brahmo faith could attract the Hindus more than Christianity because of their seeming indigeneity, though many of their traits had Christian origins. The reaction extended in two different directions— one was that any call for reforms in Hinduism was seen as being pro-Brahmo; second, such reformist zeal was also seen as anti-Brahmanism. This can be discerned in an essay by Krushnaprasad Choudhuri published in an 1897 issue of *Utkal Sahitya* under the editorship of Biswanath Kar, which caused a minor controversy too. In a succession of articles, Krushnaprasad Choudhuri discussed the ill-effects of Brahmanism on Hinduism. In an article titled the 'Revival of Hinduism', he says:

Hinduism declined due to the ill-effect [*sic*] of Buddhism, and at one point almost disappeared from India. But coming under the Wheel of Fortune, Buddhism was expelled from India and with that Hinduism rose again. But this revival of Hinduism became the cause of the decline of Aryadharma. Because, the religion that rose after the disappearance of Buddhism was not pure Hinduism—rather a perverted form of Hinduism, or Brahminism, that is, the religion based on the caste system.[59]

He concludes by saying that he was neither a Brahmo, nor a Christian nor a Muslim. This shows that he was aware of the accusation his proposition might evoke, that he was not truly a Hindu, but one of the other three communities. Elsewhere, he tried to preempt criticism by saying that the educated people of Odisha might suspect him of being a Brahmo and laugh him off.[60] Yet, many expressed unhappiness over the article; one bearing the pseudonym 'Sri Grahak' labelling Choudhury's views as 'mere whimper' and urged him to keep quiet.[61] In his autobiography Fakir Mohan too, describes many aspects of the scenario of conversion and preaching in his time which had made him and Radhanath ponder embracing Brahmoism. Whereas Radhanath held back, Fakir Mohan became a Brahmo.[62] But the Brahmo ideals continued to fascinate Radhanath.

Thus, the discourse of caste had entered the public sphere in a significant way in Odia-speaking tracts by the 1890s, if not before. The Raja of Bamanda, Sudhaldeb, had already started organizing public lectures and debates by eminent speakers and publishing the newly emerged intelligentsia's correspondence on various subjects affecting public life from the late 1880s onward. It is to the credit of Sudhaldeb that he encouraged such debates and controversies, and gave space to critics of *Mahayatra*.[63] One such debate, in keeping with the zeitgeist, was on the caste system following its critique by the Christians and Brahmos. A person using the pseudonym 'Tatwa-anusandhani' shot off a series of questions regarding the caste system, Brahminism, alcoholism, etc., in the periodical *Sambalpur Hiteisini* (5 April 1893) to which a certain 'Shri Sharma' responded with a longish piece, calling it 'Uttaramala' or 'answer series' against the proponents of the abolition of caste system (19 April 1893). By way of answering one of the questions, 'is it possible to be a successful practicing Hindu without following the caste system?', the latter replied in the affirmative, but with the caveat that it would not be wise to, therefore, oppose the caste system. Biswanath Kar, a practising Brahmo, who had already been contributing to the paper, gave a longish but hostile response on 17 May 1893. Shri Sharma was quick to respond and the exchange continued. At the end of a Biswanath Kar rejoinder, the periodical invited opinions on the subject of caste (19 July 1893). Very soon, the periodical *Sambalpur Hiteisini* was flooded with letters offering arguments and counterarguments on the subject. In his several lectures and articles, Biswanath Kar employed a kind of logic and rhetoric that is clearly modelled on the tradition of European rhetoricians; and it could clearly be seen how many of the 'learned natives' had imbibed the methodology of the new disciplines arriving from Europe. Those still trained in indigenous methods failed to grasp such arguments.

James Fergusson[64] said, albeit in a convoluted way and with a racist slant:

Wherever our influence extends, we have destroyed, or at least weakened, the influence of caste which, though, in itself, hardly conducive to virtue, simulates morals so perfectly as to become indispensable for the regulation of Indian society. In its place we have tried to introduce the loose regulations of a form of civilisation the natives can neither understand nor appreciate. Instead of the religion, which governs every action of their life, we have tried to substitute an education, which they cannot assimilate, and which in consequence remains, in almost all instances, a useless and empty platitude.[65]

The opposition to Radhanath Ray's depiction of caste, or for that matter that of Biswanath Kar and of his ilk shows the validity of the statement. Of course, Fergusson was training his gun on Rajendralal Mitra during a running battle that lasted several years as a major specialists' controversy. The same thing which sounds negative and even racist may be turned around by the slight change in perspective, from Fergusson's colonialist stance to our vantage point of the postcolonial.

It helped neither Radhanath Ray's cause, nor that of *Mahayatra* that around the same time (1892–4) a major controversy broke out in the public sphere. In fact, two new little magazines were launched one after the other in order primarily to represent two of the rival camps. This 'battle of the books' is one of the most fascinating stories of early literary modernity in Odisha, and in a way defined literary values for the next few decades. The two organs, *Indradhanu* and *Bijuli*, fought pitched battles for and against Radhanath and Upendra Bhanja backed by their respective powerful lobbies. The Gourishankar-*Indradhanu-Utkal-Dipika* group were pro-Upendra, and therefore opposed Radhanath Ray's work; those associated with *Dipika* used all their might to attack Radhanath Ray's portrayal of the caste system. That the censorious *Bijuli-Hiteisini* combine was guided by the puritanical Brahmo ideal; and their insistence on non-erotic literature in the arts got enmeshed in their other ideal of opposing the caste system, and made them support Radhanath Ray's verse can be easily understood. The latter group (led by Raja Sudhaldeb and Nilamani Bidyaratna) seemed to have been outgunned by the former, and Radhanath had to buy truce by admitting in print that he was a votary of Upendra Bhanja.

A few years later, Biswanath Kar visited Bamanda and spoke at the 'Alochana Sabha' hosted by Sudhaldeb on 4 June 1895, on 'Brahmodharmara Abhyuthan O Desha Kala Patra' (The Rise of Brahmodharma and Time, Place and Personae). In the same meeting, Madhusudan Mishra and Tarka Bachaspati spoke on the subject of the caste system, favouring its continued practice in an obvious broadside on Biswanath Kar.[66] Biswanath Kar had quoted from *Mahayatra* early on during its serialization while arguing for the veracity of his version. This explains the intensity of the caste debates conducted in the *Hiteisini*. But it took some more years before the two parallel controversies (the literary one around *Mahayatra* and the sociological one around the caste system) got entangled. Thus, it is on the body of Radhanath Ray's text *Mahayatra* that the larger debate about Brahminism and the caste system eventually got played out and the two controversies which had begun in two different contexts could no longer be conducted in exclusive domains.

Similarly, the issue of caste gets enmeshed in the fresh interest in Buddhism among Europeans and Indians. This may have been because of the popular attribution of the genesis of Buddhism to its fight against a Brahmanism-induced caste system. Now that the anti-caste movements were gaining ground, Buddhism too was increasingly seen as a way out of caste-based discrimination.

The question that arises here is whether the anti-caste discourses— already a part of the Brahmo mission in Odisha—had by now reached Odia-speaking tracts from elsewhere in India as well, especially that of Jyotirao Phule and the others from western India. Perhaps, they had, since one 'Sri Kavyabinoda' says in the *Hiteisini* that 'discussion has started on this subject of caste system almost everywhere in Bharatabarsha' (28 October 1896). In his piece titled 'The Brahmans of Kaliyuga and Buddhadeb', he gives examples from several writers and intellectuals to justify Radhanath Ray's depiction of the Hindus, including an extended quotation translated from a Bengali book called *Mahapurush Jibani*.[67] He says, 'It is not that only Radhanath Babu has ridiculed the Brahmans and praised the Buddha. People from other places have also done the same thing . . .'; and then goes on to quote from the book about the birth of Buddha and Buddhism, which reads like a prose paraphrase of the 'offensive' lines from *Mahayatra*. Before proceeding further on the subject, yet another disgression may be in order.

The New Knowledges of Power

I have already discussed, albeit briefly, the spurt in interest among British historians on Odisha/India. I need to return to the subject again. By 1890, many European historians, such as Sterling, Hunter, Arnold Toynbee and Beames had already published their works on the history of Odisha, in English.[68] More importantly, they were backed by researchers in the field of archaeology, and the remains of ancient and medieval cultures were being discovered, talked and written about.

Returning to the subject of modernity-induced interest in their own part, we notice how the latter led to the Odia intellectual class's lament and anguish over the dearth in the modern practice of history writing in their own cultures. As is evident from the Macaulay quote, if not from numerous other well-known works of the early British writing on Odisha, the practice of vernacular history-writing had come in for scathing attack. Thus it is that many Odias had started agonizing over the lack of what one might now call positivist histories of Odisha, and began writing their own histories. Of course, a similar situation prevailed in many other territories elsewhere in India.[69] This enthusiasm was spurred by the new 'nationalistic fervour'. Thus, realizing the lack of 'proper' histories in the Odia language, Fakir Mohan, Jagan Mohan Lala and Pyari Mohan Acharya started either translating or writing histories of India and Odisha. Fakir Mohan describes the circumstances under which he embarked on the task of launching one of the earliest secular printing presses in Odisha in 1868. But, as Krishna Charan Behera and Debendra Kumar Dash would say, 'Fakir Mohan had begun his writerly life by first writing "The History of Rajput", an initiative that did not see the light of day due to the lack of printing facilities'.[70] This was the foundation on which he built the edifice of his two-part *Bharatabarshara Itihasa*. The first part was published in 1869, the second in 1870. He covers a wide range from the Puranic times to the then very recent history of the 'Mutiny'. Interestingly enough, he begins by calling to question the dating of the Hindu *yugas* by one 'Bentley Sahib' saying, 'we do not know from where [Bentley Sahib] got the evidence of all this; but his words cannot be trusted more than those in the Purana'.[71] Though Bentley had studied Hindu-Sanskrit astronomical texts meticulously, and seemed to believe in a lot of them (unlike what Macaulay would call 'false astronomy' in his Minute), he also spoke of the practice of the forging of such texts by the native astronomers. Fakir Mohan quietly returns the compliment to Bentley. He also laughs at some of the civilizational claims of Athens, Babylon, China, and Burma. He mentions in passing, by way of making preliminary remarks, many of the old and ancient, religious practices have disappeared. Buddhism too 'has disappeared from Bharatabarsha and taken refuge in Singhala Dwipa and far East countries'. He spends a few pages on selecting and rejecting certain elements while depicting the episodes from the *Ramayana* and *Mahabharata* as part of India's history. In order to validate his claims, he cites European historians, 'The major historians of Europe have furnished proof to show that the Battle of Kuruskhsetra was fought 14 hundred years before Christ. . .'. Ajatashatru occupied the throne of Magadh succeeding some thirty-four generations of rulers after Jarasandha, who is connected to some episode in the *Mahabharata*. The reason for my digressive excursion into Fakir Mohan's historiographic methods here is to suggest how, he, like many other native intellectuals, would not easily let go of the historical veracity of the puranic texts, which will explain for us the tendency among Odia readers to take Radhanath Ray's history through the *Mahabharata* rather seriously and challenge it in parts where it deviates from the known versions.[72]

The need for history-writing among the 'learned natives' was formally recognized in government circles too. As Pyari Mohan Acharya says, 'the Joint Inspector of Odisha Schools of Bengal Division announced a prize of rupees three hundred to anyone who wrote a History of Odisha in Odia'.[73] He wrote a history of Odisha himself, as he goes on to say, in response to this, won the prize and published it in 1879. Given the new interest in Buddhism, in his book, he highlights Odisha's Buddhist cultural past. Though the Odia historians themselves were yet to be trained in methods of archaeology, they, especially Pyari Mohan Acharya, borrowed a lot from archaeologists' findings published in book form.

His methodology comprised the culling of evidence from scriptural texts and indigenous historical chronicles such as those in *Madala Panji* as well as from modern historians, Hunter, Sterling and Rajendralal Mitra; but discriminating between what to his mind seemed plausible and incredible. Even while being this selective in his choice to ensure that his ideological Brahmo bias was justified, he tried to ensure that his conclusions—part deduction, part assumptive, and guess work—appeared to be scientific and rational, all the while maintaining his anti-brahmanical postures while tracing the history of Buddhism in Odisha, its popularity, and decline. For example, while drawing on and invoking *Madala Panji*, he dismissed as tall tale, the lives and tenures of rulers that stretched endlessly beyond centuries.[74]

Whether it was Fakir Mohan's history of India or Pyari Mohan Acharya's history of Odisha, tales of foreign conquest, Indians' or Odias' bravery, the latter's glorious past and the reasons for their decline were concerns that were common to all, placing the blame for the real or imagined downfall on the foreign invaders, the *yavans*. In these somewhat clichéd nationalist narratives, the images of the other were constructed. In an unpublished paper, I have dealt with the emergence of a new discourse that I call the Odia Jeremiad following the formulation of 'the American Jeremiad' by Sacvan Bercovitch.[75] One of the strains in this new discourse was the finding of reasons, even scapegoats, for the decline of the Odia/Arya 'race'. This leads to occasional self-introspection within the self-other binary. It was not that only the so-called *yavans* were to be blamed for the decline of the Odia *jati*, it could have also been because of the problems within the Arya fold. This is where lessons in history-writing learnt from Europeans enabled the vernacular historians—now that they were inspired by nationalist ambitions—to identify the 'enemy' within, due no doubt to the parallel happenstance of missionary activity, as the Brahminism-induced caste system.

Buddhist Revivalism and Curiosity over the History of Buddhism in India

The genesis and histories of Buddhism and the *varnashram*/caste system became inextricably linked issues. It may be difficult to figure out at this point of time which came first—interest in Buddhism or in caste (a veritable chicken and egg puzzle). But this need not detain us here in the context of the *Mahayatra* controversy. What is beyond doubt is that the renewed interest in Buddhism received a major fillip from the excavations in Bodh Gaya.[76]

From among the 'learned natives', Rajendralal Mitra followed in Alexander Cunningham's footsteps, and by the 1880s they had both produced an impressive body of work pertaining to Odisha and neighbouring regions of Bihar.[77] Their researches claimed, among other things, evidence of the immense spread of Buddhism in the region in the pre-modern period. As a result of the information that emerged, the curiosity spread to an international audience and many started visiting and showing interest in finding out more about the past. Among these was Edwin Arnold, who upon visiting Bodh Gaya in 1886, emphasized the need for the Buddhists to reclaim Bodh

Gaya. The theosophists were also attracted and the revival of interest in Buddhism coincided with the anti-caste reformist zeal of the intellectual class.

Consequent upon these researches, unprecedented curiosity and enthusiasm to study the life of the Buddha and the history of Buddhism swept through the intellectual circles of Bengal and Odisha in the second half of the twentieth century. Following Arnold's *Light of Asia* (1879), and books such as Sarvanand Baruah's *Jeevajyoti* and Nabinchandra Sen's *Amitabh* (1896), Fakir Mohan too would render an Odia version of the life of the Buddha in the form of the poem, *Bouddhavatar* (1908).

In what follows, I shall cite and discuss two instances of controversies around Buddhism vis-à-vis casteism. One is about the attempt to reclaim Bodh Gaya in the late 1880s and early 1890s that was effectively thwarted by the dominant Hindus. The second one was in and around Puri. About ten years before the Bodh Gaya incident, in the 1880s, a community of dissident believers (*Alekhdharmis*) visited the Jagannath temple of Puri, a visit that was then represented in the print media as an 'attack'.

Different versions of this incident have been circulating. It is impossible to adjudicate between the warring versions. The one which is in popular circulation occurs in J.P. Das's *Time Elsewhere*, and it runs as follows:

On 1 March 1881, a group of people came from Sambalpur about a week ago in obedience to their master's orders. The guru had instructed them to desecrate the temple by scattering left over food there, and to take the idols to the main street of Puri and burn them down. Alekh himself, their deity, had allegedly appeared to the guru in a dream and had set him this task. They had taken part in a riot according to section 143. In view of this, the magistrate sentenced Maya, Bhaja, Jeera and Heera seven days' rigorous imprisonment and acquitted the others. The verdict on the first case (Jagua Singh versus fifteen defendants including Dhani, Situ, Bhagat, Mayaram) was given on 14 March 1881.[78]

This version extracted by J.P. Das, from the newspaper reports and court records, is seen by some as distorted. As Nagendranath Basu, who conducted his research under the patronage of the Maharaja of Mayurbhanj, and published his 'findings' in book form in 1911, says in a note, 'Various false statements about this sect were made by the English and Vernacular papers of the time'.[79]

That Buddhism lay dormant, even under subterfuge is a narrative that surfaced in the late nineteenth century. His version of the revival of Buddhism in the nineteenth century runs, 'Thus we learn that the revival of Buddhism in the name of Mahima-dharma took place in the twenty-first year of the reign of Divya-Simha, late King of Puri, i.e. in 1875. Soon after, Bhima Bhoi appears on the scene, and proclaimed Mahima.' One of the most important spiritual leaders of the time was this blind, Kondh poet Bhima Bhoi. It seems he had heard a voice from heaven to the effect that with the revival of the *Mahima dharma*,[80] the hidden state of Jagannatha as Buddha would again be brought to light.

...The villagers heard of this, laughed at the queer idea and thought 'What religion is this that *aims at the abolition of the time-honoured caste-system*, by making its followers live upon alms of boiled rice, irrespective of the caste or creed of the giver!' They then conferred together and determined that this new religion, a much dreaded leveller of castes, should be allowed no room whatsoever in the village. And they translated their resolution into practice by beating him off the village [emphasis mine].[81]

Bhima Bhoi called 'upon his numerous disciples to come and join their forces with him. Fired with the zeal of devotion and piety, his followers madly obeyed his call and mustered strong under his standard'.[82]

In spite of the variations, there is no doubt about the anti-caste nature of Bhima Bhoi's spiritual leadership. It is well-known that the blind Kondh poet and spiritual leader, whether or not of Buddhist orientation, had received no European education and was, therefore, beyond the pale of 'modern' caste discourses.

These incidents preceded the caste controversies and the ones around *Mahayatra* by less than a decade. But contemporaneous to the years that *Mahayatra* came under fire for its depiction of Hinduism vis-à-vis Buddhism, another controversy verging on a communal conflict, broke out in neighbouring Bihar, in Bodh Gaya—the best-known Buddhist shrine, where Buddha is said to have attained enlightenment. The circumstances leading to the incident were as follows: members of the Theosophical Society were drawn towards India and Buddhism as part of their syncretic agenda. Its founding members were Henry Steel Olcott; the Russian, Helena Petrovna (Madam) Blavatsky; Anagarika Dharmapala,[83] a Christian-educated Sinhala Buddhist, who became a close associate of Olcott. After Madam Blavatsky's death in 1891, the Society broke into groups. Be that as it may.

Let it be said here that in the revered Buddhist shrine, a Hindu temple had been set up, and turned into a place of Shaivite worship

over a period of 300 years. In a way, this should have been an ideal
symbol of the kind of syncretism that the Theosophical Society was
aiming for. But Dharmapala had gradually moved away from that
ideal, a 'desire for universal brotherhood'. In 1892, Olcott had
delivered a lecture on 'The Kinship between Hinduism and
Buddhism' about the '"baseless antagonism and inexcusable
prejudice" perpetuated by the Brahminical Hindus toward Buddhism.
He appealed to the common roots of the two "sister cults"' and
'argued that it was not only possible for the two religions to coexist
in peace and harmony at Bodhgaya, but it was natural for them to
do so, because for Olcott, Hinduism and Buddhism were in essence
the same'.[84] He had hoped that the two related belief systems would
coexist harmoniously at Bodh Gaya. However, Dharmapala had
been completely steeped in the Orientalist stereotyping of Hinduism,
reducing it to the sole element of Brahminism. 'India by right
belongs to Buddha';[85] 'Brahmans through sheer selfishness ejected
the Noble Aryan Dharma from its native soil and India fell';[86]
'(W)hen the Kshatriya Dharma was supplanted by Brahminical
priestcraft and ritualism, when rulers became victims of sensuality,
and illegitimate luxury, when duty was perverted for satisfaction of
one's own self, the teachings of the Lord Buddha were abandoned
for idiotic superstitions and insane sensualism.'[87]

Dharmapala was convinced about the 'idea of restoring the
Buddhist Jerusalem into Buddhism'. But, of course, Dharmapala
had already read Arnold's *The Light of Asia* and was enraged by the
plight of Buddhism at Bodh Gaya, where it had been subsumed by
the dominant identity as a Shaiva shrine that it had by now acquired.
As he says, 'It was [Arnold] who gave me the impulse to visit the
shrine, and since 1891, I have done all I could to make the
Buddhists of all lands interested in the scheme of restoration'.[88] In
May 1891, Dharmapala founded the Maha Bodhi Society, ostensibly
to restore Bodh Gaya to its former state and to establish the site
as the sacred centre of pilgrimage for the world's Buddhists.
Dharmapala's Bodh Gaya 'mission' was also inspired by a vicious
anti-brahmanical polemic. Thus, in January 1891, reflecting on the
sorry state of Bodh Gaya, he wrote in his journal that 'a powerful
Buddhist's eloquent voice is needed to show the knavery of the
selfish bigoted Brahman priests'.

This may seem to be the single most natural provocation for his
rash action one fine morning, when he entered the precincts of the
main structure of the Mahabodhi Temple on 25 February 1895. He
was accompanied by several assistants, who were carrying with them
a piece of stone sculpture, that of the Buddha. Then they started

setting up the statue for worship with flowers and incense sticks. Just then, two other men appeared on the scene—Hossain Baksh and Jagganath Singh. Along with a few other accomplices, they disturbed the arrangements through physical force. After some altercation, calm prevailed and the intruders left. As Dharmapala began to meditate before the image, the group re-entered, snatched the statue and flung it on the temple lawn. This was one of the most significant moments in the history of Buddhism in India and, in the light of what would come to pass in Independent India, a mild intimation of the violence in 1992—almost exactly a hundred years later.

Dharmapala went to court over the incident. As per court records, the case was fought in two stages. The first one was won by Dharmapala,[89] and the three convicted who appealed to the higher court (under 'Criminal Revision' against the order of Dr Macpherson, Esq., District Magistrate of Gaya, dated the 9 June 1894) were found not guilty. The juridical proceedings were captioned as 'Before Mr. Justice Macpherson and Mr. Justice Banerjee. Jaipal Gir and Others (Petitioners) *v*. H. Dharmapala (Opposite Party).* [22nd August, 1895.] Religion, Offence relating to—Penal Code (Act XLV of 1860), s. 296—disturbing a religious assembly'.

The three petitioners were convicted by the district magistrate of Gaya, under Section 296 of the Penal Code, of the offence of voluntarily causing disturbance to the complainant and his associates while lawfully engaged in the performance of religious ceremonies and religious worship, and sentenced to undergo one month's simple imprisonment and to pay a fine of Rs.100 each. On appeal, the sessions judge affirmed the convictions and the sentences of fine, but set aside the sentences of imprisonment. The facts connected with the occurrence, which gave rise to this case, were fully stated in the judgements of the High Court.[90] Employing a long circuitous logic, the verdict was delivered as

I, therefore, think that it is not established that the complainant and his associates were lawfully engaged in religious worship when they were disturbed, and that the accused, therefore, in causing the disturbance have committed no offence under section 296 of the Indian Penal Code. I agree with my learned colleague in holding that this rule should be made absolute, the convictions and sentences set aside, and the fines, if realised, refunded.

Conclusion

There is little doubt that Radhanath Ray had internalized contemporary European discourses then circulating about Buddhism vis-à-vis brahmanical Hinduism of the kind Dharmapala had been influenced by. For, the general nineteenth-century attitude towards Hinduism, in the memorable words of the early nineteenth-century archeologist Francis Buchanan, 'the most abominable, and degrading system of oppression, ever invented by the craft of designing men'. Buddhism, by contrast, was celebrated as a highly rational religion rivaling Protestant Christianity. The 'status of the Buddha was enhanced enormously by the perception that he had been an opponent of Hinduism, for in this he was aligning himself with the vast majority of Victorians'. Cunningham described him as 'a great social reformer who dared to preach the perfect equality of all mankind and the *consequent abolition of caste*, in spite of the menaces of the most powerful and arrogant priesthood in the world' [emphasis mine].[91]

The foregoing discussion helps me conclude that, like Milton's *Paradise Lost*, there was a context for the composition of *Mahayatra*, and there was a context for its reception. It is significant to note that Radhanath Ray began publishing the epic literally 'in medias res' first in *Odia O Nabasambad* and then in *Utkalprabha* since the first episodes from the epic to be published were from the fifth *sarga*, where the 'controversial' parts figured. The poet had already gained a reputation for currying favour from patrons such as the three rulers—Sriramchandra Bhanj Deo, the Maharaja of Mayurbhanj; Baikunthanath De,[92] the Raja of Balasore; and Sudhaldeb, the Raja of Bamanda. It is quite possible that Radhanath was in a hurry to please the first one, since the latter had taken a bride from Bengal's well-known Brahmo family, that of Keshobchandra Sen. The Raja (actually a local satrap) of Balasore too, was then turning towards Brahmo *upasana* as described in Fakir Mohan's autobiography. Brahmoism justified its breaking away from Hinduism primarily for reasons of the fissiparous caste system. Though Radhanath was too timid or too committed to Hinduism in his personal and family life (witness his weaning away of a young man who had fought with his parents, and whose father had approached Radhanath to prevent him from leaving the Hindu fold),[93] he must have thought, there was nothing wrong in indirectly singing the glory of anti-brahmanical-Hinduism, Brahmoism by attacking the caste system vehemently, the way he does in the fifth section. This helped in the long run as both Baikunthanath and Sudhaldeb extended their support to him during the Upendra Bhanja controversy (1840–93).

At the level of reception, those among the strong, orthodox Hindu lobby (mostly, but not all were brahmans) had felt jittery about the strength of the Brahmo-Christian missionary combine which threatened to break their hegemony. These groups who had already been part of the *jati* controversy suddenly saw in the work of a popular poet, an ally abetting the opposition camp of intellectual rationalists with a strong anti-Hindu-brahmanical bias. Not a few targeted Radhanath even using his Achilles heel, his Bengali identity, at the time of the hey-day of Odia nationalism. But as has been seen, historians and archeologists had already prepared the ground for such a cultural production as *Mahayatra* and the casteism-Buddhism controversies, and court cases had prepared the stage for its reception.

Notes

1. Thomas Babington Macaulay, 'Minute on Education', <http://home.iitk.ac.in/~hcverma/Article/Macaulay-Minutes.pdf>, accessed 20 June 2016.
2. Ibid.
3. Ibid.
4. Vinay Dharwadker, 'The Historical Formation of Indian-English Literature', in *Literary Cultures in History: Reconstructions from South Asia*, ed. Sheldon Pollock, New Delhi: OUP, 2003, p. 226.
5. He learnt Hindi at a mature age and had read and memorized Tulsidas's *Ramcharitmanas*. See, Durgacharan Ray, *Radhanath Jibani* (1941), Cuttack: Friends Publishers, 1998, pp. 28–30, 186.
6. Natabar Samantaray, *Odia Sahityara Itihasa (1803-1920)*, Bhubaneshwar: Bani Bhavan, 1964, p. 303.
7. John Milton, *Paradise Lost*, ed. Thomas Newton, London: J. and R. Tonson and S. Draper, 1750, Book X. No English translations of *Mahayatra* are available. All references to the text are from the edition, *Kabibar Granthabali*, and are in my translation. Quotations from Michael Madhusudan Dutt's *Meghnadbadh Kavya* are from William Radice, tr., *The Poem of the Killing of Meghnad*, New Delhi: Penguin India, 2010.
8. 'Sarga Six' of *Mahayatra*, in *Kabibar Radhanath Granthabali*, ed. Prasanna Kumar Mishra and Debendra Kumar Dash, Cuttack: Grantha Mandir, 1998, p. 141.
9. Milton, *Paradise Lost*, Book I.
10. Mishra and Dash, *Kabibar Radhanath Granthabali*, pp. 114–16.
11. Ibid.
12. Ibid., p. 338.
13. Fakir Mohan Senapati, *Granthabali, Trutiya Khand or Complete Works of Fakir Mohan Senapati*, vol. 3, ed. Debendra Dash, Cuttack: Grantha Mandir, 2008, pp. 358–62.
14. Ibid.

15. Gangadhar Meher, *Kichak Badh* (1904); repr. in *Gangadhar* Granthabali (1951), 3rd edn., Berhampur: Das Brothers, 1961, pp. 129–64.
16. Quoted in Introduction, Michael Madhusudan Dutt, 'Introduction', *Meghnadbadh Kavya* (Bangla), <http://www.banglainternet.com/pdf-legend/michael_madhusudan_dutt_meghnad_badh_kabya.pdf>, accessed 21 September 2015.
17. Partha Chatterjee, *The Partha Chatterjee Omnibus* (I), New Delhi: OUP, 1985; 1999, p. 55.
18. Ray, *Radhanath Jibani*, p. 100.
19. Ibid.
20. Ibid., pp. 402–43.
21. Macaulay, 'Minute on Education'.
22. Nilakantha Das, *Odia Sahityara Krama Parinama* (1953), Cuttack: Grantha Mandir, 2011, pp. 268–300.
23. Quoted in Partha Chatterjee, *The Nation and its Fragments: Colonial and Postcolonial Histories*, Princeton: Princeton University Press, 1993.
24. John Milton, *History of Great Britain*, MDCLXXI, London: St. Paul's Church-Yard, 1671. See, <http://www.ebay.com/itm/John-Milton-The-History-of-Britain-1671-Second-Edition-Frontispiece-No-Reserve-/222089316462?rmvSB=true>, accessed 10 May 2016. The full title reads as follows: 'The History of Britain, That part especially now called England. / From the first Traditional Beginning, Continued to the Norman Conquest. Collected out of the Antientest and best Authors thereof: / By John Milton. London, Printed by J.M. for Spencer Hickman, at the Rose in St. Paul's Church-Yard, MDCLXXI [1671]'. In Hindu scriptures the only equivalent can be found in the *Vishwarupadarshan* through which the future is revealed by Krishna, but the futures are mythical not historical.
25. Milton, *Paradise Lost,* Book X.
26. Mishra and Dash, *Kabibar Radhanath Granthabali*, p. 127.
27. Ray, *Radhanath Jibani*.
28. Raziuddin Aquil and Partha Chatterjee, eds., *History in the Vernacular*, Ranikhet: Permanent Black, 2008, pp. 449–81.
29. Departing from usual practice, I use Arya instead of Aryan throughout the book in order to distinguish the Indian context from the fascist use of the term in Europe.
30. Sudipta Kaviraj, *The Unhappy Consciousness*, New Delhi: OUP, 1995, p. 145.
31. See his oblique references to colonial histories of India/Odisha in *Mahayatra*.
32. Chatterjee, *The Partha Chatterjee Omnibus* (I).
33. Ibid., p. 82.
34. Ibid.
35. It is doubtful whether Milton's *The History of Britain, that Part especially now called England; from the first traditional Beginning, continued to the Norman Conquest. Collected out of the antientest and*

best Authours thereof, was available in India in Radhanath Ray's time. Milton's unfinished history was first published in 1670. His methodology, which he himself distrusted, uses history based on dubious sources and popular fables.

36. Kaviraj, *The Unhappy Consciousness*, p. 110.

37. John Beames, *Memoirs of a Bengal Civilian*, London: Chatto & Windus, 1961, p. 197.

38. Mishra and Dash, *Kabibar Radhanath Granthabali*, pp. 117–56.

39. Fakir Mohan Senapati, *Chha Mana Atha Guntha (Six Acres and a Third)*, 1902; repr. in *Granthabali: Complete Works of Fakir Mohan Senapati.*, vol. 3, ed. Debendra Dash, Cuttack: Grantha Mandir, 2008, p. 17.

40. B. Rajan, *Under Western Eyes: India from Milton to Macaulay*, Durham: Duke University Press, 1999.

41. Aquil and Chatterjee, eds., *History in the Vernacular*, pp. 449–81.

42. Following the decision of the Brahmo leader R.C. Dutt, to marry his under-age daughter to the son of the Maharaja of Cooch Bihar.

43. Natabar Samantaray, *History of Modern Odia Literature*, Cuttack: Self Published, 1963.

44. It was alleged that Radhanath Ray had masterminded the undermining of the iconic seventeenth-century *Riti* poet on account of his extreme eroticism in order to further his own reputation as poet.

45. 'Odishara Dukkha' (Odisha's Grief), 1887, was about his alleged discrimination against Odias (Mishra and Dash, *Kabibar Radhanath Granthabali*, p. 455); and 'Bakacharita' (Life of a Heron), 1894, was about Radhanath Ray's alleged machinations in order to enhance his reputation (ibid., 459; published in *Bijuli*).

46. Mishra and Dash, *Kabibar Radhanath Granthabali*, p. 457.

47. Ibid., pp. 114–16.

48. Rabindranath Tagore, 'Meghanadavadha kavya' (The Slaying of Meghanada), in *Rabindra-racanavali, Acalita Samgraha* (The Collected Works of Rabindranath Tagore: Out-of-Print Material), Calcutta: Visva-Bharati, 1962; first published in Bharati, August 1882, 2:80.

49. Pramatha Chaudhuri, 'Sabuja patrera mukhapatra' [Sabuj Patra's Manifesto], in Nana-katha [Miscellany], Kolkata: Self Published, 1919, pp. 109–10.

50. This is discussed at some length by Rosinka Chaudhuri. See, Rosinka Chaudhuri, *The Literary Thing: History, Poetry And The Making Of A Modern Cultural Sphere*, New Delhi: OUP, 2014, pp. 234–40. As I have already pointed out, Radhanath Ray was close to Nabinchandra Sen, whose letters to the former have been reproduced by Durgacharan Ray. It is quite possible that Radhanath Ray learnt to use history as literature from Bengali models. On reading his Bangla verses in the collection *Lekhabali* (1902), Nabinchandra showers high praise on the poet comparing his verses with those of Michael Madhusudan Dutt's 'Birangana'. See, Ray, *Radhanath Jibani*, pp. 402–3.

51. Radhanath Ray, *Mahayatra*; quoted in Mishra and Dash, *Kabibar Radhanath Granthabali*, pp. 134–5.
52. *Sambalpur Hiteisini*, 22 April 1896.
53. Sadashiv Mishra, *Sambalpur Hiteisini*, 13 May 1986.
54. Madhusudan Mishra, *Sambalpur Hiteisini*, 10 October 1896.
55. Nagendranath Basu, *Buddhism and its Followers in Orissa*, Calcutta: Self Published, 1911.
56. Ray, *Radhanath Jibani*, pp. 180–2.
57. Paramananda Acharya, *Dagar* (Special Issue on Radhanath Ray); quoted in Gaganendranath Das, *Nirbachita Prabandha Samkalana*, Cuttack: Vidyapuri, 2005, pp. 1–45.
58. Samantaray, *Odia Sahityara Itihasa*, pp. 301–50.
59. *Utkal Sahitya*, vol. I, p. 20.
60. Ibid., p. 189.
61. Ibid., p. 254.
62 Ibid., p. 455.
63. How far this was induced by the circumstances outlined in Nicholas Dirks is a moot point. For Dirks argues, 'By 1858 there was nevertheless general recognition that caste was the foundational fact of Indian society, fundamental both to Hinduism (as Hinduism was to it) and to the Indian subcontinent as a civilizational region. Caste emerged, stronger than ever, from the legacy of Orientalist forms of knowledge'; Nicholas Dirks, *Castes of Mind: Colonialism and the Making of Modern India*, Princeton and Oxford: Princeton University Press, 2001, pp. 154–6.
64. James Fergusson (22 January 1808–9 January 1886) was a Scottish architectural historian, mainly known for his interest in Indian antiquities, architecture, etc. He was an important figure in the nineteenth-century rediscovery of ancient India.
65. James Fergusson, 'Preface', in *Archaeology in India, With Especial Reference to the Works* of *Babu Rajendralal Mitra*, London: Trubner & Co., 1884, p. vii. The Preface is itself polemical and part of the specialists' controversy on the subject.
66. As described in a piece of his travel writing by Biswanath Kar himself in *Sambalpur Hiteisini* in a double issue, 6–13 November 1895.
67. The Bengali book dealt with the lives of Buddha and Mahatma John Howard. Author and publication dates unknown.
68. Many of these were about Buddhism—Rajendralal Mitra, *The Antiquities of Orissa*, vol. 1, Calcutta: Baptist Mission Press, 1875 and Rajendralal Mitra, *The Antiquities of Orissa*, vol. 2, Calcutta: W. Newman & Co., 1880 [both illustrated with photographic plates and a similarly illustrated work on Bodhgaya (1878), the hermitage of Sakya Muni]; Rajendralal Mitra, *Indo-Aryans: Contributions towards the Elucidation of Their Ancient and Mediaeval History*, 2 vols., Calcutta: W. Newman, 1881; Rajendralal Mitra, *The Sanskrit Buddhist Literature of Nepal*, Calcutta: Asiatic Society of Bengal, 1882; and Alexander Cunningham,

Mahabodhi or The Great Buddhist Temple Under The Bodhi Tree At Buddha-Gaya, London: W.H. Allen & Co., 1892.

69. Aquil and Chatterjee, *History in the Vernacular*, pp. 10–11.

70. Fakir Mohan, *Granthabali*, p. 249.

71. Turns out to be John Bentley, the British astronomer; John Bentley, *A Historical View of the Hindu Astronomy, from the Earliest Dawn of that Science in India to the Present Time*, London: Smith, Elder, & Co., 1835. Bentley doubts the veracity of the texts. As the reviewer says, 'Bentley adduces note p 175 proof in the confession of a Hindu astronomer upon grounds stated by him avowed that i would put his name to an work wherein the epoch from which the calculations were made proceed 1000 years back but have added in such cases it usual was put the name of some ancient sage to it or that of some fictitious astronomer with an account of his birth parentage connexions and country in to give it the plausible appearance of being ancient and royal which to modern notions would much enhance its value it is proper to that Mr Colebrooke himself admits that the affixing the name of a celebrated author to a work composed in later times is a common practice which is too in India as in many other countries'. See, <https://books.google.co.in/books?id=8CYYAAAAYAAJ&pg=PA210&lpg=PA210&dq=bentley+on+hindu+eras&source=bl&ots=fQERBS2jE5&sig=GP4s61CsVc8wp2NmkS_xcooB59c&hl=en&sa=X&ved=0ahUKEwjDrtvkqrvNAhWHwI8KHYPuDbkQ6AEIKDAC#v=onepage&q=bentley%20on%20hindu%20eras&f=true>, accessed 22 June 2016.

72. Aquil and Chatterjee speak of the two kinds of vernacular history—one that when translated into English might be comparable to the historiographical methods of the British historians; the other, a hybrid of the two. Both the pioneering efforts of Fakir Mohan and Pyari Mohan Acharya represent the latter variety. Most parts of the latter's work appears to be more of the first kind. See, Partha Chatterjee, 'Introduction', in *History in the Vernacular*, ed. Riazuddin Aquil and Partha Chatterjee, Ranikhet: Permanent Black, 2008, p. 18.

73. Pyari Mohan Acharya, 'Bhumika' [Foreword], in *Odishara Itihas*, Cuttack: Cuttack Printing Company, 1879, pp. 1–3. If not in the specific instance of Acharya's pioneering work, a similar interest in the Hindu past, especially its caste system and the treatises such as Manu's, received scholarly attention. A brief digression in the form of reiterating the caste issue might be in order here. Dirks studies in detail the various landmarks that lead to the consolidation and reinforcement of caste. He argues how, 'The last half of the nineteenth century witnessed the development of a new kind of curiosity about and knowledge of the Indian social world, exhibited first in the manuals and gazetteers that began to encode official local knowledge, then in the materials that developed around the census, which led to Risley's great ambition for an ethnographic survey of all of India'. He argues how the category

'caste' was a British invention that was necessitated on the declaration of a policy of non-interference into Indian culture and tradition in 1858, and used census' to universalize and ethnicize caste in order to guard that tradition. In the same period, 'missionaries continued to play a role, contesting official policies of nonintervention and continuing their critique of caste and religion. But the critique of caste that was heard loudest now came from a very different place, mobilized by Indian critics and activists as varied as Rammohun Roy and Dayananda Saraswati, M.G. Ranade and G.K. Gokhale, J.G. Phule and Rabindranath Tagore. . . .'

Basing my study on the Odia archives from roughly the 1870s onward, I find Dirks's generalizations rather sweeping and not discriminating enough. First, he does not seem to take into account the state of caste consciousness among Indians during the Islamic period; second, and more to our context here, the critique of caste is pervasive in the Odia public sphere under Christian and Brahmo influence and also due to the other pan-Indian discourses emerging from Maharashtra, the latter not clearly mentioned—but as we have just seen, Christian and Brahmo intellectuals like Madhusudan Rao and Biswanath Kar. The Brahmos were themselves an elite class in the sense that very few Dalit converts ever became prominent Brahmos. The case against brahmanical Hinduism gets stronger with the consolidation of the history and archaeology of Buddhism. Even those who were far removed from the discursive spaces of colonial modernity challenged Hindu orthodoxies. Among these latter were the *mahima dharmi*s.

74. Pyari Mohan Acharya, *Odishara Itihas*, Cuttack: Cuttack Printing Company, 1879, pp. 23–4.

75. Sacvan Bercovitch has traced this model of the American patriot's modern consciousness. He uses John Winthrop's work [*Models of Christian Charity*; quoted in Sacvan Bercovitch, *The American Jeremiad* (1978), London: University of Wisconsin Press, 2012] to describe the American jeremiad, that originally meant a sermon that sought to unify people by creating a tension between ideal social life and its real manifestation. The 'jeremiad' is named after the biblical lamentations of Jeremiah also known as 'the weeping prophet', 'Yet I had planted thee a noble vine, wholly a right seed: how then art thou turned into the degenerate plant of a strange vine unto me?' (Chapter 2, verse 21). Bercovitch's interpretation of the jeremiad does not strictly follow its original religious connotation. Rather, his understanding is around the jeremiad's role in the construction and the critique of public life. He seeks to distinguish between the American version from the earlier European model of the jeremiad. Without going into the details of that difference, and using Bercovitch's model of the jeremiad as a trope, one can see its role in identity formation in certain cultures, especially during their coming to nationalist consciousness. The fact that I appropriate the term only as a trope, and in a non-Christian context,

helps the further secularization of the term, while the remnants of the religious trappings undergo some further 'conversion' (this intended pun is used as a synonym for revision). In what follows, I define the mutant model of the jeremiad, what I call the 'Oriya Jeremiad' in contradistinction with the European and American jeremiads. By the Oriya jeremiad I mean a recurrent mode of self-expression practiced by a community of middle-class, English-educated Odias during what is generally recognized as the period of Oriya nationalism, *circa* 1866 to 1936. I see, that is, how a new linguistic consciousness gave rise to a certain political consciousness which in turn began constructing a new kind of political subjectivity. I examine the role it plays in the evolution and rise of identity discourses, and which in turns fuels Odia nationalism during the late nineteenth and early twentieth centuries.

76. Haraprasad Shastri says, 'The sixties and the seventies were periods of the greatest activity for archaeological researches under Sir Alexander Cunningham. His researches, his excavations, and his discoveries all over Northern India, showed in unmistakable terms that Buddhism lingered in many parts of Northern India for hundred years after the Muhammadan conquest. From the early eighties commenced the minute and scholarly investigations in all matters that related to India, both in Europe and in this country. The credit of initiating this accurate and sympathetic movement belongs to Hofrath Buhler. He and his numerous followers investigated very carefully all the available sources of information about India and then pronounced their opinions. The late lamented 'Prof. Bendal examined the wonderful collection of Palm-leaf Mss. in the University of Cambridge and found that many of them belonged to the Pala period. Babu Carat Chandra Das travelled in Tibet and showed from Tibetan sources that a large number of Pandits, especially, from Eastern India, went to Tibet in the Pala period.' Also see, Nagendranath Basu, 'Introduction', in *Buddhism and its Followers in Orissa*, Calcutta: Self Published, 1911, p. 2.

77. Cunningham, *Mahabodhi or the Great Buddhist Temple.*
   Cunningham says in his Preface: 'In 1878, when Dr. Rajendra Lala Mitra published his work on the Temple of Buddha Gaya, the only excavations which had then been made were the trenches dug by Major Meade in 1863 at my suggestion, and the subsequent surface clearances by the Burmese. The former had exposed the foundation lines of the original Buddhist Bailing, which once surrounded the Temple, while the latter had brought to light several small Temples, besides many votive Stupas and Buddhist Statues. I visited Buddha Gaya in 1879 for the express purpose of seeing what had been done by the Burmese. Their clearances had not been carried deep enough to expose the more ancient monuments which still existed on or near the original level of the ground on which the Temple was built. The clearances also had not been made with any discrimination. Everything was removed as it became exposed; and thus many of the hemispherical domes of the

rows of early votive Stupas were thrown down. Fortunately they were not carried away, and when the great clearance of the ruins was subsequently made by Mr. Beglar, many of these stone hemispheres were restored to their original Stupas, the remains of which had not been disturbed.'

78. J.P. Das, *Time Elsewhere*, tr. Jatindra K. Nayak, Delhi: Penguin, 2009, pp. 271–6. The hugely popular Odia original is *Desha, Kala, Patra*.

79. Basu, *Buddhism and its Followers in Orissa*, p. 166.

80. Ibid., p. 165.

81. Basu, *Buddhism and its Followers in Orissa*, p. 163.

82. Nagendranath Basu's version reads thus, 'Having equipped themselves, as best as they could, with the weapons of war, the people of about 30 villages marched upon Puri under the leadership of their preceptor. The news of their advance had already reached Puri, and the Raja with his personal guards, was waiting to receive them duly. It was rumoured that the object of the Kumbhapatia invaders was to burn the images of Jagannatha, Balarama and Subhadra and spread the doctrine of Nirakara among the people of Puri. No little consternation was caused by this. But the Raja was determined to fight to the last; and he was reinforced by a body of police officers from Pipli. No sooner had Bhirna Bhoi set his foot within the limits of Puri than both the parties fell upon one another. and a fierce fight ensued. The holy city of Puri became polluted with the blood of the heroes of both sides. At length Bhima Bhoi became convinced of the unrealizable character of his ambition, and so proclaimed amongst his warring disciples that the avoidance from doing any harm to others was the first principle of religion; and so they should not commit sin by injuring others. He did further announce that Jagannatha had already left Puri in the guise of Buddha and he now understood that it was not Buddha's intention that his image be brought to light again. What, then, was the necessity for continuing this bloody and sinful fight? Upon this instruction falling from the lips of their leader, the Mahima-dharmins took to flight. Some of them were, however, captured by the enemy and imprisoned, and some were transported for life on charges of murder by the British Government. At this juncture Bhima Bhoi declared that no true religion had ever been established without self-renunciation and self-sacrifice. So the followers of Mahima-dharma should not mourn the loss of those who had suffered persecutions at the hands of the infidels; they should rather bless and ennoble themselves by cherishing their stainless memories. After this, for fear of persecutions by the Government they took shelter in the hills and forests of the Gadajats of Utkala.'

83. Anagarika Dharmapala was born Don David Hewavitarne in Colombo, Sri Lanka, in 1864, to a middle class Buddhist family.

84. Ananda W.P. Guruge, *Return to Righteousness: A Collection of Speeches, Essays, and Letters of the Anagarika Dharmapala*, Colombo: Government Press, 1965, pp. 368–86; reprinted in Jacob N. Kinnard,

'When is the Buddha Not the Buddha? The Hindu-Buddhist Battle over Bodhgaya and its Buddha Image', *Journal of the American Academy of Religion*, vol. 66, no. 4, 1998, pp. 817–39. I have made extensive use of Kinnard's article.
85. Guruge, *Return to Righteousness*, p. 571.
86. Ibid., p. 580.
87. Ibid.
88. Ibid., p. 336.
89. During the course of the trial that followed Dharmapala's attempt to install the image in the Mahabodhi Temple, a commission was set up by the Lieutenant Governor of Bengal Bourdillon, at the request of the Viceroy Lord Curzon, to prove that the Buddhists did indeed have a rightful claim to Bodh Gaya.
90. I have drawn liberally on the court records. See, <http://www.southasiaarchive.com/Content/sarf.100025/212197/002>, accessed 8 June 2015.
91. Kinnard, 'When is the Buddha Not the Buddha?', p. 825.
92. Baikunthanath De (1852–1913), the Raja of Balasore, was a patron of literature and around him was formed the nucleus of writers in Balasore.
93. Ray, *Radhanath Jibani.*

4

Sarala Das's *Mahabharata*
Questions of Textuality and Authorship

Since there is a prior text called the *Mahabharata* by Vyasa (which is itself not one but many texts), the relationship that the Odia *Mahabharata* by Sarala Das has with the putative original is problematic. The problem is even more acute as the question of the authenticity of the Odia *Mahabharata* by Sarala Das and the identity of the author is itself a fraught field. The issues plaguing the Odia text, in comparison with the Sanskrit original, are less only in degree, but not in kind.[1] As Nilakantha Das says, 'what had happened to the Sanskrit *Mahabharata* about a thousand or fifteen hundred years ago has also happened to Sarala *Mahabharata* in the past five hundred years, during which period different versions had been scribed in palm leaf manuscripts which now lay scattered all over Odisha'.[2] The text, with all its variants prospered and proliferated, circulated unhindered and unhampered with no evidence of anyone questioning their authenticity since, in the pre-modern cultural ethos, Odia readers did not seem to believe in the concept of arresting and restricting the proliferation of a text.

As for the text so for the author. For over a century, or more, hagiographic accounts of the author's life and circumstances kept circulating. Myths and legends have been passed on as historical facts about the author. One of the earliest biographers, writing what is arguably the first biography in the Odia language, Mrutyunjay Rath—generally considered to be more of a rationalist than a traditionalist—also tends to present myths as facts.[3] Modern scholars have tried to remedy the situation by deploying 'scientific' methods to date the author. They have admitted that the author may have been one Sarala Das, but interpolations by unknown authors have added to or modified the text down the ages. The combination of an historically elusive author, whose life and times are shrouded in mystery, and who has been the subject of centuries-old folklore, credited further with having written an even more elusive text with numerous versions, is a perfect recipe for controversy—generating waves of exciting scholarly engagement at the hands of generations of modern scholars armed with imported methodologies of investigation.

Unsurprisingly, after having been dogged by controversies for decades, the text finally saw the production of a 'definitive' edition through work carried out by a team of eleven scholars, led by Artaballabha Mohanty, on the basis of twenty-one different palm-leaf manuscripts carefully sorted out from among numerous others collected from different parts of Odisha, courtesy of the Department of Culture, Government of Odisha.[4] The final volumes, to which all references here are made, appeared in 1965. However, the editorial job carried out by the scholars on the Sarala's *Mahabharata* lacked the thorough professionalism of its Sanskrit (Bombay) counterpart[5] in the sense that it neither carried any editorial apparatus indicating the methodology the editor-in-chief had followed, nor did it try to argue why it should be treated as a definitive edition. It did not even have an Introduction, not to speak of notes and other explanatory material. One can only deduce from different sources the methodology followed by the team and its leader. Consequently, as in the case of its Sanskrit original, the efficacy of such an enterprise was immediately questioned. J.M. Mohanty, a literary historian, said, 'How far [Artaballabha] Mohanty was successful in his efforts is a moot point. For, the methodology adopted while putting together this definitive edition is itself replete with errors.'[6] No wonder then that disagreements over what is authentic, what is apocryphal or spurious have persisted and controversies have been part of the history of the printed book, and its author.

This chapter traces the way certain questions about the text and its author begin to emerge and modify the way traditional notions of textuality and authorship undergo transformation in Odia literary culture. It also attempts to chart the fraught field of textual history of the Odia epic and the historicity of its author in terms of their affective as well as political value. The fulcrum around which my discussion moves, in spite of the limited space I accord it, is the mid-twentieth-century controversy on the dating and place of birth of the epic poet, the immediate provocations for which were offered by the arch controversialist Gopinath Mohanty,[7] known primarily as a pre-eminent Odia novelist. It was to his provocations that the renowned historian of Odisha, Krishnachandra Panigrahi, responded and provided high-strung rejoinders in the form of over half a dozen essays. Çounter-rejoinders followed.[8] In 1956, Gopinath Mohanty suggested what many thought was an absurd date and location for Sarala Das's birth. The controversy, to the details of which I shall return by and by, lasted several years, and kept resurfacing every now and then; it has just been revisited as recently as in 2014 during the Gopinath Mohanty centenary celebrations.[9] But, the question that suggests itself here is what factors contributed to the new approaches to a text, versions of which had been in circulation for almost four centuries?

I shall present a genealogy and contexts of the debates that culminated in the controversies of the 1950s, which I shall then proceed to contextualize if only to indicate how the controversies seemingly conducted in the philological and aesthetic realm were actually predicated on and overdetermined by certain ideological concerns of interested parties.

From Vyasa's to Sarala Das's *Mahabharata*

Sarala Das's *Mahabharata* (*c.*mid-fifteenth century) is the first complete vernacular rendering of the epic composed by a single author in the geopolitical region now known as India. Its spread was so spectacular across the Odia-knowing tracts that people knew many parts of it by heart and it was transcribed frequently, keeping in view local tastes and immediate needs of censorship. It was transmitted orally, and copied and transcribed on palm leaves through scribes for over three centuries.[10] The Sanskrit *Mahabharata*— the great Indian epic—took its present form around the fourth century AD. Composed in Sanskrit, it is said to be the longest poem in world literature. The result of this medieval Odia intervention in the *Mahabharata* is that, instead of a remote and high brahmanical Sanskrit text, we have a version in the vernacular that is intimate and easily accessible to the common Odia reader and listener, which accounts for its unprecedented popularity.

That at the reception level no one disapproved such liberties as Sarala Das took with the Sanskrit original becomes clear from the Odia *Mahabharata*'s popularity. At no point of time in the history of the work's reception was anxiety expressed over its likely corruption. Its fame spread to non-Odia regions as well, and even Telugu and Bangla versions are said to have circulated.[11] It eventually enjoyed great popularity, virtually displacing the original. There are instances of the work's popularity through centuries—mainly at the level of dissemination through innumerable copies and reiteration of unique Sarala Das inventions, one example of which is the figure of 'Navagunjara'.[12] As the art historian Joanna Williams says, 'This substitution of the pan-Indian Jatayu may reflect the popularity of the enigmatic creature in Odisha, which goes back to Sarala Das's *Mahabharata*'. She also says that there are three more or less 'faithful' translations of the epic, none of which equaled Sarala Das's in popularity.

The late-nineteenth century saw the emergence of print culture in Odisha and attempts to arrest the proliferation of the text. This rapid textualization of numerous extant versions in a way changed its traditional status as a 'text'. Kaviraj argues how the advent of print culture immediately created pressures towards standardization; towards the privileging of a particular dialect among the variety of regional forms that had flourished traditionally side by side. In the case of Bengali, he says, the non-standardized form was marked 'low type'.[13] However, there was another kind of standardization that Kaviraj does not take into account—the standardization of *texts*. This took newer forms culminating in the cry for 'definitive' editions. One of the first to receive attention in this regard was the Odia *Mahabharata*, and its first print version of the text was published in 1898.

Surprisingly enough at a time when Odia 'nationalism' was on the rise, instead of glorifying the old work, which predated similar works in rest of the country, Odia nationalist writers like Fakir Mohan attempted to translate into Odia the original Vyasa version, saying that Sarala Das's version was not faithful to the original. It took him nineteen years of intermittent work (1886–1905), to translate four of the eighteen *parvas*. Raja Krushna Singh had proudly translated the Sanskrit *Mahabharata* in 1790s jettisoning the Sarala's version, which he said was not a translation of the original but a re-rendering. A printed version was brought out in the 1890s. Though it earned a wide readership in modern Odisha, its popularity was nowhere near Sarala Das's. However, references to Sarala Das and his *Mahabharata* had begun appearing in the Odia periodicals from the late-nineteenth century onward such as *Utkal Dipika*, *Bodhadayini*, *Sambalpur Hiteisini*, etc. Fakir Mohan also refers to the work in his autobiography, and says that 'even now religious scriptures in Odia such as the *Bhagabata* by Jagannath Das, the *Mahabharata* by Sarala Das, and the *Ramayana* by Balaram Das are read out every evening in important households in these parts'.

Audience

Sarala Das's text is known for its many innovations and variations, which infused a new aesthetic dimension to it, adding local colour through the use of Odishan topography. Images such as that of the *Navagunjara* began travelling soon after, and one can see its representations in remote Rajasthani paintings as suggested by the art historian Joanna Williams. These facts indicate the widening reception of the translated text.

The objectionable changes in the Sarala *Mahabharata* are more recent in origin, and at the advent of print culture. Nilakantha Das says, 'For example, the "dandi bruta"—the Sarala Das text's identity marker, has been regularized in some versions.[14] We are not concerned with the variations in the print version. John Boulton has argued strongly though briefly, and almost idealistically, in favour of tolerating the various versions.[15] The Odia *Mahabharata* in question is part of a much larger social, cultural, and political response to the Sanskrit *Mahabharata*. As Pollock has argued, for reasons that in each case demand careful historical analysis, at different times and in different places but increasingly everywhere, it became more important—politically, socially, and aesthetically, more urgent—to speak locally rather than globally. Sanskrit, the idiom of a cosmopolitan literature, died over the course of the long vernacular millennium in part, it seems, because cosmopolitan talk made less and less sense in an increasingly regionalized world.[16]

William Smith[17] spoke of the Odia *Mahabharata* as one of the popular *Mahabharata*s of eastern India. It is his contention that since Sanskrit could only be comprehended by the educated, new versions of the epic began to appear in the spoken languages of eastern India around 1,000 years later. These include the Odia *Mahabharata* of Sarala Das (1475?), the Bengali *Mahabharata*s of Kashiram Das (seventeenth century) and Kabi Sanjay (early sixteenth century), and the Assamese *Mahabharata* of Rama Saraswati (mid-sixteenth century). Though these works are classified by literary historians as translation literature, they are, in fact, essentially new works which reflect the many changes which had taken place in Indian society since the original epic first appeared.

What Kind of a Text is Sarala Das's?

Sarala Das's *Mahabharata*, like its putative original, and many other epics, claims to be history from creation onward, with realistic references to contemporary places, names, rivers, and mountains.

The claim that the events are historical is, of course, disputable and has been disputed. What kind of a text is it? Is it history? Is it an imaginative history in the absence of a history of the kind we now recognize and respect? The text further raises the issue of the historicity of the fight over the control of the upper Gangetic plains. Sarala Das, of course, tried to connect the history of Odisha or 'Odrarastra' to the events in the *Mahabharata*, which explains the localization of many of the incidents in his version.[18] Then there is another kind of history, the history of the epic as a text, which too is uncertain. All these issues have been raised with regard to the putative original *Mahabharata* as well.

As already remarked upon, Odias, like the rest of their vernacular brethren, are never known to have felt the need to standardize their sacred or secular texts, and no questions regarding their corruption were ever raised. The text owed its popularity and circulation, across the region over centuries, to its narrative economy—combining enjoyment and instruction. But it was always received and treated with reverence as a holy text, a 'canon' in the original, non-secular sense of the term. It was yet to be treated as 'literature'. So, when the shrill controversy broke out in the latter half of the nineteenth century between the 'ancient' and 'modern' (the 'battle of books' as Animesh Mohapatra calls it)[19] literatures, the 'ancient' belonged to a poet of no earlier antiquity than that of Upendra Bhanja (early-eighteenth century). Sarala Das and the *Panchasakha* who had composed the 'holy' texts of the *Ramayana*, *Mahabharata*, and *Bhagabats* in Odia, were nowhere in the reckoning. The definition and emergence of the category 'literary' was as yet in a nascent stage going by the evidence in the periodical press. The battle between the two groups was so vehement that two little magazines emerged to speak for the two camps and fight out the battle of books—one in favour of the *adi rasa* of the ancients represented by the erotic verse of Upendra, and the 'moderns' represented by the poetry of Radhanath Ray and his contemporaries. The details of this battle are too complex to outline within a limited space. In fact, a detailed history will merit a whole book, if not more.[20] Suffice it to say that Sarala Das figured nowhere in the debate as a 'literary' figure, and therefore, did not belong to the 'literary field' in the sense in which Pierre Bourdieu uses the term.[21]

Until the advent of modernity in the nineteenth century, the sacred texts were signifiers of the Odia identity. As against this traditional and centuries-old awareness, there grew another kind of identity-conscious subnationalism towards the end of the nineteenth century and beginning of the twentieth century—a response to what

Kaviraj calls 'sub-imperialist delusions' of Bengalis.[22] It is in the latter half of the nineteenth century that the public intellectuals of this region consciously began to see people of the region primarily as speakers of a particular language, i.e. Odia (then called, Utkal *bhasa*, in the periodical press).[23] Since language became the key identity-marker (among several others such as caste, gender, religion, tribe, etc.), literature being the best specimen of language played a crucial part in its construction.[24] In their anxiety to show off a larger body of literature and books, the Odia intellectuals tried to augment the mass of Odia 'literature', fulfilling the 'imagining' of the Odia 'sub-nation'. Thus, the newly educated class began to take it upon themselves to date Sarala Das in their works of history of the culture of the Odias. The deployment of scientific methods also happens to coincide with the advent and spread of new European disciplines such as archaeology, sociology, history-writing, as well as philology. The Odia intelligentsia had a different perception of the threat to their autonomy, which had hitherto been militaristic—that now the threat is hegemonic and not military, that cultural hegemony, true to its nature, had started making inroads surreptitiously. The resistance of the Odia intellectual class in the form of imagining the Odia community too followed the model of Anderson closely.[25] Not to forget the compulsions of print economy vis-à-vis textbook production. The old threat of Persian and Marathi had been replaced by Bengali, Hindi, and English cultures. The bulwark needed was the resurrection of the Odia heritage; and the antiquity of the Sarala *Mahabharata* provided an opportunity to consolidate the retrieval of the glorious past, already strengthened by the discovery of temple architecture through the by now expanding catalogue of archaeological and historical findings. This is when the search for Sarala Das begins, and controversies and debates begin amidst the warnings against such an enterprise that both the text and its author seem to have issued, already preempting as it were, from within their narratorial logic.

The (?) Text and its Author

What are the text's own notions of what kind of a text it is? Does its teleology inhere in the text? Does the text tell us anything about the version it presents, and about the language in which it does so? I think these questions are in far more urgent need of being addressed than the question of the production of an authentic text called the Sarala *Mahabharata* and the reconstruction of the poet's historicity. Also, the moment we attribute an authorship, we also assume the 'authority' of the author. We also then need to situate our notion of authorship in the context from which the text has emerged.

The lineage of authorship of the 'original' Sanskrit *Mahabharata* is complicated. For, neither a single author nor a single date can be assigned to the great epic. Indian tradition attributes the composition to the name Krishna Dvaipayana (another name for Vyasa), a kind of immortal brahmin who appears between generations of a particular dynasty. But this may have been intended more as a symbolic authorship.[26] Dvaipayana taught the text to his son Suka, and later on the master passed it on to other students who were fit for the task. Narada recited it to the gods. Nilakantha Das gives a brief account of accepted mythologies around the composition of the Sanskrit *Mahabharata*, which had begun as a song of victory (*Jai*) of the Pandavas by Vyasa; and the way Vyasa got it expanded by his followers who added more verses to it, finally calling it the *Mahabharata*. Over centuries, more episodes were added, incorporating cultural beliefs current at that time. Every addition had a purpose—the establishment, consolidation of Vedic and brahmanical dharma and the integration of Jain and Buddhist religious practices.[27] Nilakantha Das astutely points out 'it is difficult to say whether there was someone called Vyasa and whether all the changes were carried out in his lifetime'.[28]

In India and elsewhere, the same text(s) has/have been adapted and rendered into many of the modern languages. As J.A.B. van Buitenen says, the text was copied out endlessly by scribes, and in between many interpolated their own versions. In fact, the original text encourages such interpolations. After the composition of the *Mahabharata*, 'The Bard' said, 'I shall speak the entire thought of that great seer and saint who is venerated in all the world, Vyasa of limitless brilliance. Poets have told it before, poets are telling it now, other poets shall tell this history on earth in the future.'[29] 'For the wise wish to retain it for this world, in its parts and in its entirety . . . there are those who are experienced in explaining it, others in retaining it.'[30] Thus, it can be argued that the *Mahabharata* textual tradition is too complex, and too rooted in living tradition to be amenable to editorial mediation by following Western models of scholarship. It is not surprising to note that the idea of the authenticity of the Sanskrit text, and the need for a definitive edition of the original was first felt by European Indologists.[31]

Many of the issues which come up for discussion in the context of the Sanskrit text are equally applicable to Sarala Das's text. That, for example, changes to the putative original text were made possibly while copying out, adding and deleting lines due to exigencies of memory, comprehension, or sensibility. Some lines which may have proved recalcitrant may have been simplified, such as the one about Sarala Das's brother and father. The Khalyakara episode involving Krishna and the Duti has also been sanitized by a later culture which may have found the depiction of Krishna's amorous play offensive. But such interventions are integral to the mnemonic-oral-textual tradition at a pan-Indian level. After all, the author himself made startling changes in the mythography of the epic. What he did was in keeping with the principles of reproduction laid down in the Sanskrit text. His genius lay in the retelling of the text to suit the needs of his audience and culture, and to make it relevant to them. Thus, several versions are extant. The now objectionable corruptions are more recent in origin and at the advent of print culture. For example, the *dandi bruta* that is Sarala Das's text's identity marker has been regularized in some printed versions.

The Self-Image of the Sarala *Mahabharata*

Sarala Das is among the earliest of self-conscious Odia writers, and his text is one of the most self-reflexive works in medieval India. The first verses of Mangalacharana and invocation leave the reader in no doubt concerning the ambivalence of the author and the text—even while defending the enterprise by taking recourse to divine intervention and inspiration. He assumes a name and a title (Sarala Das and Shudramuni, respectively) and constructs an identity for himself. He even constructs a role for himself, which is somewhat ambiguous, and makes the modern-day reader wonder if he is the author or the translator? Such questions proliferate to which answers are seldom given. When answers come, they often annul each other. Then, the poet calls his work the *Mahabharata*, without any warning that he is retelling the epic in Odia. He, in fact, offers his own version of what the genesis of the original *Mahabharata* is, who the author was, and so on. In so doing, he is destabilizing the text he is himself creating by simultaneously giving rise to the illusion of sameness as well as difference. First of all, he feels the need to assert the fact that he is writing the *Mahabharata*, and he does this by following some textual strategies. One of these is an act of repetition of the symbolic constant of the invocation in Sanskrit addressed to *Nara* (the universal man), *Narayana* (God) and Saraswati (the Goddess of Learning). In textual-material terms, he is maintaining the identity of the 'original text' through the number of *parvas* which is eighteen. Substantively, he maintains the identity of the epic through the retention of the main protagonists in the narrative, as well as in the teleology of the narrative. So that Sarala Das's *Mahabharata*, with all its new episodes, sub-plots, and departures (the biggest being the omission of the Gita), is still the *Mahabharata*.

The journey of its own identity begins with the Odia inscription juxtaposed with the Sanskrit invocation (which is the highest common factor), and is closely followed by the invocation to Ganesha and then the local goddess, Sarala. The second invocation is more direct—Ganesha, and here he is Bighnaraj. He clearly distinguishes between *grantha* (treatise) and *kavita* (poetry), credits Vyasa for having wrought this transformation with permission from Viswabasa, the all-pervasive or omnipresent. Words such as writing and poetry are self-reflexively used. 'The ancient treatise you disseminated', he invokes, crediting Lord Ganesha who supposedly held the stylus. The task is ridden, forbiddingly, with *bighnas* (pitfalls); hence, the destroyer of all *bighnas*, Ganesha is invoked. 'The subject and its ingredients are interesting, steeped as they are in *ranga* and *rasa*. Be satisfied and permit me to tell the story of the *Mahabharata*. In beginnings and ends, also in decline you [are] all-pervasive.'

The invocation to Ganesha is followed by the invocation to Goddess Sarala, who after all, had ordained his fate to be the teller of the *Mahabharata*. Though a mere shudra, he was granted the ability to narrate the *Mahabharata* at great length.[32] In the very next section, Agasthi is urged to recount the circumstances under which the *grantha* came to be called *Mahabharata*. In fact, every section begins with a similar refrain. Also, there is a frequent reiteration of the fact that he was reworking a prior text. It is possible that he used the text of the Sanskrit *Mahabharata*, available to him in script or oral form. As the text unfolds, it begins to diverge and depart so radically from the 'original', that it is hard to keep track of the reinventions. A whole range of new signifiers feed the narrative, and its difference from the original begin to proliferate. At the same time, the poet is able to persuade the reader into believing that they are still reading or reciting the *Mahabharata*. Though scholars have highlighted the inventions he had introduced, it is even more remarkable how close he was to many of the original passages. Why the work is called *Mahabharata*, for example, is an elaboration of what is said in the Sanskrit version. Sarala Das was also perhaps aware of where he was deviating, and why. As any self-conscious writer, he seems to have been aware of criticisms he was likely to encounter if he deviated from the Shastras. Hence, his repeated apologia that whatever he was saying was not his, but as he was prompted by the presiding deity of his village, 'I do not know the *shastras*', he would insist repeatedly; 'I am an ignoramus'. But at places, he justifies how he has composed in accordance with the Shastras, 'I have thus recounted Sri-Madhya parva/in accordance with the *shastra*, for the good of the world, o men!

At a later point, he even thinks of himself as part of the reincarnative self. Like Vishnu himself, Sarala Das claims to have been born as Kalidasa in an earlier birth, and will be born again. So, his self-image ranges from being a humble 'Das' of 'Ma' Sarala to a reincarnative avatar of Kalidasa. All these go to show two things. One, that Sarala Das is self-conscious about his role as a writer and a poet. Two, that he constantly tries to fictionalize himself—from assuming a name for himself to offering metamorphosed identities. This had implications for the kind of text he was writing. Sometimes, it was the word of God, versified Shastra or law, with the promise that listening to it might wash away the sins of the listeners. Sometimes, it is a great history of the Bharatas. It also is an instruction manual for practical affairs of men as there are direct instructions on everyday matters such as governance, marriage, sex, inheritance, childbearing, and so on. Worldly success and salvation go hand in hand is the internal teleology that propels the text. There is a third dimension to Sarala Das's attempt at role-playing through his name. And this might prove to be disturbing to the sociologist. His social conformism displayed at places in the text compels him to project a low self-image as a shudra writer, as a result of which he performs a constant erasure of the self.

The Pre-History of Debates

Now, let us return to the early debates around the poet and his work. The mid-nineteenth century anxieties emerge, as we have seen, when modern notions of textuality and authorship are deployed to understand texts that were scribed in the pre-print era. It would be appropriate here to provide a brief account of the reception of Sarala Das's *Mahabharata* in the mid-nineteenth century when Odia literary culture was in the cusp of modernity. The earliest known disagreement in print with Sarala Das's *Mahabharata* surfaces in October 1867, in a pre-publication notice (in the form of a letter) in *Utkal Dipika* of a more recent translation (1797) of the epic. The rival re-rendering in question of the Sanskrit 'original' was by Krushna Singh, the Raja of Dharakot, with the assistance of chief poets of the period such as Kavisurya and Bharatbhushan.[33] The announcement said, among other things, that 'the vernacular *Mahabharata* by Sarala Das that is now in currency, when compared with the Sanskrit *Mahabharata*, nowhere does one find there any similarity between the two; rather, knowledgeable readers do find it enjoyable due to its many impurities'.[34] The timing of the letter is significant since *c.*1866, following the great famine, the Odia Bhasa Andolan (or the local linguistic movement to save the Odia language from the perceived hostility of a section of Bengali officials and intelligentsia) was just beginning to gain ground. Naturally, the announcement underscores the relevance of the Odia epic to the contemporary political context by urging the literate class among Odias to follow the example of Bengalis and work towards the development of 'our mother tongue' and the pride of 'our territory'.

The letter goes into some practical aspects and advantages of the new in terms of print economy over traditional palm-leaf versions. While a palm-leaf version of the text with many *impurities* is available for Rs.50, a printed version of the text containing 1,500 leaves would be priced at around Rs.20 if the publishers could receive the consent of at least 1,000 customers [emphasis mine].[35] Yet another claim of authenticity surfaces almost three decades later when a notice appears in the July 1898 issue of *Utkal Sahitya* and touts Fakir Mohan's new translation of the *Mahabharata*. The notice sees both Sarala Das's and Krushna Singh's versions as rivals and tries to explain the reasons for which the new version should be preferred by the readers.

However, these petty squabbles can hardly be called controversies since they did not provoke any angry reaction from those who continued to adore Sarala Das, nor did they carry any easily identifiable nationalist motives. In all this, there was a subtle subtext of a parallel move to appropriate Sarala Das and his work (hitherto treated in sacral terms) into the secular domain of the Odia literary canon. This is an understandable strategy on the part of the new intelligentsia at a time when, as part of the linguistic-nationalist fervour, they tried to establish their literary heritage by drawing on the earlier lists of major poets and their oeuvre prepared by colonial historians (Hunter, for instance), and the essays on the literary history of the region (Beames and Manmohan Chakravarty). Sometimes, the dating went wrong and later, Bijoy Chandra Mazumdar was to own up his mistake and attribute his misascription of dates to Manmohan Chakravarty.[36]

In a first attempt of its kind, Hunter appended 'an analytical catalogue of 107 Odia writers, alphabetically arranged' with a brief sequential description and the titles of their works to his *Orissa*.[37] In Hunter's chronology, Balaram Das, Sarala Das and Upendra Bhanja were contemporaries who lived three centuries ago and Jagannatha Das lived fifty years prior to them. Hunter's timeline was contested by subsequent historians. Ironically, these minor contestations were followed by the first printed version of Sarala Das's *Mahabharata* and advertised in the 28 May 1898 issue of *Utkal Dipika*. None of these details, important as they are, can rival the next development—a response in the form of a letter to the editor of the same paper from an anonymous reader, published a few weeks later (23 July 1898). The reader, while welcoming the move by the publisher, anticipates likely opposition to the version for the dilemma the publisher was faced with:

Generally, the palm-leaf manuscripts that are available are replete with errors; thus printing them verbatim is not advisable. However, editorial interventions to bring out an error-free version would result in the production of a drastically different version. In such a situation, even though it might be desirable to print in accordance with the *pothis*, these should be printed after incorporating necessary editorial corrections.

What is noteworthy here is the writer's prescient observation that in view of the existence of multiple palm-leaf versions, the publisher of 'an error free version' of epic might face serious objections, thus anticipating the more fierce controversy of the mid-twentieth century. But it was not as if the matter was laid to rest in the interregnum.

Odia scholars like Shyamsundar Rajguru, Gopinath Nanda, Mrutyunjay Rath, Tarinicharan Rath and others continued to write short essays on Sarala Das (and other poets), trying to situate him in the mid-fifteenth century (citing internal textual evidence) and to project him as the *adikavi* (the first poet) of the language. They also, in their own way, tried to justify the poet's digressions and divagations from Vyasa's version or the metrical limitations of his verse. Shyamsundar Rajguru,[38] for instance, not only placed the poet for the first time in the fifteenth century but also explained the poet's 'metrical indiscipline' by suggesting that the poet followed the *dhaga brutta* (or the rhythm of the proverbs). He also approves of the poet's departure from the original and lauds him for his imaginative prowess. Mrutyunjay Rath[39] analyses Sarala Das's departure from the Sanskrit 'original' thus, 'compared with the original, its descriptions are abridged at some places and expanded at others; at yet others transformed, imagination-laden or transported to a different location'. Mrutyunjay Rath also followed the lead of Shyamsundar Rajguru and placed Sarala Das in the fifteenth century. The most significant work on the poet, however, was by Gopinath Nanda who in his monumental *Bharat Darpana* (serialized in *Utkal Sahitya* between April 1911 and July 1915, in thirty instalments) discussed the departures of the Sarala Das version from the Sanskrit version and compared the text with Bengali and Telugu versions. The combined effort of such scholars helped place Sarala Das as the first major poet in Odia and consolidated his status in the Odia literary-canon.

All this took place in the colonial period when Odias were carving their identity on linguistic grounds. In the late colonial period, one of the most significant observations appeared in an address by the then preeminent scholar Artaballabha Mohanty, who in the year of the formation of the Odisha[40] state bemoaned the lack of any initiative on the part of Odia scholars to put together and publish a definitive version of Sarala Das's *Mahabharata*.[41] Artaballabha Mohanty said:

Unfortunately, one doubts how much of Sarala Das is present in the versions of Sarala *Mahabharata* now available in print. No one has, unfortunately, attempted so far to bring out an uncorrupted version of the Sarala *Mahabharata*. What can be more unfortunate than this? Is there a work more ancient and bigger than this in any other regional language of India? . . . Have we Odias proved to be a cowardly race? (Presidential Address, 1936).

One cannot miss the political significance of this forceful observation as it was made at a meeting of the Utkal Sahitya Samaj, a cultural organization that had become inseparable since 1903 from the political Utkal Sammilani. For, eleven years before India achieved its independence, the identitarian struggle of Odias was. Naturally, the Odia intellectual class wanted to showcase the preeminent Odia literary artefact to the world and to themselves by bringing out the unblemished edition. Is it also possible that the speaker was inspired by the effort that was already under way about the putative original, by the Sukhthankar team started in 1925?[42]

Yet another salvo was fired on the corrupted versions and uncertainties of the existing versions by Pandit Nilakantha Das who by 1936 had been involved directly and deeply in practical politics, both of Odisha and India. Nilakantha Das wrote a non-linear history of Odia literary-culture, calling it '*Kramaparinama*' (evolution) rather than *kramabikasha* (linear history) of Odia literature. He argues—through several examples and display of immense learning and scholarship—that the printed versions in the market differed significantly from the way he was familiar with the epic that was part of traditional institutions in his village. It is clear that Nilakantha Das had come to share the tendency to demonize Muslims in India; and though he does not bring it within the purview of his discussion, it might be necessary to give from his influential and otherwise scholarly study a few instances of the discourse if only to contextualize the controversy that follows. He outlines how the Odia script had not evolved into its modern form prior to King Kapilendra Dev's time. He goes to great lengths in providing a detailed contextual and linguistic history leading to King Kapilendra's reign and Sarala Das.

Enter Gopinath Mohanty

As we have seen, no one seems to have ever dated Sarala Das further back than the fifteenth century. Against the backdrop of almost a hundred odd years of modern scholarship identifying Sarala Das as a fifteenth-century figure who was born in village Jhankada (in the modern district Cuttack, Odisha), Gopinath Mohanty offered radical alternatives that triggered a major controversy. He argued that Sarala Das lived between the late-ninth and early-tenth centuries, and *not* during the reign of King Kapilendra as had been traditionally believed. He also tried to prove that the poet was born in village Kania near the temple of Chitreswari on the bank of the river Prachi in the modern-day district of Puri.[43] This caused nothing short of an uproar in scholarly circles. Had Gopinath Mohanty been an upcoming or anonymous scholar, these claims would not have found an audience. But by 1956, Gopinath Mohanty had already established himself firmly as a novelist and a sound scholar to boot—for by then he had bagged the Sahitya Akademi award. But, as it turned out, one of the most powerful cultural and political icons of Odisha (as associate of Nehru and Vallabhbhai Patel), Harekrushna Mahatab, the editor of the journal where these startling claims were made, himself dismissed these arguments in his editorial in *Jhankar*, vol. III, July. It is perfectly possible that soon after he asked Krishnachandra Panigrahi, the noted historian, to embark on the project of studying Gopinath Mohanty's claims. Obtaining a grant to study Sarala Das's *Mahabharata* in Delhi, Krishnachandra Panigrahi admits to using the printed version of the epic supplied by the Prajatantra Prachar Samiti (owned by Harekrushna Mahatab) in order to reconstruct the history of Odisha from the Odia epic and because of the generosity of his patrons, Krishnachandra Panigrahi publishes a series of essays in the same periodical (*Jhankar*) owned by Mahatab but without taking cognizance of Gopinath Mohanty's claims, published a few months earlier. After the first four parts in the series had appeared, the novelist sends rejoinders refuting Krishnachandra Panigrahi's claims, which too were published in the same journal. Other scholars also participate in the debate and the controversy assumes a rather virulent form.[44] The chief bones of contention between the two were:

1. The versions to use, the authenticity thereof (printed versions and those in palm-leaf manuscripts).
2. The time and place of the birth of the poet.
3. The Raja Kapileswar mentioned in the epic ('*pranamitey khatai Shri Kapileswara Maharaja*' of the Adya Parva, not the one who lived in the fifteenth century, as believed by Krishnachandra Panigrahi and many others before him; but, according to Gopinath Mohanty, could have been some other Raja by the same or similar name who lived in the ninth century).
4. The use of certain proper names of people and places, words and their etymology.
5. Misuse of logic to draw erroneous conclusions.

Much else was nitpicking which even led to personal attacks. But even beneath these lay subtler subtexts. Krishnachandra Panigrahi studied the epic with a view to extracting evidence of the poet's engagement with the Muslim rulers, culture and the Perso-Arabic idiom. This could be validated only if the period of the poet was indeed that of the fifteenth century. Gopinath Mohanty's contention was that these names and idioms were indigenous, Sanskritic and even Buddhist—predating Muslim rule. Gopinath Mohanty cited two printed versions as the chief culprits in the misrepresentation— 1917, Arunodaya Press and 'the one published by the Utkal Trading Co'.[45] His study reveals to him that the epic poet of Odisha was born in the ninth century or earlier.

Such proper names as 'Yamagoshtha', 'Daradasen', 'Surasahi', Munehi', etc., and terms as 'Kotwal', 'Brahmasahi' and 'Chokhar', etc., which Krishnachandra Panigrahi says are 'truly yavanic' are dismissed as belonging to the pre-Muslim era. One example will suffice. In the epic Daradasen had destroyed 'Brahmasahi' in his battle with Arjuna. According to Krishnachandra Panigrahi, the suffix 'Shahi' was derived from the Perso-Arabic term 'Shah' or Raja. But for Gopinath Mohanty, 'Shahi' always signified a village quarter or locality. He emphatically declares that 'The term, "Shahi" in Sarala Das can never be Yavanic'.[46] Similarly, according to Krishnachandra Panigrahi, the historic event of King Kapilendra's attack on Bahmani to free Sultan Humayun's fort is allegorized as the episode between Yamaprusta and Daradasen. For Krishnachandra Panigrahi, this is an example of Hindu-Muslim amity in the fifteenth century. Gopinath Mohanty argues that the two episodes are not comparable; and also that King Kapilendra was not the only king in his time who fought battles. Similarly, Krishnachandra Panigrahi argues that the two place names, Vijay Nagar and Udaygiri are both frequently mentioned in all the versions of the Odia epic. 'Since these places were non-existent in the 9th century Mohanty avoids mentioning them. There was no Udaygiri prior to the 15th century. Mohanty does not mention these since he is out to prove that Sarala Das lived in the 9th-10th century.'[47]

On studying the two sets of arguments, one might come to the conclusion that the differences, for their scholarly trappings are heavily coloured by their respective ideologies. It is possible that there is a strong subtext of a rivalry between a professional scholar of history and a writer of imaginative fiction practising amateur scholarship—between an academic and a bureaucrat. But if Krishnachandra Panigrahi comes across as a trained historian believing in 'scientific' methodology, he also comes across as someone with a liberal outlook, who would eschew any jingoistic tendentiousness. But, for all that, his logic sometimes goes askew. As the historian-linguist Gaganendranath Das has pointed out, at the end of the battle, the last piece was by Krishnachandra Panigrahi, which gave the impression that he was the victor, and Gopinath Mohanty, the vanquished. But the fact of the matter was that Krishnachandra Panigrahi's dating of Sarala Das went along accepted lines established by scholars of the eminence of Mrutyunjay Rath and Nilakantha Das during the previous half a century of scholarship.[48] Though there seemed to be few takers for Gopinath Mohanty's arguments, they appear, nonetheless more cogent of the two, even when his claims about the possible period of the epic poet appeared preposterous to many in the end.

I have mentioned above that Nilakantha Das offers a demonized version of the Muslims in India. He says, 'Indians had seen demons like Sikander or Alexander; but they had never seen Muslims. . . . Muslims! they surpassed the wildest imagination of the *bharatiyas*. . . . When the Muslims came, they lusted after Hindu women, and killed their men and took away or raped them. . . .'[49] That Nilakantha Das moved away from the INC after Gandhi's assassination and came closer to the fold of the Jana Sangh is a well-known fact in Odisha intellectual circles. Natrually, some of these subtexts plague the debate between the two stalwarts. In his rejoinder to Gopinath Mohanty, Krishnachandra Panigrahi tries to establish the context of Islamic rule in Sarala Das's *Mahabharata*, and seems to counter the prevalent negative representation of the Muslims. His discussion of what he thought was Sarala Das's representation of the Muslim rule was sympathetic. He says that where Sarala Das speaks of the '*Alekh Purush*' or '*Mahabrahma*', he actually is speaking of the monotheistic Muslim. But Gopinath Mohanty's Sarala Das lived in the pre-Islamic period of the region's history and Gopinath Mohanty himself appears to be less tolerant. In his response to Krishnachandra Panigrahi, Gopinath Mohanty scoffs at the idea,

If Panigrahi could prove that any Hindu religious text has ever shown any respect to Islamic religion or culture even by mistake, then it would be a great discovery. Even though the Hindu is broad-minded like the sky, in none of his scriptures has he either mentioned believers of any other faith, or allowed their shadow to touch any of his temples. It is not necessary to go into this; today Bharat is Bharat, Pakistan is Pakistan.[50]

He goes on to ask, 'where does Panigrahi get the proof that "*Alekh Purush*" meant *Pathan*?'[51] Later, he shows another aspect of his ideological mooring, and betrays a streak of postcolonial Odia nationalism in his main argument. Obviously, as a dig at Krishnachandra Panigrahi he says that he notices a tendency among scholars that, 'if they could prove that the greatest Odia poet was stupid, the culture or literature of this *desha* was not that ancient, or that Jaydeva was not an Odia, a great purpose could be served'.[52] Krishnachandra Panigrahi remembered this unkind cut much later when he would give several examples of how among many Odias of his time he noticed a tendency to claim antiquity for characters and events to prove their nationalistic zeal. In his autobiography published a few years later, Krishnachandra Panigrahi is pained to point out how it had become a profitable business for many scholars to show off their Odia identity by making absurd claims about

Jayadeva being an Odia. He points out that he had tried to call the bluff on such people by saying that no one had taken the trouble of proving this to the world by writing anything in English. Similarly, eighty years after Radhanath Ray and Yogeshchandra Ray had brought to light the achievement of Samanta Chandrasekhar, no Odia scholar had done any further work to enhance his reputation.[53]

More to the point, Krishnachandra Panigrahi had not forgotten the controversy and returned to the subject of the authenticity of Sarala Das's *Mahabharata* after thirty long years. In his autobiography, he points out how the Artaballabha Mohanty edition produced after a prolonged delay by the Ministry of Culture, Government of Odisha, was not trustworthy. Produced ten years after Artaballabha Mohanty's death, he says, 'it is not a faithful reproduction of the manuscript he had prepared. Many significant parts have been deleted; and some others have been so distorted that they do not seem like Mohanty's.'[54] In fact, he went on to accuse the authorities of having manipulated those passages, terms and phrases which proved his point. These, he said, had been deleted systematically to prove his thesis wrong. He alleged that the *pothis* that Gopinath Mohanty used were faked by Pandit Sadashiva Rathasharma, a master faker of old texts.[55]

The Importance of Being Sarala Das

Around the time of the Gopinath Mohanty-Krishnachandra Panigrahi controversy, the poet Gyanindra Verma felt impelled to enter the fray and intervene, in a way that only a poet could, through '*Sarala Dasara Ghara*' (Where Did Sarala Das Live). It is worth quoting the poem at some length in prose paraphrase (if only because it captures the essence of the futile controversy):

> A hectic search is going on to find out where Sarala lived.
> Did he belong to Jankahar or Jhankad?
> Or did his village lie on the banks of river Prachi or the Chandrabhaga,
>   river Chitroptala or the Brudhamata? The search goes on.
> Again, the search extends to the period he had lived in.
> Dates, months and years will have to be fixed.[56]

The poem can be seen as an exasperated response to the obsession of scholars with the 'authentic' text and the 'true' identity of the author and his place of birth. It touches upon the key issues of the debate; but dismisses them as irrelevant to the larger question of the poet's greatness and transcendence beyond specificities of birth and death. Significantly, the lines also touch upon the issue of the *jati* and nation, which is also the reason for claiming him (or Jayadeva) as 'one of our own'.

Mayadhar Mansinha in his *History of Odia Literature* not only gives him ample space for discussion, but calls the work 'a national epic'.[57] Surendra Mohanty devotes almost the entire first volume (Adi Parva) of his *History of Odia Literature* to a discussion of Sarala Das's *Mahabharata*.[58] No wonder, the essential point in the entire controversy is Sarala Das's Odia identity which is what makes his time and place of birth a bone of contention. Every time the need for asserting Odia identity arose, Sarala Das was invoked, as indeed he was during the recent claims of 'classical status' for the Odia language. The volume prepared by the protagonists of the movement to stake the claim carried an abstract with the lines:

Such a tradition accounts for the emergence in the 15th century AD of a grand epic like the Odia *Mahabharata*, consisting of one hundred and forty thousand couplets. It may be mentioned here that this epic is written in an innovative verse form known as *dandi bruta*. This is the only [complete] *Mahabharata* among the modern Indian languages written by a *single author* in a life time [emphasis mine].[59]

To conclude the history of Sarala Das's *Mahabharata* as a text can test even the most sophisticated theories emanating from the West. In a way, the growth of the *Mahabharata*, whether the Sanskrit or Odia version as a text, owes its present vitality to the lack of closure or finitude, made possible through its invitation to re-rendering. Much of it was unconscious and part of the culture in which it has grown, namely, the oral tradition, and the near-free-for-all re-inscribing, and multiple representation. To return to Nilakantha Das's account cited earlier, that 'the practice of exaggeration and interpolation was quite popular and widespread even during Sarala Das's time, there can be no doubt'.[60] While copying the epic out from stacks of palm-leaf manuscripts onto fresh stacks, the scribes, especially the sellers among them, would vastly exaggerate and interpolate fresh episodes, and tout them as what is now called the unique selling point of their versions. There was no limit to such hyperboles and interpolations in the text, according to Nilakantha Das. He goes on to give examples of such episodes, and says these versions can never be Sarala Das's. But, all interpolations and alterations went in his name. The idea of arresting its growth is foreign to the very culture which engendered the text. It is not the relative authenticity of a given text which is in question. In this sense, the completion of an editorial job which results in a perfect text is not a cause for celebration, just as the confusion over a text's authenticity and its author's identity is no cause for despair. This nonchalance towards the sacrosanctity of the text may sound typical of Eastern/Hindu mysticism, and quite incomprehensible to a Western audience but the changing attitude in the Western philosophical tradition may eventually find the idea quite acceptable. In his recent study of Geoffrey Chaucer's *Canterbury Tales*, Andrew Higl invokes the work of Henry Jenkins on the 'convergence culture' of the new-media to offer a formulation that could take on the issue of the authenticity of the oldest and one of the most canonical of all the works in the English literary canon. The *Canterbury Tales*, Higl says, 'has a history of transmission and reception in which acts of consumption and production converged. Though often ignored, these post-Chaucer continuations and additions to the *Tales* remain in the extant manuscripts and early printed editions but unseen in the modern editions of Chaucer's works because editors have condemned them as spurious and apocryphal.'[61] In the context of discussions above, these issues sound quite familiar to scholars of the *Mahabharata*. Higl says:

When most scholars and students imagine the *Canterbury Tales*, they likely have in mind a set of very specific tales by Chaucer perhaps in a specific order. Oftentimes, the text of the *Tales* that most imagine is that of a modern critical edition such as the Riverside, which presents only one version of the *Tales*, and that version is largely a modern editorial construct. Such editions only include those tales that we assume Chaucer wrote. As far as we know, there is no surviving manuscript in Chaucer's hand, so there have been some tenuous assumptions involved in the selection of what ought to be and what ought not to be in Chaucer's oeuvre since his death. . . .

One just needs to substitute terms like Canterbury Tales/Tales, Geoffrey Chaucer/Chaucer, Riverside, etc., by terms such as Sarala Mahabharata, Sarala Das and Artaballabha Mohanty edition, respectively, that would yield a passage that is as valid to the Odia epic as it is to Chaucer's *Tales*. The statement will still hold good. Given its genesis, and its continued oral and free-for-all scribal fluidity, reception and circulation, any attempt to erect an authentic, well-defined and identifiable author called Sarala Das by using the text, and to simultaneously resurrect an authentic text actually written by one Sarala Das, will constitute a fallacious methodology.

In any case, this double enterprise goes against the very dynamics of the culture which has produced the text. I shall go into some of the internal logic of the text that shows this to be the case. The English scholar, John Boulton (then a professor at the University of London) too argued against the idea when the edition was finally published. He drew a comparison with Shakespeare and said:

It is no longer possible to bring out one definitive edition of Sarala Das's *Mahabharata*. . . . Unfortunately, in this country (India) too, like in our country (England), critics concentrate on the 'text'. Through enactment, interpretation and editing, every now and then Shakespeare appears in a new version. It will be difficult for Shakespeare himself to identify the definitive edition of Shakespeare. . . .[62]

It is ironic that such discourses from the West have to be invoked now to derive conclusions about the textuality and authorship of an Odia text that were available for centuries as has been seen in the instances cited from Sarala Das's *Mahabharata*. In spite of such knowledge, Odia scholars from the late nineteenth century onward, and more vigorously in mid-twentieth century, have clamoured for an authoritative version under the rising influence of modernity. As Mayadhar Mansinha says, the Odia masses who loved Sarala Das 'care little for pedantic accuracy'.[63] Going by the contemporary trend among informed scholars, the use of the 'authenticated' edition by Artaballabha Mohanty continues to be preferred over other available versions. But there are, and there will continue to be, questions about its authenticity, whenever a new historical/literary/linguistic view will emerge. This is no reason to not perpetuate in print the tradition of the *pothi* form—a willingness to accept diversity of reading and rewriting. The question to ask is why the textuality of the other Odia classics and their authorship has not been questioned, given that these texts have also been copied out variously? To the best of my knowledge, no one has even bothered to compare the diverse versions, let alone compare the differences in them. Though, Natabar Samantaray questioned the temporal and spatial disparities of the five comrades, who were thought to be contemporaries, the same was never challenged and no controversies ensued. Their printed texts are also in circulation unproblematically.[64] One reason could be that Sarala Das's has been perceived as the foundational text of the Odias ever since the modern concept of Odia identity emerged in the late-colonial period. No wonder, Boulton invoked Shakespeare to add to his comparatist dimension with regard to the authenticity of the text. Apart from the authorized version of the Bible, it is Shakespeare or Milton as 'national' poets, not so much Chaucer (who is much older and whose textual 'purity' is more suspect) who is pressed into service to assert *English* identity.

Notes

1. For a detailed discussion on the preparation of the definitive edition of the Sanskrit *Mahabharata* by V.S. Sukthankar and his team. See, Arjun Mahey, 'Epic Mediations: Text, Book, and Authority in the Organization of the *Mahabharata*', in *Reflections and Variations on the Mahabharata*, ed. T.R.S. Sharma, New Delhi: Sahitya Akademi, 2009, pp. 165–386; V.S. Sukthankar et al., eds., *The Critical Edition of the Sanskrit Text: The Mahabharata for the First Time Critically Edited*, 19 vols., Poona: BORI, 1939–59; and J.A.B. van Buitenen, tr. and ed., *The Mahabharata*, Chicago and London: University of Chicago Press, 1973.

2. Nilkantha Das, *Odia Sahityara Krama Parinama*, Cuttack: Grantha Mandir, 2011, p. 346.

3. Ashutosh Mukherjee, comp., *Odia Sahitya Parichaya*, Calcutta: Baptist Mission Press, n.d., p. 85; and Labanya Nayak, *Odia Charita-Sahitya*, Cuttack: Friends Publishers, 1988, p. 147.

4. Gourangacharan Das, ed., *Artaballav Rachana Samagra*, vol. II, Cuttack: Ravenshaw College, 2015.

5. Sukthankar et al., eds., *The Critical Edition of the Sanskrit Text*.

6. Jatindra Mohan Mohanty, *History of Odia Literature*, Bhubaneshwar: Vidya Prakashan, 2006, p. 289.

7. Jatindra Mohan Mohanty had previously and subsequently challenged poets like Sachi Rautray with charges of plagiarism or 'unpoetic' verse, also accusing Odia translators of Tagore of incompetence, among other things, through letters to editors of periodicals—steadily from 1930s to 1980s.

8. Among the other scholars who made significant interventions were Bansidhar Mohanty and Achyutanand Das. Krishnachandra Panigrahi does not mention this issue; but Gopinath Mohanty referred to Sarala Das as a poet belonging to the ninth–tenth centuries in his brief survey in his monograph on Radhanath Ray for the same series (*Makers of Indian Literature*, New Delhi: Sahitya Akademi, 1975).

9. Basant Panda tried to be even-shaded in his discussion of Gopinath Mohanty's claims.

10. As Mayadhar Mansinha says, the Odia version predated the Bangla version by nearly 200 years; Mayadhar Mansinha, *History of Odia Literature*, New Delhi: Sahitya Akademi, 1962.

11. Das, *Odia Sahityara Krama Parinama*; and Mansinha, *History of Odia Literature*, pp. 61–2.

12. In his version, Sarala Das presents an episode where Arjuna is confronted by a strange figure, an animal with limbs and parts from

nine (hence nava) different animals. As he discovers, it was none other than Vishnu/Sri Krishna in disguise to test whether Arjuna could recognize him. The episode occurs in the 'Madhyaparva, Prathama Khanada', in *Sāralā Mahābhārata*, Cuttack: Sarala Sahitay Sansad, 2007, pp. 428–33. Also see, J.P. Das, *Puri Paintings*, New Delhi: Arnold-Heinemann, 1982, pp. 136–7. He thinks that since the Odisha temples predate Sarala Das, the iconography of Navagunjara is conspicuous by its absence in these. They are seen in the patachitra of succeeding centuries.

13. Sudipta Kaviraj, 'The Two Histories of Literary Culture in Bengal', in *Literary Cultures in History: Reconstructions from South Asia*, ed. Sheldon Pollock, New Delhi: OUP, 2003.

14. Das, *Odia Sahityara Krama Parinama*.

15. John Boulton, 'Sarala Dasa: His Audience, His Critics and His Mahabharata', in *Essays on Oriya Literature*, compiled and with an afterword by Ganeswar Mishra, Prafulla Pathagara, 2003, pp. 7–38.

16. Sheldon Pollock, *Literary Cultures in History: Reconstructions from South Asia*, New Delhi: OUP, 2003.

17. William Smith was a scholar teaching Hindi, Bengali and Cultural history. See, <http://sasnet.lu.se.asiaportal.info/node/590391>, accessed 12 November 2012.

18. The *Sāralā Mahābhārata* attributes the naming of Odisha as 'Odorasthra' to 'Gopal Nrupati'; quoted in Das, *Odia Sahityara Krama Parinama*, pp. 199–200.

19. Partly due to the exigencies of textbook production as Natabar Samantaray argues; Natabar Samantaray, *History of Modern Odia Literature*, Cuttack: Self Published, 1963. Also see, Animesh Mohapatra, 'The Local and the Global in Oriya Public Sphere: 1866–1948', Unpublished Ph.D. dissertation, University of Delhi, 2016.

20. Sudarshan Acharya's edition of extant editions of *Indradhanu* with a detailed introduction is most informative of all studies on the subject.

21. Pierre Bourdieu et al., *The Rules of Art: Genesis and Structure of the Literary Field*, tr. Susan Emanuel, California: Stanford University Press, 1996.

22. Kaviraj, 'The Two Histories of Literary Culture in Bengal', pp. 537–8.

23. Nivedita Mohanty, *Oriya Nationalism: Quest for a United Orissa, 1866-1956*, revised and enlarged edn., Jagatsinghpur: Prafulla, 2005; Gaganendranath Das, 'Soma-vamsi Yayati in Tradition and Medieval Odia Literature', *Studies in History*, vol. 28, no. 2, 2012; Subhakant Behera.

24. Das, '*Soma-vamsi* Yayati in Tradition and Medieval Odia Literature', pp. 151–77.

25. In the form of the search, retrieval and even invention of a glorious past. Elsewhere, I have spoken of the emergence of a new discourse, which I call the 'Odia Jeremiad' following Sacvan Bercovitch's formulation of the American Jeremiad.

26. Buitenen, *The Mahabharata*, p. xxiii.
27. Das, *Odia Sahityara Krama Parinama*, p. 301.
28. Ibid.
29. Buitenen, *The Mahabharata*, p. 21.
30. Ibid., p. 22.
31. Ibid., p. 20.
32. It is to be noted here that his assumed name is derived from this presiding deity, 'Ma' or Mother Sarala: the poet, originally Siddheswar Parida, is the 'Dasa', i.e. servant of Sarala.
33. Mayadhar Mansinha describes this version of the epic thus, 'Of the *Mahabharatas* [produced in the eighteenth century], the best known is the authenticated translation of Krishna Simha, the Raja of Dharakot, a principality in Ganjam district. Known all over Odisha as Krishna Simha *Mahabharata*, this work is only next in popularity to the vibrant epic of Sarala Das; Mansingh, *History of Odia Literature*, p. 114.
34. Ibid., p. 234.
35. Mohanty, *Odiā Bhāshā Āndolana*, p. 234.
36. However, as discussed by Animesh Mohapatra, Bijoy Chandra Mazumdar's chronological mistake can be attributed to his misreading of Manmohan Chakravarty's essay. All contemporary historians arrange the same poets in the following order: Sāralā Das (mid-fifteenth century), Balarām Das, and Jagannāth Das (sixteenth century), and Upendra Bhanja (late seventeenth and early eighteenth centuries).
37. W.W. Hunter, *Odisha or the Vicissitudes of an Indian Province under Native and British Rule*, London: Smith, Elder & Co., 1872.
38. Shyamsundar Rajguru, 'Shudramuni Sarala Das (the *Mahabharata*-writer)', *Utkal Sahitya*, vol. 7, no. 4, 1903, pp. 112–15.
39. Mrutyunjay Rath's essay was serialized in three episodes in the literary periodical *Mukura* in 1911.
40. The first one to be linguistically formed, and thirty-three years after the launching of the formal demand in 1903, with the setting up of Utkal Sammilani.
41. Fakir Mohan Senapati, *Sabhapati Abhibhasan*, 1914; repr. in *Granthabali: Complete Works of Fakir Mohan Senapati*, vol. 3, ed. Debendra Dash, Cuttack: Grantha Mandir, 2008.
42. Sukthankar et al., eds., *The Critical Edition of the Sanskrit Text*.
43. Gopinath Mohanty, 'Sarala Dasnka Samaya O Sabhaparva', *Jhankara*, vol. 5, no. 4, 1958, pp. 363–71 and 'Sarala Dasnka Ghara Keunthi', *Jhankara*, vol. 8, no. 2, 1957, pp. 249–58.
44. Contrary to existing scholarship, it was Gopinath Mohanty who first stirred the hornet's nest by asking 'Sarala Dasnka Ghara Keunthi?'. Also see, Panigrahi, 'Sarala Sahityara Rachannakala O Aitihashika Chitra', *Jhankara*, vol. 8, no. 9, 1956, pp. 1–10. To these Gopinath Mohanty responded by writing a few rejoinders one after the other and Krishnachandra responded in successive issues of the same periodical.
45. *Jhankara*, vol. 8, no. 2, 1956, p. 251.

46. Ibid., vol. 9, no. 5, 1957, p. 367.

47. Ibid., vol. 9, no. 6, 1957, p. 587.

48. Gaganendranath Das, 'Sarala Mahabharata o Itihasa', in *Nirbachita Prabandha Samkalana*, Cuttack: Vidyapuri, 2005.

49. Das, *Odiya Sahityara Krama Parinama*, p. 171.

50. *Jhankara*, vol. 9, no. 4, 1957, p. 363.

51. Ibid. The term *pathan* is pejorative in Odia.

52. Ibid., p. 366. Interestingly enough, the issue of Jayadeva's Odia or Bengali identity continues to surface in lectures and newspapers even today.

53. Krishnachandra Panigrahi, *Mo Samayara Odisha* (Odisha of My Time), Cuttack: Kitab Mahal, 1978, p. 198.

54. Ibid., p. 191.

55. Ibid., pp. 157–72. Krishnachandra Panigrahi deals with the process of faking in his autobiography. The revival of 'Utkala Brahmins' is attributed to Pandit Shri Sadashiva Rathasharma who, in the mid-twentieth century, re-established Sanskrit education in around Odisha. Also see, J.P. Das, 'Micchha Itihasa', in *Ama Odia Amara Odisha*, Bhubaneswar: Shikshasandan, 2016, pp. 116–22. He had personal experience of such unethical practices of the Pandit.

56. The rest of the poem in free prose translation runs thus:

> Information on *King Kapilendra* whose subject he was must be looked for.
> These are but bubbles in the river of time but debates on them rage on.
> What goddess did this poet pay his worship to?
> Was it Sarala or Sarola Chandi? Or was it Hengula or Mangala?
> All these however *belong to Odisha*.
> Somewhere here had Sarala built his house.
> There is no doubt it has crumbled, or has been washed away by a river.
> May be all that is left of it is a patch of sun burnt rocky ground.
> Who knows, someone may locate it one day.
> But this son of clay who rose like a lotus from mud vanishes
> if you seek to confine him to a house or in a prison of years or months.
> Who cares where the poet Jayadeva was born, in Kenduli or in Kendubilva? Singing of divine ecstasy he belongs to the *whole of India*.
> Listen to me, oh! you residents of Kania and Jhankad.
> The gifted have met the death fit for worms here.
> No one knows if the poet who wrote the *history of his race*
> *and created a literature for it died of starvation.*
> No record of which village he had breathed his last in has been kept.
> All we are left with are *worm eaten pothis* written by him and we have not even begun to study them properly.

Why then do you disturb him lying fast asleep in his quiet grave?
Stop trying to find him in the feeble light of glow worms.
Let the setting sun rest in peace.
He belongs to everyone.
He has made every home, every city his own.
Go and sing his story in every house, in every city (Jatindra K. Nayak's translation).

57. Mansinha, *History of Odia Literature*, p. 60.
58. Surendra Mohanty, *Odiya Sahityara Kramabikasha*, Cuttack: Agraduta, 1978.
59. *Classical Odia in Historical Perspective*, Department of Culture, Government of Odisha (The Document Submitted for Classical Status of Odia Language to the Ministry of Culture Government of India), 2015. It may be pointed out here that in 2004, the Government of India declared that languages that met certain requirements could be accorded the status of a 'Classical Language in India'. In a 2006 press release, the then Minister of Tourism & Culture Ambika Soni told the Rajya Sabha the following criteria were laid down to determine the eligibility of languages to be considered for classification as a 'Classical Language': High antiquity of its early texts/recorded history over a period of 1,500–2,000 years; a body of ancient literature/texts, which is considered a valuable heritage by generations of speakers; the literary tradition be original and not borrowed from another speech community; the classical language and literature being distinct from modern, there may also be a discontinuity between the classical language and its later forms or its offshoots.
60. Das, *Odia Sahityara Krama Parinama*, p. 345.
61. Andrew Higl, *Playing the Canterbury Tales: The Continuations and Additions*, Surrey: Ashgate, 2012.
62. John Boulton, *Jhankara*, 1975, pp. 178–9; quoted in Panigrahi, *Mo Samayara Odisha*, p. 154.
63. Mansinha, *History of Odia Literature*, p. 60.
64. Natabar Samantaray, 'Panchasakha: A Myth?', in *Adhunika Odia Sahityara Bhittibhumi*, Cuttack: Friends Publishers, 1964.

5

Mahabharata's Chitrangada Redux
Contemporary Queer Appropriations of Tagore

The same year in which Radhanath Ray's experimental reinvention of the *Mahabharata* began to be serialized in at least two periodicals, Tagore's radical reinvention of an episode from the same epic was published in the form of a *gitinatya* or poetic play—*Chitrangada* (1892). The Odia experiment caused quite a stir in the public sphere, whereas *Chitrangada* made a relatively quiet entry into the Bangla literary canon, with a few contemporaries like Dwijendralal Ray (19 July 1863–17 May 1913) accusing Tagore of the distortions he subjected the noble character of Arjuna to, and for his depiction of the princess as 'a prostitute-like profligate woman self-indulging with her lover Arjun and therewith desecrating the virtuous chastity of daughter and wife depicted by the original epic'.[1] Almost a century after Tagore won the Nobel Prize, Rituparno Ghosh produced a film that was a radical (and one might say, controversial) take on the ambiguous sexuality of Tagore's heroine. Why did *not* his film *Chitrangada* (a queer reinvention of Tagore's iconic dance-drama of the same title, itself drawn on the *Mahabharata*), generate a heated debate on the controversial queer content in it, especially at a time when Article 377 itself is in the middle of fierce controversy? After all, Tagore's *Chitrangada* was itself a radical reinvention in its time of the character in the *Mahabharata*. There could be two reasons—one that the film catered to a niche audience; the second reason could be that discussion on the theme of the film itself was overshadowed by the controversies for nearly two decades over *Fire*, *Girlfriend*, and over Article 377, the court verdicts, pride marches, etc.

However, this chapter does not deal directly with such larger questions; rather, it takes up the subject of contemporary queer appropriations of a writer who has seldom been seen in terms of the rainbow thrown on the wall by the queer prism. The point I wish to make in this chapter is that homoerotically inclined subjects can and do 'misread' signs pertaining to the heteronormative world around them in order to derive pleasures and seek out a larger body of affective community. Also, in so doing, creative artists and critics extend a range of aesthetic possibilities. This may be because they are forced to spectate an overabundance of dominant cultural productions that are different from their own sexual proclivities. After all, until recently, the range of choices the queer subjects have had for entertainment—on the popular electronic and print media, cinema, etc.—has been extremely limited, and they have had to dip into the underground for queer art, that is not always of unquestionable merit, for succour. In the sphere of literature, similarly, it has been only a couple of decades since discussions of queer elements in established and celebrated authors such as Shakespeare, Walt Whitman, E.M. Forster, Virginia Woolf, W.H. Auden, and so on has gained ground. But these are mostly writers from the West. For Indians with a queer orientation or for queer people with an orientalist bias, India does not afford many gay or lesbian icons or iconic texts—one reason why dissident critics in India are often seen as over-interpreting traditional texts either by critics and reviewers with a right-wing bias or simply by straight critics.

In this context, it might be salutary to look at the gay reception of India's preeminent poet, Tagore. Though Indian admirers of Tagore are generally homophobic, queer interpretations of the man and his work are not entirely unknown. I have no intentions whatsoever of adding to the meagre corpus of the queer Tagore; rather, in what follows, I shall examine, especially citing the instance of his *Chitrangada*, how irrespective of the original intentions of Tagore, latter-day gay readers and spectators have attempted to appropriate and read his poetry and plays in ways that the mainstream audience might find offensive.

I

To begin with, I accidentally came across one such gay appropriation on a blog maintained by an American blogger, Kenneth Hill, who juxtaposes sepia photos of pairs of same-sex lovers from the late nineteenth century with literary texts from entirely different contexts to narrate what, according to him, the couples might be saying, doing, feeling, with the note, *'Photographer, sitters, unknown'*.[2] These pieces are from confirmed gay or gay-friendly, lesbian writers/ poets/artists such as C.P. Cavafy and Alexander Pushkin as well as from non-homoerotic writers and poets such as Charles Dickens. Hill justifies his enterprise as 'Assembling these Imagined Histories creates a gay ancestry of sorts that I have always longed to know —*even if I have had to make it up myself.* This is the lineage I wish had been passed down to me like so much treasure, like other cultures do to honour a common identity' [emphasis mine].[3] I did not find anything surprising about his exhibits except when I encountered one of Tagore's poems, 'Unending Love', in William Radice's translation, excerpts from which I quote:

> I seem to have loved you in numberless forms, numberless times
> In life after life, in age after age, forever.
> My spellbound heart has made and remade the necklace of songs,
> That you take as a gift, wear round your neck in your many forms,
> In life after life, in age after age, forever.[4]

Taken somewhat aback by this exhibit, I quickly tried to guess what may have encouraged Hill to read these lines as expression of homoerotic love is the incidence of gender-neutral pronouns such as 'you' and 'I'. Also, references to 'universal love' echoing Auden's valorization of the vision and feast of Agape, and the deployment of Whitmanesque rhetoric about '[t]he love of all man's days both past and forever' as well as of phrases like 'numberless forms' make it easy for the blogger to relocate the lines in a homoerotic ambience. If they had been given a different context, such as the sepia photograph of a man and woman in a similar posture, the same lines would have been read as part of the tradition of the heterosexual love lyric. Obviously, visual repositioning of a written/printed text involves a certain degree of semiotic figuration and reconfiguration.

But, to anyone familiar with Tagore's intellectual growth, the lines would appear not as poetic assertions of any queer identity, they would rather be perceived as belonging to the intertwining traditions stretching back to the Upanishadic teachings through the medieval Bhakti[5] to the rural folk traditions of the Baul[6] that Tagore knew only too well, including Kabir's *dohas*[7] which he had co-translated with the American mystic poet, Evelyn Underhill. For instance, Tagore's debt to the Maithili poet, Vidyapati[8] is well-known. One of Vidyapati's verses is well worth quoting here:

All my inhibition left me in a flash,
When he robbed me of my clothes,
But his body became my new dress.
Like a bee hovering on a lotus leaf
He was there in my night, on me!

Here, Vidyapati's graphic description notwithstanding, the traditional semiotic would insist that the poet's bhaktic persona assumes the garb of Radha and imagines being embraced by Krishna. But Vidyapati's is not the only instance. In his *The Religion of Man*, Tagore quotes several other poet-saints of medieval India who help in our understanding and placing Tagore's views on the subject. Tagore may have been aware of the then newly emergent sexological discourses engaging in conflicting views about 'inversion' and 'third sex'; but instead of invoking these, he chooses to highlight and work within the indigenous traditions.

Recently, J. Edgar Bauer has put these traditional instances to slightly different use. Offering readings that were totally secular, he says in his article that their 'ecstatic homoeroticism can hardly be overlooked'.[9] Further, referring to Tagore's quotation from one of them, he comments how one of the bhaktic poet-saints exclaims without subterfuge, 'Thou seest me, O Divine Man (*narahari*), and I see thee, and our love becomes mutual'.[10] This queer critic refers to another of Tagore's quotation from a Baul, 'Man seeks the man in me and I lose myself and run out'.[11] Soon Bauer takes over and goes on to pile quotation upon quotation from more of the poet-saints including Kabir. Kabir utters his unconditional surrender as *wife* to the exalted male Beloved, 'I meet my husband, and leave at His feet the offering of my body and my mind'. More importantly, Kabir reasserts his rapturous sex-crossing when acknowledging the shortcomings of 'her' bridal love, 'When people say I am Thy bride, I am ashamed; for I have not touched Thy heart with my heart'.[12]

Bauer, it seems, gets carried away by his 'discovery', and wonders why Tagore does not do enough to articulate what appears to be obvious to the modern reader. Obviously, apart from his propensity to secularize Indian mysticism, Bauer is looking for evidence in English translation of all these lines in order to be able to isolate strands of homoeroticism, without realizing that in their original context and language register the semantic structures are different. For example, in the first quote from the Baul mystic, man is generic rather than a gendered subject. But in the English translation, it sounds conveniently homoerotic.

Similarly, even in his own time, Tagore's views and Whitmanesque deportment had prompted certain Western intellectuals to see similarities between Tagore's views and their own on human sexuality, as was then emergent. For instance, Magnus Hirschfeld (1868–1935; a well-known sexologist, who had met and recorded his conversations with Tagore), read in Tagore's public persona certain feminine features and gleefully reproduces observations by a teacher (who may have himself imbibed Western values) at Santiniketan, to the effect that Tagore resembled a *prima donna*. Here again, Bauer deals with the views of Hirschfeld at some length and is surprised how Tagore does not extend some of his own ideas regarding the continuum of creation to the sphere of human sexual binary.[13] This puzzlement on the part of Bauer may have been caused by his inability to grasp the indigenous tradition within which Tagore was meditating both in his discursive, philosophical prose as well as his poetry and plays. What Bauer seems to be missing out on is the pervasive evidence, in Tagore, of the immaterial, mystical self, the inner-outer binary, the inner essence, and outer garment of gender identity entrenched in Hindu mysticism. Finding Tagore's mysticism too elusive, Bauer, the queer critic, tries to construct and 'imagine a history' where he would have liked to place Tagore, very much like Hill does.

It is in the performative aspect of Tagore's art, however, that one is faced with more complex issues. For, from reading a printed text to spectating a performative one, the process of cultural translation might interfere with questions of intersubjectivity. Though, in his poetry Tagore successfully elides issues related to the materiality of the body, whether male or female, and shrouds his lines in impenetrable mysticism, in his dramatic art (because of its very performative nature) he meets with a serious challenge. His play *Chitrangada* (1935) is a case in point. When the dance-drama is performed on stage, the body's materiality cannot be elided even though Tagore deploys metaphors for external, bodily endowment as clothing, as also through the semiotica of costume and body language, even though such symbols and imageries are not as pervasive as those in his poetic drama. Thus, any sensitive and intelligent choreographer who attempts to stage Tagore's dance-drama will have to contend with several questions about costume, choice of actors with certain kinds of bodily features and their body language, arising out of the contradictions between the visual-semantic and the thematic-epistemological. It is not only necessary for us to see how Tagore has interpreted the apparently innocuous Chitrangada episode from the Indian epic in revolutionary ways, but it might also prove to be a revelation in the context of the point I am trying to make, if we examine how his own representations of human sexuality and gender have inseminated fertile minds and helped proliferate even more radical representations.

That the Chitrangada episode from the Sanskrit epic held much significance for Tagore there is no doubt, since he returned to it again and again, having first composed a poetic play (*Chitrangada*; 1892), and then supervise its translation (if he did not translate it himself) into English as *Chitra*—for the English stage and with elaborate stage instructions. Then he got it published as *Chitra* (1914) without the stage directions, finally reworking it into a dance-drama in 1935. Why is Tagore interested, almost obsessed with the episode so as to inflect it to almost an unacceptable level of irreverence?[14] What does he do with it that prompts a queer film-maker like Rituparno Ghosh, more than a hundred years later, to reprise Tagore's play through his film *Chitrangada: The Crowning Wish* and in such a way as to give it a major queer twist nearly unacceptable to an average Tagore fan? A large part of this chapter is preoccupied with these and similar questions.

As an aside, one might note that such adventurous reinvention on Tagore's part was made possible partly because the Chitrangada episode is embedded in the scriptural text of the *Mahabharata*, and may be said to have been imbued in 'cult value'. When Tagore reinvents it on the modern stage, it is as yet unaided by technology, and its cult value ought to be intact. This enables Tagore to exploit, and subtly modernize the narrative. But, in the process, Arjuna and Chitrangada's father no longer remain the focal point, but are retrenched as they are to the background, diminishing the cult value. There is a parallel between Hill's effort to the cult of remembrance by using nineteenth-century photographs and excerpts from canonical literary pieces, that even when secularization of a cult is in process, through technology, an attempt is being made to retain the cult value.

Just as Tagore was poised on the cusp of modernity, Rituparno Ghosh's context is that of the globalized, postmodern epistemic moment. He lives in a time when Indian cinema has already fought its first battles with its homophobic audience (from *Fire* and *Girlfriend* onward). Though both films are not free from essentialism and sexual stereotypes, they pave the way for a more open discussion of queer identity, the representation of which continues to grow in mainstream Hindi cinema. Thus, when Rituparno Ghosh falls back on the cult value of the episode, he can afford to dispense with the cushion of the *Mahabharata*, and go straight to Tagore's dance-drama, *Chitrangada*. In spite of this denial of sacrality to his text,

the cult value derives by way of Tagore's own iconic status, even as
it (cult value)[15] relocates itself from the sacral to the secular context.

II

Vyasa's narration runs thus: in the Arjuna-*vanavasa* section of
Adiparva, Arjuna crosses the country of Kalinga and goes to
Manipura, where he meets Chitrangada, the daughter of Chitravahana,
the ruler of Manipura. He desires to possess her, and requests the
king for her hand. After satisfying himself about Arjuna's lineage,
the king gives the background to her birth and his future plans for
her. He says, 'there was in our race a king of the name of Prabhanjana,
who was childless . . . [after he performed severe penance, Mahadeva]
granted him the boon that each successive descendant of his race
should have one child only. In consequence of that boon . . . [a]ll
my ancestors . . . had each a male child. I, however, have only a
daughter to perpetuate my race.'[16] Then follow the crucial lines:

> *Ekacha mama kanyeyam kuloshyutpadinibhrusam*
> *Putromamayemiti mebhav anapurusharshava*
> *Putrika hetubidhina sangita bharatarshva*
> *Tatmadekahsuto joshyamjayate bharatashyoya*

The passage has been paraphrased by Kisari Mohan Ganguly.
Chitravahana says, 'But, o bull amongst men, I ever look upon this
daughter of mine as my son. O bull of Bharata's race, I have duly
made her a *Putrika*.' In another edition, the annotations are
somewhat different, though here too the cryptic Chitrangada section
(Chap. 214; verses 14 to 27) is silent about her upbringing. Far from
being 'manly' in any way, she is portrayed as a beautiful woman
right from when (and as) first seen by Arjuna. The two adjectives
used to describe her are '*charudarshana*' (good looking; verse 14)
and '*Bararoha*' (curvaceous; verse 15), i.e. well-proportioned, in
particular with beautiful waist and hips. She is just taken to be (not
even treated like) a son by Chitravahana; she does not look in any
way like a son. As the king puts it, it is his '*bhavana*' (fancy) that she
is his '*putra*'. The '*putrika*' line, which is held up by many as a
gender-neutral term for a child, follows immediately after and runs
as '*putrika hetubidhina samjita bharatarsava*', i.e. 'O Arjuna, she is
named/called by me *putrika* by *hetuvidhi*'. '*Hetuvidhi*', which
Professor Harish Trivedi explains in a personal communication to
me as 'maybe a technical term; literally, it means for a reason'. This
reason, explained parenthetically in the edition is—for the reason

that her first son will be regarded/recognized as my own son—in terms of succession to the throne. Chitravahana eventually agrees to give away his daughter to Arjuna with the proviso that after the son is born to them, he would leave both his wife and son behind and leave Manipura. Arjuna duly agrees and fulfils his promise subsequently.

Thus, the manly aspect and the boon that transforms Chitrangada into a lovely ultra-feminine beauty seem to be entirely the creation of Tagore. We see in the *Mahabharata*, that the boon from Shiva was for a sole child (*pradadeky ekam prasabey kule*, i.e. progenetate one each, with gender-neutral overtones) for each of the descendants, and a son was born to successive kings, whereas Tagore changes the plot significantly and consciously so that 'Lord Shiva promised to [her] royal grandsires an unbroken line of male descent'[17] but even this divine word 'proved powerless to change the spark of life in [her] mother's womb—so invincible was my nature, woman though I be'.[18] Tagore, after giving deft touches of signifiers for masculinity at crucial junctures, turns to the traditional Hindu view of *maya* (reality as illusion). 'Alas, that this frail disguise, the body, should make one blind to the deathless spirit!'[19] Arjuna realizes this much later, almost at the end of the one year of feminine beauty granted to Chitra, 'Illusion is the first appearance of Truth. Then she advances towards her lover in disguise. But a time comes when she throws off her ornaments and veils and stands clothed in naked dignity. I grope for that ultimate you, that bare simplicity of truth.'[20] In a way, Tagore here seems to be influenced by the following lines from the *Gita*:

vasamsijirnaniyathavihaya
navanigrhnatinaro'parani
tathasariranivihayajirnany
anyanisamyatinavanidehi[21]

[As a person puts on new garments, giving up old ones, similarly, the soul accepts new material bodies, giving up the old and useless ones]

To my mind, Tagore simply exploits the aporetic moment in the original episode, and he (or his as yet unknown source) interprets the terms *santana* and *putrika* (used instead of *putra* along with the difficult, *hetubidhina*) as male child to suit his need, and provides for a potential queer reading of the transformation. The only known account of the play's genesis is Tagore's own. In 1940, Tagore recalls his experience of a train journey of many years ago from Santiniketan to Kolkata when certain thoughts occurred to him and it was then that he remembered and recalled the Chitrangada episode as 'the episode, having taken different forms (he uses the term *rupantar*), had been playing in my mind'. He clearly states that his intention was to pit 'strength of character against external beauty', human value against natural value or '*Suchana*'.[22] But, of course, in his rendering, he does more than that as he delves deep into questions of masculinity and femininity often blurring the boundaries between the two, and insists on the essential core of humanness, the generic man or human, rather than the manly-man. My point, however, is that this strategic recasting by Tagore, of the characters, generates a kind of sexual polyvalence in the text that subsequent queer readers and spectators seem to have felt tempted to exploit, befitting their disposition.

Within the radical recasting of the tropes, however, in all his versions, Tagore portrays the original and metamorphosed Chitrangada most stereotypically. She is first manly and, therefore, *kurupa* (or ugly). She is brought up as a man of the warrior caste. She is also shown as failing to court Arjuna because of her manly features, even when she puts on women's garb. In fact, when she later recounts her encounter with Arjuna, she describes herself as having behaved shamelessly 'as though she were a man';[23] for a woman with *lajja* (shame), a *bhadramahila* (well-mannered woman),[24] would not make the first overture to a man (which could be Tagore's half wink to his contemporary audience). Chitrangada is further represented in terms of the then existing stereotype of a beautiful woman when she is metamorphosed by Madana into a feminine—and therefore exquisitely beautiful—woman. There is hardly any difference between the first version of 1892 and the 1935 version of Tagore's emphasis on the masculine-feminine binary, suggesting some sort of androgyny as an ideal. In the first, the stereotype of the woman as *abala* (bereft of strength) or the weaker sex appears again and again, 'I know no feminine wiles for winning hearts. My hands are strong to bend the bow. . .'.[25] After being ignored by Arjuna, she lays aside her 'man's clothing . . . the unaccustomed dress clung about my shrinking shame. . .'.[26] In the dance-drama version too, Tagore brings it up. In both, the attempt continues to be the valorization of the inner, essential self and the neglect of the outer cover of illusion of the body. 'Alas, I have failed the woman in me/thus far in my life/shame to the bow and arrow/shame to my strong arms.'[27]

In the original version as depicted in the *Mahabharata*, the coercive transaction over Chitrangada's body is between two dominant males—the father and the would-be husband, completely denying any agency to the woman. Tagore turns this on its head, and accords marginal agency to Arjuna and none to her father, who is not even a character in any of the versions. She desires Arjuna; it is she who arouses Arjuna's desire for her, and it is on her terms and conditions and not her father's that she agrees to accept him. Noteworthy are the series of imperative verbs that Chitrangada uses in her dialogues with Arjuna.

III

Generations of theatre directors have given various interpretations of the earlier and later Chitrangada by gendering her vis-à-vis Arjuna and her *sakhi*s. These interpretations are iterated and visibilized through costume, or as in the case of Arjuna, through a muscular body with or without facial hair, moustache, etc., and, accordingly, they have asked their actors to use appropriate body language and dance forms. Whereas, in most productions, then and even now, the heterosexual audience's titillatory expectations are kept alive, in minimalist sartorial make-up of the female actor as the manly Chitrangada, by merely adorning her with a man's headgear and, her prominent body language is used to iterate female sexuality through a kind of faux simulacra.

While in a heterosexual environment such violation of theatrical *auchitya* (propriety) is accepted without protest, a queer, phantasmic spectator might respond differently. One can see an example of this when a queer auteur like Rituparno Ghosh critiques such performative misappropriation in the dance-drama within his film *Chitrangada*. His reprisal of *Chitrangada*, by way of contemporanizing it with a sharp dose of intertextuality, sees a queer twist in the tale he receives from his idol, Tagore. Even more significantly, Rituparno Ghosh, who is himself a cross-dressing male in real life, plays the role of Rudra, the choreographer in the film. While rehearsing the opening scene (within the frame narrative) where Chitrangada and her friends are shown capturing Arjuna, the bare-chested actor playing Arjuna is revealed as a young man with long hair and a six-pack body, and the actor playing the role of Chitrangada (Kasturi) as the 'manly' princess. The hyperreal Ghosh/Rudra so deeply identifies with the character of Tagore's heroine that he is upset with the actor playing Chitrangada, because she acts too dainty to be mistaken for a man by Arjuna or even the spectators. First, he yells at the actor, 'not so dainty'. Failing to drive home the point, in a moment of black humour, he then accuses Kasturi of expressing the body language of a Radha playing Holi instead of behaving like a manly princess, as if in answer to Dwijendralal Ray's attack.[28]

Ghosh/Rudra goes on to explain Tagore's purpose by saying that Chitrangada was conditioned to be a man by her father, and so her body language needed to be shown to be that of a man. 'It was only when she saw Arjuna that she wished to be a woman'. Ghosh/ Rudra goes on to declaim that the story of Chitrangada is about desire, '*aur baabar icche versus Aur icche*' (her wish *v.* her father's wish); '*Chitrangada ekta iccher golpo*' (*Chitrangada* is the story of a wish) that 'you can choose your gender'. For Ghosh/Rudra this is *the* queer moment in Tagore that he sets out to unpack in his film. For us, this is *the* queer spectatorial phantasma that Ghosh/Rudra's queer subjectivity gazes and seizes upon. Self-reflexive to the hilt, the film even introduces a scene where a laudatory review of the dance-drama speaks of the novelty in the production. Later, of course, Rudra's own experiences in life convince him that he had failed to do justice to Tagore's *Chitrangada*, leading him to admit to Subho that he had not understood the character fully and, by implication, is critical of the ending of Tagore's dance-drama.

IV

So far in our discussion, we notice the imbrication of issues of performativity and spectatorship. I shall now deploy Brett Farmer's formulation of the 'fantasmatic spectator',[29] by which he tries to

. . . demonstrate how gay spectators can engage in queer fantasmatic negotiations of mainstream film. [He] suggest[s] that, in their readings of the Hollywood musical, gay spectators latch on to those points of rupture or excess to which the musical is so spectacularly prone and mobilize them to construct patently queer forms of fantasmatic desire.[30]

While analysing a few of the early movies to illustrate his point, he takes up a few plays which were turned into screenplays in the 1940s such as *The Pirate*, originally clearly fitting into the heteronormative format of early cinema. Originally written as a play, it was turned into a screenplay for the musical, which is how it became famous, especially among the gay spectators; and, as discussed by Farmer, Judy Garland became a gay icon. The gay blogger Hill too talks about how his 'reading a biography of Judy Garland in 1974 at the age of twelve' outed him.[31] Looking at the reasons why the movie and its heroine become gay icons, Farmer cites certain features of the movie such as its opulence (a characteristic feature of the director), the real-life image of the main character Garland, and the then prevailing homophobia-enforced public-private existence of gays.

Like *The Pirate* and other contemporary musicals, Tagore's dance-drama too can be seen as a theatrical 'musical' in the sense that the story is put to music with the characters acting out their parts through dance. It also enables a kind of visualization on stage, but with the difference that the spectator's perceptions are not aided by the technology of the movie camera. The naked eye is all that he/she uses. But traditionally, the play is enacted through various forms of dance such as Manipuri and Odissi, where the *mudra*s of the hand and eyes constitute the principal elements of body language which add to the textual language of the original author. This semiotic of the stage enables the director of the play, to read, and interpret it in certain ways that is not available to the reader of the printed text. What is true of films applies no less to the visualizing of printed texts.

Recently, in answer to a question by Shohini Ghosh, Rituparno Ghosh says that he identifies with Binodini of Tagore's *Chokher Bali*, which he had directed. The film ostensibly has nothing to do with the question of homosexuality, but even here the principle of phantasmatic spectator is equally applicable.[32] For Rituparno Ghosh says:

I identify with parts of all my films, but if I had to choose a character that was closest to my heart, it would be Binodini, played by Aishwarya Rai in *Chokher Bali*, because she stands on the threshold of transformation. Binodini becomes a widow when widow remarriage has been legislated (by the British) but has yet to find social acceptance. There is tragic isolation in being caught in the half-light of legitimacy. I feel a strong sense of identification with that.[33]

He did not have to try hard to identify with Chitrangada. When his film *Chitrangada* begins with a heavily drugged Rudra half way through his gender correction surgery, he tells the story of Chitrangada to Subho, a product of his hallucinated imagination. Soon, Rudra's hallucinatory interlocutor questions Rudra's production of Tagore's play by asking him 'Will it not be too autobiographical?' To this, Rudra/Ghosh replies, 'It is because you know me'. Yet, a few scenes later, Subho is so taken aback by Rudra's radical reprisal of the play within the film that he asks him, '*Eita je Tagorer Chitrangada seta kibojhajabe?*' (Will it be possible to recognize this as Tagore's *Chitrangada*?). Rudra/Ghosh's identification with Chitrangada was easy because, no matter what were Tagore's stated or implicit intentions, certain dialogues and the form of *Chitrangada* seem overdetermined by elements of sexual dissidence. These elements in Tagore's play start appearing in quick succession as Arjuna becomes increasingly curious about the identity of Chitrangada upon hearing details from the villagers, 'In affection', he was told, 'she is mother, in armed might she is king;' and 'in bravery she is manly/. . . on throne she is a lion-rider'.[34] The best examples of the queer potentiality of the Tagore text can be culled from the scenes where the *sakhis* are surprised at the 'unnatural' longing of Arjuna for the manly Chitrangada. They ask Arjuna pointedly whether he was already weary of womanly temptations, and has now started indulging in absurd longing, looking for 'a man in woman'.[35]

However, unlike Chitrangada, Rudra is born male. Unlike Chitrangada who is raised as a woman, and assumes manly features, Rudra's parents want him to go for counselling to cure his effeminacy and save them social embarrassment. The major invention, however, is that of Rudra's love interest for the male percussionist in his drama group—heroin addict, Partho, another name for Arjuna, and happily, a common Bengali name; the allegorization and contemporization of the Chitrangada episode could hardly be more obvious. To drive home the allegory, Rituparno Ghosh weaves scenes and lines from the play into the fabric of the screenplay. After having aroused the female passion in Rudra, and holding out hope for companionship, the relationship goes awry. When Subho asks him later why he should be in love with a heroin addict, he says that it is precisely because of that reason. After all, Partho is also ostracized by the society. Thus, very much like Garland's escapades providing the gay spectators of *The Pirate* with an image of their own dissidence, Rudra sees in Partho's drug addiction, images of his own ostracization within the heteronormative regime.

However, Subho's misgivings notwithstanding, the allegorical resonances are never a far cry, in terms of exact parallels or major discrepancies. For, the two fathers, Chitrangada's and Rudra's, wanted their child to fulfil their wish for inheritance. Though both in the epic and Tagore's play, the mother of Chitrangada is invisible, in Rituparno Ghosh, Rudra's mother plays a crucial and sympathetic role, and helps her gay son 'come out'. The transformation of Chitrangada in Tagore's play takes recourse to Ovidian narrative techniques,[36] so that the supernatural Kamadeva brings about the metamorphoses; but in Rituparno Ghosh's film, the plastic surgeon is responsible for Rudra's bodily transformations. Thus, Chitrangada's ambisexual body in Tagore becomes a palimpsest where Rituparno Ghosh overwrites a completely unambiguous queer text.

The allegorical plot in the screenplay takes an entirely different course from the original plot of Tagore's Chitrangada when Partho deserts Rudra because the latter cannot give him a child. Rudra receives a rude shock with the discovery of the materiality of his body, and yet at another level its immateriality. He almost expresses a Tagorean interpretation of the body, that of the illusion of the bodily reality. When he is asked by his father to sign bank papers saying that he has no claims to the property by virtue of not being a son, Rudra says, 'Have I now ceased to be the person who was your child. Have I disappeared just because I have undergone surgery?' The imagery of clothing and ornamentation is pervasive whenever Chitrangada talks about bedecking herself or, and even more so, when Rituparno Ghosh focuses on Rudra's bodily changes for he too interprets Tagore's Chitrangada in terms of bodily deceit and the triumph of the plain truth.

The cultural conditioning of the dance form as feminine, too, helps Rituparno Ghosh in his interpretation as Rudra frequently expresses his emotions through the dance moves and hand-body language. Rudra's parents, especially the father, are aghast that their son has opted for a feminine career as a dancer. But it is to Partho that he explains this, 'My art is not gender bound. Neither is my identity'. In an interview, Rituparno Ghosh says, 'That's where Anjan asks me how I would like to be remembered—as an artist or as *surupa*. At that moment, I realise that I don't need a woman's body to realise my feminine desires. Because the body is not about physical boundaries, it is about the relationship between me and the person perceiving it.'[37]

In the climax of the play, Chitrangada pleads with Arjun to ignore the bodily beauty and accept her for her essential, true self as the spell of Madana for one year comes to an end. Rudra has similarly undergone bodily transformation at the hands of the plastic surgeon in order not to become more beautiful, but technically a woman so that he and Partho could adopt a child. In contrast to Chitrangada, he undergoes tremendous amount of psychological trauma, trying to cope with the change (from identifying himself as a man to accepting herself as a woman), as if to bring out the lack of psychological depth and psychological realism in the portrayal of Chitrangada, from being coerced into imagining herself as a man first and then realizing the reality of her female desire. Thus, though within the film, Rudra's theatrical interpretation is lauded by the press, he is himself deeply dissatisfied with his handling of the theme. He is able to realize this only through his personal situation in relation to his homophobic father, the culture in which he lives, and finally through Partho saying, 'if I am to marry why not marry a real woman, why marry this strange half-way creature?' It is at this juncture that Rudra gives up his desperate attempt to become, 'technically' a woman, and thereby returning to his original condition. Though this is exactly similar to Chitrangada's return to her original self, Rudra instead of being united to Partho, is united to his family. He stands vindicated when his parents, and Chitrangada's father accept him and takes him home, thus reconciling himself to Rudra's desire to be what he is. The most gay-affirmative, and heart-rending scenes are those when he is with his mother, and finally with both the parents. In fact, the profoundest moments of love and tragedy are in the context of Rudra's relationship with his parents, climaxed by some sort of a rapprochement between father and son. Thus, the ending is queer-affirmative through the agency of the queer subject just as Tagore's *Chitrangada* is feminist through the agency of the woman subject.

Rituparno Ghosh succeeds in a thorough contemporization of Chitrangada, with the obvious message that queer existence is realizable within the framework of the family, and not by rejecting it. Whether this is a conservative resolution to the contemporary Indian context or not, he certainly has chosen his options clearly. As he says in his interview, he loves to have the freedom to do what he likes with his body in terms of looks, dress, and so on. He has to be accepted on his own terms and not through any bodily disguise. In sharp contrast to the fun and frolic and the happy resolution, all through Tagore's play, when the audience is barely, if ever, given any occasion to pity Chitrangada, his film invites the audience to empathize with Rudra's abjection.[38] In an interview he gave in 2010 to *The Telegraph*, he has said:

. . . I consider myself privileged because of my gender fluidity, the fact that I am in between. I don't consider myself a woman and I don't want to become a woman. I can wear kurta-pyjama and can also wear kajal and jewellery and attend a social do. . . . The concept of unisex has been monopolised by women. Women can wear men's clothes. The problem arises when men wear women's clothes. Whatever I wear has always been worn by men. Wearing things like earrings and necklaces has always been a part of our sartorial history and tradition. . . . My point is why shouldn't I celebrate my sexuality?[39]

In this interview given long before he did *Chitrangada*, his personal predilections are clearly stated. It also reveals how two kinds of personal circumstances remind two artists of one character in vastly different ways—Tagore's 'train' of thought from a railway carriage upon spectating a natural scene, and Rudra/Ghosh's train of thought from spectating Tagore's *Chitrangada*.

Notes

1. Esha Niyogi De, 'Gender, Nation, and the Vicissitudes of *Kalpana:* Choreographing Womanly Beauty in Tagore's Dance Dramas', in *Rabindranath Tagore in the 21st Century: Theoretical Renewals*, ed. Debashish Banerji, New Delhi: Springer, 2015, p. 161; originally published in *Journal of Contemporary Thought*, vol. 34, 2011, pp. 135–50.
2. Kenneth Hill, <http://woolfandwilde.com/2013/02/im-not-coming-with-you/>, accessed 12 November 2013.
3. Ibid.
4. Ibid.
5. Bhakti is a medieval movement in Indian culture. A.K. Ramanujan discusses the Kannada movement of Bhakti; see A.K. Ramanujan, *Speaking of Siva*, Middlesex: Penguin, 1978, pp. 27–9. Here, for example, is the Vachana poet, Dasjmayya:

   If they see
   breasts and long hair coming
   they call it woman,
   if beard and whiskers
   they call it man:
   but, look, the self that hovers
   in between
   is neither man
   nor woman
   0 Rimanitha!
   And, here is Vasavanna:
   Look here, dear fellow:
   I wear these men's clothes
   only for you.
   Sometimes I am man.
   Sometimes I am woman.
   O lord of the meeting rivers
   I'll make wars for you
   but I'll be your devotees' bride.

   It is a peculiar irony that the advent of colonial modernity made Indian readers and believers homophobic, denying fluidity of gender identity in the face of traditions such as Bhakti and Vachana poets.

6. Baul is a mystical Vaishnava tradition that combines with it the Muslim Sufi tradition of devotion. It is also a musical tradition of a particular kind. Tagore was deeply influenced by this tradition.
7. Kabir was a fifteenth-century saint poet of north India, largely known for his oral poetry, where he criticized the evil practices prevalent in both contemporary Hinduism and Islam. His oral poetry, which had an overt reformist message, was produced as *doha* in the written composition. *Doha* is a type of couplet composed in verse, that rhyme together. A poet like Kabir, whose poetry is often associated with this form, being unaware of alphabet, never wrote anything in his lifetime. This form was chosen by his followers when they decided to commit his oral poetry into written form.
8. Maithili is a language with its own rich literary tradition which dates back to the fourteenth century and has its own script known as Mithilakshar, spoken in Mithila, the north-eastern region of Bihar and some parts of Nepal. It is often misunderstood as a dialect of Hindi. Vidyapati Thakkura was a fifteenth-century poet of Mithila, who composed in both Sanskrit and in Maithili, but is popularly known for his Maithili love songs about Radha and Krishna. Grierson was the first colonial administrator to collect and publish some of the popular songs of Vidyapati in late nineteenth century.
9. Edgar Bauer, 'The Sexologist and the Poet: On Magnus Hirschfeld, Rabindranath Tagore, and the Critique of Sexual Binarity', *Rupkatha Journal on Interdisciplinary Studies in Humanities*, vol. 2, no. 4, 2010, p. 456; special issue on Rabindranath Tagore, ed. Amrit Sen, <http://rupkatha.com/v2n4.php>, accessed 12 September 2012.
10. Ibid.
11. Ibid.
12. Ibid., p. 457.
13. Ibid., pp. 455–6.
14. I have checked versions of the *Mahabharata*, including the Bengali version by Kashi Das, for this episode, and there seems to be no precedent to the innovations we notice in Tagore. It is impossible to ascertain whether there had been newer versions in folk *yatras* or Baul songs that Tagore knew. Even to this date the episode exists as an Odia *pala*.
15. Walter Benjamin, 'Art in the Age of Mechanical Reproduction', in *Illuminations: Essays and Reflections*, tr. Harry Zohn, New York: Knopf Doubleday Publishing Group, 1968, pp. 218–55.
16. Kisari Mohan Ganguly, tr., *The Mahabharata of Krishna-Dwaipayana Vyasa*, translated into English prose from Sanskrit, New Delhi: Munshiram Manoharlal, 1998, p. 421.
17. Rabindranath Tagore, *Chitra*, New York: Macmillan, 1914, p. 2.
18. Ibid., pp. 2–3.
19. Ibid., p. 18.
20. Ibid., p. 52.

21. *Gita*, Chapter 2.
22. Rabindranath Tagore, *Rabindra Rachanabali*, Calcutta: Saraswati Press, 1961.
23. Tagore, *Chitra*, pp. 5–6.
24. De, 'Gender, Nation, and the Vicissitudes of *Kalpana*', p. 168.
25. Tagore, *Chitra*, p. 3.
26. Ibid., p. 6.
27. Translation mine.
28. Quoted by De, 'Gender, Nation, and the Vicissitudes of *Kalpana*', p. 170.
29. I borrow this from Brett Farmer, *Spectacular Passions: Cinema, Fantasy, Gay Male Spectatorship*, Durham: Duke University Press, 2000.
30. Ibid., p. 17.
31. Kenneth Hill, <http://woolfandwilde.com/2009/07/the-day-judy-garland-outed-me/>, 2009, accessed 12 November 2013.
32. Shohini Ghosh, a queer critic herself, looks at another text by Tagore, *Streer Patra* [Rabindranath Tagore, *Streer Patra* (*The Wife's Letter*), tr. Prasanjit Gupta, <http://www.parabass.com/translations/stories/Streer Patra1.html>, accessed 28 May 2015] especially, the film version by Purnednu Patrea (1976) in the same way. See, Shohini Ghosh, 'Forbidden Love and Passionate Denial: A Dialogue in Queer Love and Domesticities', in *Handbook of Gender*, ed. Raka Ray, New Delhi: OUP, 2012, pp. 428–52.
33. Rituparno Ghosh in an interview with Shohini Ghosh for *Marie Claire*, December 2012.
34. An allusion to Goddess Durga, the annihilator of the evil demon, Mahisasura.
35. Rabindranath Tagore, *Tagore's Dance Drama Omnibus*, tr. Utpal K. Banerjee, Delhi: Niyogi Books, 2013, pp. 108–9.
36. Though physical transformation through supernatural intervention is not unknown in Indian mythology and folk narratives, I call such transformation in the context of Tagore 'Ovidian' because such metamorphosis is central to all of Ovid's tales as is the case with Tagore's text.
37. Rituparno Ghosh, Interview: *The Telegraph*, 20 September 2012.
38. I borrow this term from Julia Kristeva, *The Powers of Horror: An Essay on Abjection*, tr. Leon S. Roudiez, Oxford: Columbia University Press, 1982.
39. Rituparno Ghosh, Interview: *The Telegraph*, 22 December 2010.

6

Gandhi before Gandhi
Two Little Pre-histories of the Great Soul

The views are mine, and yet not mine. They are mine because I hope to act according to them. They are almost a part of my being. But, yet, they are not mine, because I lay no claim to originality.

—MAHATMA GANDHI

Whereas Richard Attenborough's film *Gandhi* had got embroiled in a minor controversy in India at the time when the cast was announced, it went on to be a runaway hit after its release at the box office without any further controversy. It is possible that the constant vigil that the Indian government exercised during the making of the film, in the form of leading politicians, including the then Prime Minister Indira Gandhi, being taken into confidence through frequent peeps into the script and not a few cuts here and there, ensured the film's smooth run in India. It is unthinkable what would have happened if some of the more controversial aspects of Mahatma Gandhi's life, vividly described in his autobiography, which were either elided or sanitized beyond recognition, had been part of the final version.

In the US, however, a controversy erupted over the film. One of the most savage attacks on the film titled *The Gandhi Nobody Knows* came from Richard Grenier, a neo-conservative senator in the US. Grenier began by denigrating Mahatma Gandhi, not the film, but the historical figure, and then went on to attack Hinduism and Indian politics, stirring a controversy of considerable nature in the English speaking world.[1] An American Gandhian, Jason de Parle followed the controversy and came up with what many thought was a 'balanced' view on the subject in which he conceded many of the charges levelled against Mahatma Gandhi. Suffice it to say, that in his appropriately titled 'Why Gandhi Drives Neo-Conservatives Mad', he contextualized the Grenier review in America by drawing attention to the aftermath of the Vietnam war and then the debate within the American policymakers and advisers on the use of force in central America. He said, 'The fear that America has too much force fuels the passions of nuclear freeze supporters, while the fear that America has too little guides their opponents. The debate about "Gandhi"—and Gandhi the man—thus quickly becomes a debate about American politics.'

This controversy, which only a few in India noticed, did not otherwise seriously affect its success in India as the positive reception in the subject-country ensured that stray Western criticism could not dent Mahatma Gandhi's reputation. Some intellectuals, though, responded to the criticism rather belatedly. Even as late as 2000, Ashis Nandy refers to Grenier's essay in his article on Mahatma Gandhi in *The Little Magazine*. He said:

Some year ago, an American columnist, Grenier, taken aback by the immense popularity of Richard Attenborough's *Mahatma Gandhi*, tried to debunk Mahatma Gandhi by pointing out major discrepancies between his life and philosophy. (Grenier of course did not have anything to say about whether he rejected Milton and Beethoven because they had a record of child abuse or Plato because he justified it in the context of homosexuality.) But such attempts at demystification do not work because the Greniers of the world confront the need to believe in human potentialities and a curious compulsion to intercede in situations of manmade suffering that often seems basic to human nature.[2]

In fact, even while controversies around Mahatma Gandhi, of varying intensities, have dogged him, his stature, far from diminishing, has only continued to grow.

The 'Father of the [Indian] Nation', Mahatma Gandhi continues to enjoy state patronage and recedes to the background of the nationalist imaginary, unless occasionally revived through popular culture—such as the lovable Munnabhai sequel—and goes on acquiring the mythical, deificatory status in the backdrop of more recent happenings in African nations, especially in the aftermath of the dismantling of apartheid regime in South Africa, and the frequent references to Mahatma Gandhi as a spiritual force behind Nelson Mandela, and the Gandhian antecedents of the African National Congress (ANC). Mahatma Gandhi is invoked on many occasions in the public sphere in Africa. Yet, the African media continues to carry stories of his dubious stance towards European racism. Though numerous examples can be culled from the recent media coverage of these controversies, one or two examples might suffice. First, 'Gandhi branded racist as Johannesburg honours freedom fighter', screamed a headline on 17 March 2003. It said, 'it was supposed to honour his resistance to racism in South Africa, but a new statue of Mahatma Gandhi in Johannesburg has triggered a row over his alleged contempt for black people'. Newspapers continue to publish letters from indignant readers, 'Gandhi had no love for Africans. To him, Africans were no better than the untouchables of India . . . the Indian embassy in Pretoria declined to comment.'[3] And so on. A whole underground anti-Mahatma Gandhi literature thrives in the censor-proof cyberspace. A page of *The Christian Party* is entitled 'The Racist Gandhi'[4] which then goes on to arrange quotes from Mahatma Gandhi's writing now freely made available by the Government of India on the internet. Another says, 'Gandhi was loyal to Imperialism'.[5] These charges of racism against Mahatma Gandhi, many of them based on straightforward quotations from his unambiguously worded writings, surely merit juxtaposition with Achebe's charge of racism against Joseph Conrad. If such are the underground radical murmurings about Mahatma Gandhi in Africa, serious intellectual/academic engagements seem to be competing to sustain and nurture a more positive and healthy and ever increasing tendency to credit him with exclusive qualities. The question to ask is whether we are going overboard with such an enterprise, or whether we are handicapped as cultural historians with availability of limited archives from the sprawling evidence hidden from view across inaccessible vernacular domains.

While there is no gainsaying that certain practices and symbols became prominent and came to be recognized as pan-Indian only after their association with Mahatma Gandhi (and are, therefore, always referred to as Gandhian), to completely elide earlier instances of similar practices adopted by local heroes in various parts of India, would be historically unwise, especially in view of the Mahatma's declaration quoted as epigraph. Yet, it is not uncommon to come across such conscious or inadvertent elisions on the part of overenthusiastic cultural historians. This is tantamount to lapsing back to the traditional *charitamrita* (hagiographic) mode of life-writing. What surprises one is the incidence of overstatement in the seminal works of redoubtable historians when it comes to Mahatma Gandhi. An observation by Emma Tarlo about khadi is a case in point, 'It was this stipulation that the yarn must be handspun that *distinguished Gandhi's promotion of home industry from the efforts of earlier* Swadeshi (home industry) *activists* in Bengal who had contented themselves with the promotion of Indian produced mill cloth' [emphasis mine].[6] Dipesh Chakrabarty too, while describing khadi as '*the Gandhian dress* of the male politician in India',[7] claims that 'Gandhi's is, in fact, *the only confessional autobiography ever to be written by a prominent Indian public leader*, and it shares much with the tradition of Augustine and Rousseau' [emphasis mine].[8] Thus, much recent scholarship that has highlighted the semiotic of khadi and the confessional mode has done so in terms of the imbrications between the biography of one man and the history of a nation.

However, Dipesh Chakrabarty goes on to develop a persuasive argument that sees a connection between the confessional mode (the material body included) and khadi, '. . . I will read as confessional what is commonly seen as obsessive in Gandhi. . . . Once we do this, we will see in clearer outlines the alternative conceptions of public life that Gandhi articulated and of which khadi now acts as an extremely condensed statement'.[9] Taking a cue from his formulation, I shall not only try to see connections between the two major Gandhian tropes—the confessional mode and khadi—in terms of their indigeneity, but explore and contextualize those connections with the help of prior instances in the hitherto obscure or neglected archives. Though this chapter is not overtly concerned with the semiotic of the khadi per se, it will take up a related trope, that of the charkha. It will also deal with an aspect of the confessional mode of self-writing. I argue here that we need to explore further the available indigenous archives across diverse Indian regions before making any sweeping generalization. I also wish to instantiate and discuss a few of the antecedents in colonial Odisha among lesser(-known) mortals. My intention is not to undermine Mahatma Gandhi's singularity; far from it. My aim, rather, is to bring the Mahatma Gandhi-phenomenon into sharper relief by tracing how what were common became exclusive through their reiterative association with the Mahatma. For, never again after Mahatma Gandhi were these signs to be dissociated from him.

I

The Confessional Mode of Self-Writing

We begin with the point about Mahatma Gandhi's being 'the only confessional autobiography ever to be written by a prominent

Indian public leader'. Insofar as his autobiography is concerned, the confessions in question, are about his petty thieving, meat-eating, smoking, and copulating with his wife when his father was ill. But nowhere does he directly mention, let alone elaborate, the most sensational of his affairs of the heart, i.e. his relationship with Sarala Devi of the illustrious Tagore family.[10] However, a few years after the appearance of his *An Autobiography*, he confessed to a friend that a public confession of his relationship with Sarala Devi[11] 'was not possible [since it was a matter] which he thought was so personal [I] did not put it into [my] autobiography'. This, like a few of his other confessions, was made in personal conversations.

But unbeknown to Mahatma Gandhi and his biographers, around the time he was most likely seeing Sarala Devi for the first time in Kolkata (1901), a major Odia poet—Radhanath Ray,[12] aged fifty-two—was seeing a bright Bengali woman poet, Saraswati Nagendrabala (Mustophi) from a modest background in Hooghly.[13] Of course, his relationship with Sarala Devi would turn passionate and complicate his life much later, in 1919, whereas Radhanath Ray's had already been quite turbulent between 1900 and 1907.[14] Otherwise, the parallels between the two love lives are too striking to be ignored. As we shall see, both Radhanath Ray and Mahatma Gandhi developed, subsequently, feelings of revulsion towards the two women. What were their reasons for doing so? How did they represent the relationship in retrospect? Can one read, as Dipesh Chakrabarty does, '[Mahatma Gandhi's] obsessive descriptions of his guilt ridden sexual experiences as so many confessions of his sin'?[15] Why did Radhanath Ray decide to take the unusual step of making a detailed public confession? How is his confession different from the Christian or European modern on the one hand, and from the 'colonial modern' of Mahatma Gandhi?[16] Though these are large questions, I shall attempt to throw some light on them by tracing the story of Radhanath Ray and Nagendrabala.

Sometime in 1899, Radhanath Ray was posted to Bengal's Bardhaman district division as school inspector in which capacity he served in Hooghly from 1899 to 1903. It was during his stay there that Saraswati met him ostensibly because she had read the latter's poetry and was deeply enamoured of it. The meeting that is said to have taken place in 1900 led to an initial phase of *guru-shishya* relationship. Saraswati was then only twenty-two years of age, thirty years younger than Radhanath Ray. In 1901, she composed a eulogy addressed to him entitled, '*Bhutaler Swarga*' or 'Heaven on Earth' which ran thus:

What I have seen is incomparable
in this world full of selfish men
there lives in the form of a sacred spirit
Radhanath Ray: an image of heaven on earth
master of the fine arts!
You are the mentor, I the disciple
At every touch of yours dross turns gold
come you who want to see heaven on earth. . . . (translation mine)[17]

The full version of the panegyric was later incorporated in the first edition of Radhanath Ray's *Granthabali* or *Complete Works* (1903).[18] When still at Hooghly, he wrote to Gangadhar[19] referring to Saraswati as his 'dear student' and quoting her words of wisdom.[20] He also informed Gangadhar that she highly commended his poetry,[21] especially *Kichakbadh* rendered in *amitrakhshar* meter that Radhanath Ray had introduced into Odia poetry under the influence of Michael Madhusudan Dutt's *Meghnadbadh Kavya* (1861). In 1901, Radhanath Ray also praised Saraswati's *Naridharma* (1900) as an invaluable Bangla publication.[22] The same year, on New Year's day, Radhanath Ray wrote a brief biography of the poet for her 1902 collection, *Amiya Gatha* which Saraswati, in turn, dedicated to Radhanath Ray inscribing the words, '*guru-tulya Utkaler kabiguru* Srijukta Ray Radhanath Raibahadur, School Inspector *mohodayer prati*'. The poem began, 'What can I give you that has remained ungiven . . .?' Radhanath Ray sent copies of the book to many of his friends introducing the poet to them. These expressions of mutual admiration continued when Saraswati's *Brajgatha* (1902) appeared and to which Radhanath Ray contributed an effusive Foreword, under the title 'Bhumika'.[23]

Meanwhile, their *guru-shishya* relationship had changed to that of lovers. It was possible that Radhanath Ray was briefly carried away by the attitudes prevalent in liberal circles of Bengal.[24] By 1902, Saraswati seems to have become a family friend of his. So much so, in October that year, Radhanath Ray's wife Parasmani invited Saraswati to their newly built house at Dhabaleswar, a scenic river island that lies close to Cuttack. Later, in 1903, Saraswati dedicated her poem *Dhabaleswar Kavya* to Parasmani, calling her a 'mother-like' figure. Radhanath Ray returned from Hooghly to Odisha in 1903. At some point of time, thereafter, things seem to have gone wrong between the two. Radhanath Ray, who had been brought up by his strict disciplinarian father, and had, therefore, a 'puritanical' upbringing, regretted his 'fallen' state. Soon, his body already frail and disease-prone, began feeling deeply remorseful. This seems to have caused psychosomatic ailment, an early symptom of which is discernible in the letter he wrote to a correspondent, 'For more than a year now I have been living in extreme ill-health'.[25] Finally, he decided to unilaterally terminate his relationship with Saraswati. She, on her part, refused to give up and revisited Odisha in January 1905. A few months later, on 13 April 1906, she committed suicide in her room in Hooghly. She had consigned all her letters and manuscripts to fire.[26]

The news must have shaken the already miserable Radhanath Ray further; and in 1906, he started writing a 'confessional' autobiography, only a fragment of which is extant.[27] Not content with merely this behind for posthumous circulation, he also wrote a shorter public confession entitled 'A Grievous Sinner's Most Humble and Piteous Entreaty to the General Public' in Odia, for immediate publication.[28] This appeared on 26 July 1906 in various newspapers and public forums with the further note that whosoever gets a copy must give it the widest possible publicity.[29]

I shall now go into the bare facts of Mahatma Gandhi's relationship with Sarala Devi, following closely Rajmohan Gandhi's narrative. Sarala Devi, just three years younger than Mahatma Gandhi, may have seen him before her marriage to Rambhuj Dutt Chaudhuri of Lahore in December 1901.[30] Though there is no record of that meeting, it is speculated that the two had met. Indeed, in 1919, when he was the guest at the home of her jailed husband, Mahatma Gandhi, then forty-seven, remembered her when she was reintroduced to him as Rambhuj Dutt Chaudhuri's wife.[31] Soon Mahatma Gandhi would write to Anasuyaben, 'Sarala Devi's company is very endearing. She looks after me very well . . .'. The relationship grew to be a special one, which he called 'indefinable', so much so, he even 'wanted a "spiritual marriage"' with her. For four or five months—between January and May 1920—he was clearly dazzled by her personality and seemed to fantasize that Providence desired them together to shape India to a new design. He wrote to her that he often dreamt of her and that she was a great *shakti*. In 1920, *Young India* carried a song by Sarala Devi on the front page and *Navajivan* another poem by her along with Mahatma Gandhi's comment that it was 'perfect'. But his son Devadas questioned his father's growing fondness for her and asked him to think of the consequences for Kasturba, people like themselves and Mahatma Gandhi himself if he continued the special relationship with Devi. Mahadev Desai and Rajagopalachari (the 'keeper' of Mahatma Gandhi's conscience) too did not approve of the relationship. Whatever the circumstances, he finally got over the passion, and later deeply regretted his indiscretion.[32]

Whether or not he shared his innermost feelings for Sarala Devi with Kasturba, their clandestine relationship certainly told upon Kasturba's health. Devi was equally adversely affected by his lack of concern for her as can be made out from what he told her about the relationship after his withdrawal symptoms had set in, and the way he represented the facts to his confidantes. When she wanted to know why Mahatma Gandhi had gone back on his promise for a 'spiritual marriage', he wrote by saying that it was something pure, and was possible only 'between two *brahmacharis* in thought, word and deed . . . I am unworthy of that companionship with you. . .'.[33] In contrast to this evasive mumbo-jumbo, he would tell Father William Lash and E. Stanley Jones in 1933 that he had been prevented from 'rushing into hellfire by the thought of Kasturba and because of interventions by his son Devadas, Desai and another young relative. . .'.[34] In 1935, he would tell Margaret Sanger that he had *"nearly slipped"* after meeting *"a woman with a broad, cultural education"* but had fortunately been freed from a *"trance"* [emphasis mine].[35] In any case, we now know that Devi was shattered by Mahatma Gandhi's decision, and deeply regretted that she had sacrificed her all for his love.[36] Twenty years earlier, Radhanath Ray too, had described his relationship in his public confession in not very dissimilar terms, 'At fifty three I got introduced to a *woman of culture* in a foreign land. I got attracted by her *extraordinary literary acumen and creative flair*'. He had further described Saraswati's role in his 'fall' in terms of *'the charm and witchery of the enchantress'*. The emphases above bear out my point about the similarity between the two cases. In any case, Mahatma Gandhi did not make his confession public.

Looked at in terms of genre, the two Radhanath Ray texts, both the longer private and the shorter public confessions, seem to have two sets of implied readers. The autobiographical fragment was not meant for the immediate reading public; and it was philosophical-meditative in tone, content, and style. The second, shorter version seems to address directly the readers and admirers of his poetry as an attempt to 'clear his conscience', pleading mercy. The former dwells exclusively on the subject of his 'infatuation with another man's wife'. He judges himself with a frightening severity. The whole text is repetitiously self-flagellant as it goes on and on about the dreadful consequences of sin, of his own fallen state. In neither does Radhanath Ray mention Saraswati by name, even while calling her all kinds of names during the course of describing his own 'sin'. He refers to her indirectly as someone's wife who had 'degraded herself one hundred times over', or that he fell into 'bad company', or succumbed to 'vile temptation'. He is crushed with shame when he recalls that he is the author of such highly acclaimed *kavyas* as *Tulasistabaka*, *Darbar*, and *Mahayatra*. All the while, Saraswati suffered silently.[37]

Similarly, an autobiography that Devi was to write later makes no reference to the relationship,[38] nor does Mahatma Gandhi's, though a few letters and recorded conversations reveal his thoughts on it ('It was so personal I did not put it into my autobiography', he said to Sanger).[39] Rajmohan Gandhi speculates that since Sarala Devi and her son were alive when Mahatma Gandhi's autobiography was published, he could not have referred to the episode without hurting her again.[40] Radhanath Ray waited, and published his confession only after Saraswati's death. When he consulted his son, Shashibhusan and friends like Gourishankar Ray and Raja Baikunthanath, they advised him against making his confession public. The last two said, 'such things happen everywhere in the world by scores. Who goes out and tells the world about it?'[41] However, Radhanath Ray had already made up his mind and went ahead with making the public confession, in spite of such advice and remonstrations of friends. A possible reason for the unusual decision on his part to go public can only be guessed from the text itself. He asserts right at the beginning, 'Perhaps, nowhere in the world there is a book that should have been written on the subject. My character lost its purity during the last three years in Hooghly. Alas! Has anyone succumbed to temptation at the fag-end of their life!'[42] Towards the end of the text, he again says, 'Only someone who suffers can write in detail about the changes that come about slowly in a man slowly through the process of slow mental and physical agony. I am yet to read a book like that myself. I wish I had written such a book for the good of the world.' From this, one can guess that the extant piece was a prelude to a longer treatise on moral conduct, and his own example as a warning from experience. Either he never wrote this piece or, if he did, he destroyed it.

As part of his attempt to seek exoneration from the reading public, Radhanath Ray goes to the extent of retracting his public praise of Saraswati's qualities as a poet:

Complying with her request . . . I had written introductory notes for two of the books written by her. Owing to my ignorance, gullibility and other reasons I have, brought into them an element of untruth and exaggeration.

I have time and again failed to get the introduction removed from the subsequent editions of these books.

In the preface to one of my books in Odia, a poem by her was included. The time when she composed the poem she had no lustful designs on me; however by the time the poem was included, our relationship had become sensual. Therefore the book has got tainted.[43]

Radhanath Ray expressed his profound regret for having betrayed Parasmani and brought the family infamy. In fact, he wrote poems about a chaste wife and her unfaithful husband.[44] He said in his confession that while pondering over how he lost the sanctity of his character, he caused grave harm to the

Innocent members of my family and became the cause of their grief, I feel I am being consumed by a fire of remorse. An unusual reason for my remorse is that despite being aware of my frailty, *my chaste wife and my two obedient and affectionate sons* have reposed greater faith and sympathy in me, and proving to be the very epitome of forgiveness.[45]

Looking back, Mahatma Gandhi too, shared with Father Lash how his wife and son 'rescued' him during the crisis in his life, '"It was their love which chained me so tightly and strongly" and "saved him"'. Like Saraswati before her, as we have seen, Devi never accused Mahatma Gandhi in public for having betrayed her. One could easily pursue a feminist angle here, and call Radhanath Ray's conduct, or even Mahatma Gandhi's, reprehensible. But I am not overtly concerned with these, even while recognizing the importance of this line of argument.[46] I am more interested in looking at how both Mahatma Gandhi, and before him, Radhanath Ray ultimately withdrew into the traditional institution of the family and marriage rather than continuing to flirt with sexual adventurism. Tanika Sarkar argues how the adoption of the traditional family went hand in hand with the call for strengthening the nationalist cause.[47] As she says, 'the new nationalist worldview . . . reimaged the family as a contrast to and a critique of alien rule'.[48] This is equally applicable to cultures beyond Bengal, in the early decades of the twentieth century.

Insofar as their sense of sexual guilt is concerned, both Radhanath Ray and Mahatma Gandhi can be seen as having derived from non-Hindu traditions. Though, as Rajmohan Gandhi tells us, Sarala Devi accused Mahatma Gandhi as a person who had the mind of a Christo-Buddhist rather than that of a Hindu,[49] he himself dishes out an explanation to Sarala Devi that hearkens back to the high-Hindu traditions of spirituality and *brahmacharya*. Even Radhanath

Ray's confession can be construed as Christian in its inspiration. After all, he was exposed to European modernity and Christian discourses (though the first Odia translation of the Bible appeared in 1811, the first missionaries had arrived in Odisha in 1823, and the first Odia converts were a long time coming). Unsurprisingly, the two versions—the personal autobiography and the public/published confession—are replete with echoes of the Roman Catholic/puritan practice of confession. Surprisingly, however, neither in his autobiographical fragment nor his public confession does he refer to St Augustine or Rousseau, though he refers to Dante. In both, Radhanath Ray refers to his Hindu-Sanskritic sources, citing '*papam krutwa prakashayet*' (confess if you have sinned) repeatedly, and it is this piece of scriptural injunction which provides him with the inspiration to make a public confession of guilt.[50]

Why do, first Radhanath Ray, and then Mahatma Gandhi (at least at that stage of his life), avoid acknowledging the Christian moorings of the illocutionary 'speech-act' of the confession? Either, that they really believed theirs to be a part of the traditional Hindu wisdom; or, that they did so for strategic reasons, i.e. they deliberately avoided mentioning the Christian provenance of their action in public. This latter could well be the case.[51] At least the cause of Radhanath Ray's wariness can be traced to the then contemporary anxiety over conversion. As is well-known, the second half of the nineteenth century was the time for frenetic missionary activity across Odisha; but it was matched, somewhat unequally though, by Brahmo activism. Madhusudan Das and Biswanath Kar converted to Christianity and Brahmoism, respectively. Madhusudan Rao, a friend and collaborator of Radhanath Ray and Fakir Mohan, converted to Brahmoism in 1870; subsequently becoming a leading Brahmo figure and assuming the office of Secretary, Odisha Brahmo Samaj in 1879. There was a considerable controversy when the Maharaja of Mayurbhanj married a Brahmo woman. The educated Odias were familiar with these discourses around Brahmoism and Christianity. The major tenets of the faith preached by Keshobchandra Sen, were derived from orthodox Christianity—one of them being the insistence on the self-realization of sin and repentance. A Brahmo follows this up with an intimate and fervent plea with God, a speech act tantamount to 'confession'. This Christian element of Brahmoism was fused with the Vaishnavite trait 'ecstatic-fervor'.[52] The extreme manifestation of this combination was the ritual of the piteous cry, wailing, and howling among the penitential Brahmo worshippers. Successive Brahmo preachers visited and gave public discourses in various parts of Odisha during the second half of the nineteenth century. The manner in which such preaching and practices impacted Brahmos can be guessed from the interdictions imposed by the preachers in Odisha. No 'fallen' individual (not even liars and such other immoral characters) was permitted to embrace Brahmoism. If any member of the Odia Brahmo Samaj was found guilty of any of those immoral practices, the offender would be privately asked to mend his ways. If this did not work, the sinner would be urged at the time of Brahmo *upasana* (worship) to correct himself, which, again, tantamount to a public confession. If they still do not abstain from such immoral ways, they would be expelled from the Samaj.

Fakir Mohan flirted with Christianity before embracing Brahmoism. Madhusudan Das went the whole hog and converted to Christianity. Whenever an important Odia public figure converted, it caused a major controversy. Radhanath Ray resisted these trends of conversion. He even helped others avoid conversion.[53] But, he could not resist internalizing certain Christian-Brahmo discourses. Apart from the obvious fact of his public confession, several other aspects of the Brahmo practices including 'wailing and howling' can be discerned in the two texts under discussion. Radhanath Ray must have felt an 'obligation to tell the truth' arising out of 'prohibitions against sexuality'.[54] Perhaps, sensing that the knowledgeable Odia public might suspect the connection with the foreign (and therefore, anti-national) religion, he was anxious to repudiate the Christian, and the Christian aspects of Brahmoism. His confession mentions at least one European Christian poet, Dante, refraining from any explicit mention of the Christian tradition. But, what he chooses to point to is the not so obvious indigenous Sanskritc tradition through a stray quotation '*papam krutya prakashayet*' as the reason for his confession.

II

Odisha, Khadi and the Charkha

A year before the publication of *Hind Swaraj* (1909),[55] an essay by Fakir Mohan[56] appeared in an Odia newspaper, entitled 'Arata' (1908; Odia for charkha). The essay[57] is presumably addressed exclusively to the poor and semi-literate Odia peasantry. In what follows, I examine this verbal prefiguration of the charkha in the Odia public sphere and its configuration in Indian village economy, before it acquired its metonymic status as *the* Gandhian tool for

Swaraj, and the subsequent inextricability of the two—the man and his indigenous machine.

The charkha, after centuries of service to the peasantry across South Asia, had fallen into disuse by 1900 under the impact of modernization. Recently, Rebecca Brown has discussed how visual representations of the creaky contraption, for over 200 years, played a major role in its re-emergence vis-à-vis the verbal political rhetoric around it that ensued[58] following Mahatma Gandhi's dogmatic anti-modern crusade to reinvent it. But, it is necessary to remind ourselves that his tryst with it had not begun until 1915. Though, in its heyday, the swadeshi activists had harangued the need to reject British goods, especially Manchester clothes by opting for coarse khadi, the charkha was seldom talked about as an instrument of swadeshi. Any khadi, irrespective of whether or not the yarn was handspun, would do. And, of course, in spite of Mahatma Gandhi, the charkha could never regain its pristine status as an ordinary though essential everyday household article, albeit it attained tremendous political symbolism.

Returning to Fakir Mohan's essay, what strikes one at first about it is the stand alone title itself, a stark, three-letter, *matra-less*, and therefore, totally unadorned, word अरट or Arata, like the bare khadi itself through which Fakir Mohan chiefly makes the following points:

1. *The poor state of Odisha economy*: Its people do not get two square meals a day even though it produces enough food grains to spare ('There is plenty: are there any deshas in this world as prosperous as ours? . . . and [yet] our own people eat whatever rubbish they get in order to stay alive and then die of all kinds of disease').
2. *The reasons for such poverty*: The harmful effect on the village economy of using foreign clothes ('Do you understand what I mean when I say that you buy clothes by paying the foreign weaver?').
3. *Way out of the situation*: One of them was a return to the earlier self-sufficiency in clothing ('What, then, is the way out? He then calls for a return to the old practice of hand-spinning with the *charkha*').

At first, one might construe Fakir Mohan's piece as an obscure footnote in the history of the Swadeshi movement. But one must bear in mind that swadeshi was comparatively underwhelming in Odisha, though many Bengali organizations tried to arouse the

Odias into it.[59] Second, in the essay in question, he goes beyond the swadeshi call for the boycott of British goods, and pleads for discarding *all* foreign clothes. Not until much later, Mahatma Gandhi was to distinguish between the position of the earlier Swadeshi movement and his own. Bengal's *Amrita Bazar Patrika* covered a speech that he gave in Kolkata in September 1921:

At the time of the partition of Bengal, restrictions, if any, were confined to the boycott of foreign clothes. By foreign clothes it was meant clothes manufactured in London, but allowance was given for the use of goods manufactured in Japan. The present Swadeshi cult meant total boycott of foreign clothes of all descriptions and it was restricted to only hand-spun clothes.[60]

Third, even as early as 1883, i.e. twenty-five years before he wrote the piece in question, Fakir Mohan had delivered a lecture on the subject of the ill-effect of British rule, and rued the loss of vitality and the superficial 'sheen modernity' in Odisha. More significantly, he spoke of how the weavers in rural Odisha had hung up their looms and embarked on the hunt for wage-labour. In his speech, he spoke of the bane of and over-dependence on Western clothes. Employing dark humour, he said at this rate should the British withdraw and the import of their clothes is stopped, the Odias would move around as Digambaris.[61] Also, the second point that Fakir Mohan makes in his essay (about 'paying the foreign weaver', etc.) anticipates by a year, Mahatma Gandhi's formulation on the subject in *Hind Swaraj*, 'By using Manchester cloth, we would only waste our money'.[62] Further, as Rajmohan Gandhi says, 'Linking India's poverty to the destruction of Indian weaving and to British rule, Gandhi in *Hind Swaraj* had asked India's intellectuals to "take up the handloom".' In his *An Autobiography*, Mahatma Gandhi says, 'I do not remember to have seen a handloom or a spinning wheel when in 1908 I described it in *Hind Swaraj*'. He further says, '[e]ven in 1915 when I returned from South Africa I had not actually seen a spinning wheel'.[63] In 1917, Gangaben Mazumdar found hundreds of spinning wheels lying unused in Baroda.[64] In 1919, Rajmohan Gandhi states, 'Gandhi now possessed what he had hoped for from the moment of his return to India: vehicles to communicate his message: One was the spinning wheel'.[65]

Returning to Fakir Mohan's argument in 'Arata', we see how he begins by making a characteristically witty proposition:

There was a time when every house-hold in Utkala *Desha* used *arata*s. So much so, there used to be as many *arata*s as there were women in each household. Women used to spin the yarn to meet the needs of the entire family. Along with the agriculture required for producing food-grains the farmers used to grow cotton needed for household use (and also sometimes for sale). The land is still there—the women are, of course, very much there—but what is no longer there is spinning.[66]

Soon it becomes apparent that Fakir Mohan eschews the idealism of the then current rhetoric of swadeshi. In fact, he dismisses such public rhetoric with typical irony as 'the chatter of the orator or speech-makers'.[67] He feels that empty rhetoric would serve no useful purpose. He puts it quite simply, 'Forget about these days of high inflation, even in good times do *chhapana* or 35% of the population get one square meal a day? What is the way out for us in these dire times? The riddle goes, "end of spring, he does sing" [Once the harvest is done, the farmer rejoices].' His piece is also remarkable for its irony directed at the new-fangled ideas, 'Educated people convene meetings these days to save the *desha*. Fair enough, no one is complaining. But you can save the *desha* only if it is there. Let the people survive first, let the *desha* become stable; development or welfare, call what you will, can follow.'[68] This again seems to be a telling indictment of the public meetings around the Swadeshi and Utkal Sammilani movements—a sign of Fakir Mohan's pragmatism, emphasizing practice over theory. True, the pragmatism that he displays is quite unlike the rhetoric that was being offered by the swadeshi speakers. His calculations are indigenous as well as ingenious.

He presents an argument on the political economy of the contraption, and offers a simple though elaborate arithmetic to prove his point. He arrives at a figure in any poor man's reckoning using the indigenous currency of *cauri, ganda, kahan* and *pana*:[69]

Do you know what used to be the per capita expense on clothes in the past? A man needed two pieces of *dhoti*, and one piece of *gamucha*, and one *matha*. This *matha* lasted four years. The total cost of all this, including the need of cotton wool was, say, eighteen *anna*s per one *seer* and half. But cotton wool was not bought, it was obtained from cultivation. The total amount spent on tax and cultivation would add up to no more than six *anna*s. The wages for weaving per person would be no more than one *paisa*. Thus, the expenses a person would normally incur on clothes would be fourteen *anna*s only. Now you calculate: subtracting fourteen *anna*s from four rupees and two annas, you are still left with rupees three and *anna*s four, let's say, rupees two only. If savings on clothes per person would be rupees two, how much would the *desha manage to save*?[70]

Thus, going through the essay it becomes evident that Fakir Mohan is not interested in offering through it a Benthamite calculus in favour of the use of the charkha, nor is he interested in submitting a profit-making proposition. His, rather, is an argument in favour of a need-based economy that would ensure a proper gender-evening division of labour, leading to self-sufficiency. His advocacy of the cotton that men cultivated alongside foodgrains had nothing to do with the modern-day view of growing it as a cash crop; rather, it was meant to sustain a parallel economy, that of clothing, to keep the charkha moving as a self-sustaining economic activity. He is worried that, though, enough foodgrains were being produced in Odisha, Odias did not get one square meal a day; and, analysing the reasons thereof, he concludes that it was only because the Odias were now interested in acquiring money at any cost just to be able to buy colourful foreign clothes. Otherwise, Odias, he says, 'do not believe in luxury. If we get to eat belly-full of coarse rice twice a day with fried *saag* or green leaves and tamarind seeds, and find a piece of coarse loin-cloth it is enough. Nothing else is needed.' Now, however, things have changed because of the imported goods to which simple-minded villagers have fallen prey:

Once the farmer has money in his hand, what does he care for? Markets selling colourful German and Japanese clothes are everywhere in village after village. Gold-coloured *saree*s for the daughter-in-law, colourful shirts for the son, and there is, of course, vests made out of British blanket mixed with jute for himself.[71]

His main argument is that this new culture of acquiring foreign clothing at any cost must change; the Odias must revert to the old practice of being self-sufficient and self-reliant in clothing matters, in order to alleviate their economic misery.

In his *An Autobiography*, Mahatma Gandhi makes the same point without, of course, dishing out the paraphernalia and minutiae of cost analysis that Fakir Mohan is able to supply from his intimacy with the ground reality. Talking about his early (*c.*1918) experiment with the charkha, he gives details about how charkhas were arranged, expertise to run them was obtained, and how, finally, the problem of procuring slivers was solved. The first piece of khadi, Mahatma Gandhi says, manufactured at the ashram cost seventeen annas per yard.[72] In *Hind Swaraj*, too he offers Fakir-Mohan-like indictment of the new greed for money, 'Now they are enslaved by temptation of money and of the luxuries that money can buy'.[73] In contrast to Mahatma Gandhi's puritanical moral tone, Fakir Mohan deploys his characteristically subversive humour.

Even in matters of girls' education, Fakir Mohan comes across as a person with a nuanced critical view of modernity, 'These days, some girls in schools are being taught carpet-weaving, socks-knitting'. He laughs at the idea, 'I feel like laughing: What is this? On the one hand, you are starving; on the other, you are weaving carpets! *Arre*, Babu, teach the school girls how to spin on the spinning wheel. They will find it useful in future.'[74] In order to express this he deploys irony, and feigns an ironic distance. He dissociates himself from the elite and the rich, and identifies with the Odia-educated poor and their well-wishers. He is even critical of the intrusion of babu-culture in Odisha, of which he may have become a small part. He puns with the word with sarcasm—babu. He refers to the class rather derisively as 'abu' (a tumour or bulge). 'I know that the babus will not like my words.' Then he goes on to say that he is not addressing them, 'But I am not saying anything to them. Well-fed, let them lead a happy and pleasurable life. Why should they worry about the poor? But, how many *babu*s are there in the *desha*, maybe a small handful? But you and I make for the majority of the population. The *desha* exists for us. Those who are well-off don't care for the *desha*. In my opinion, they are not *babu*s but *abu*s or undesirable tumours.'[75]

It is not known what impact Fakir Mohan's call for a return to charkha had on his readers, but when Mahatma Gandhi reinvented and tried to popularize its recirculation from 1920 onward, he met with stiff opposition from his detractors. Apart from Tagore himself, Anil Baran Roy raised his concerns about swadeshi in newspapers in the mid-1920s and later published two booklets that challenged the 'dogma' surrounding the spinning wheel:

The most common critique of the Swadeshi movement at the time involved khadi's cost relative to comparable goods in the marketplace. Especially in the early years of the movement, khadi goods were substantially more expensive than their mill-made equivalents. Roy explained in a letter to Gandhi that in his region a khadi dhoti, a common form of men's clothes made of up to fifteen feet of cloth, cost six times more than one from the mills.[76]

Had Fakir Mohan been alive in the 1920s, he would have disagreed with Tagore and Anil Baran Roy and from his personal experience supported Mahatma Gandhi's move. As we have already seen, Fakir Mohan does not speak of British goods alone; he talks about the invasion of *Japanese and German* clothes providing villagers with fatally attractive clothes, 'Markets selling colourful German and Japanese clothes are everywhere in village after village'.[77] His suggestions were *organic* to the life of the villagers and were not meant to be *artificially* imposed on them for political-rhetoric effect. In any case, his detailed calculations would have proved Anil Baran Roy wrong, at least in the context he was speaking of. In his scheme of things, farmers in the family would produce the cotton and sliver, the womenfolk would do the weaving (which used actually to be the practice). In the worst case, sliver needed to be bought, 'The total amount spent on tax and cultivation would add up to no more than six *annas*. The wages for weaving per person would be no more than one *paisa*. Thus, the expense a person would normally incur on clothes would be fourteen *annas* only.' In none of the other propositions, not even in that of Anil Baran Roy, can one come across such first-hand knowledge of the everyday practice of hand-spinning with the *arata*. After all, the detractors of the Gandhian charkha were, in Fakir Mohan's eyes, all 'babus' (like Anil Baran Roy).

Sumit Sarkar has argued how the Swadeshi (1905) movement was confined mostly to the middle-class '*bhadralok*'.[78] Fakir Mohan's debunking of the babu prattle around swadeshi corroborates that argument, albeit quite obliquely. It is obvious that, irrespective of his undefined class position, Fakir Mohan's concern for the poor and deprived stands out. Though he was born into a business family, he had experience of the life of rural peasantry around him, and grew up without receiving much by way of modern education having been to a traditional *chahali* (village school), where the 'lower', untouchable caste (sitting at a distance, of course, he says in his *An Autobiography*) too received the same kind of education apart from a stint at a Persian school.[79]

Sumit Sarkar also talks about 'the complex continuum of intermediate attitudes' and 'coexistence and complex interpenetration of extremely varied type of consciousness and activity: caste, communal, class, regional or national'.[80] Perhaps Fakir Mohan himself represents one such strand—a consciousness that is at once regional, and national and anti-colonial (unintentionally, as it would turn out). The point I am trying to make is that the rhetoric of the charkha was not entirely absent during the continuum, i.e. between the time of its ubiquity, slow passing of its usage, and its magical revival by Mahatma Gandhi.[81]

Further, Fakir Mohan's espousal of the charkha as a solution to village economy was not an isolated instance. Nor was this essay an isolated critique of modernity, as we have already seen, since he had already spoken up against the gloss and veneer of modernity in

1883. In the late 1880s too, sporadic attempts were made to keep the charkha going. Tagore gives a hilarious account of his brother, Jyotindra's experiments with 'a national costume' for all of India. He had to strike a compromise between trousers and a dhoti, since dhoti was not 'deemed businesslike'; and 'trousers too foreign'. So, 'the trousers were decorated with the addition of a false dhoti-fold in front and behind'. Tagore also narrates the manufacture of 'a flimsy country towel' that one of the enthusiasts had tied around his head, exclaiming 'made in our loom'.[82] Yogeshchandra Ray's introduction of handicrafts much before the Swadeshi movement erupted is yet another case in point. He narrates in his autobiography *Ja Manepade*, how he had set up, with the help of a few friends, a cooperative enterprise called 'Udyogi Samiti Bhandar' in connection with which he carried out some research and experiment on the charkha and published his findings in the journal *Prabashi*—the period in question: 1898–1905.[83] Around the same time (1901?), when Gopabandhu Das, a younger contemporary of Radhanath Ray, Fakir Mohan, and Madhusudan Das, was studying law, he insisted on wearing crude rather than refined khadi. He was known to wear crude khadi even when he was in school. Unlike Fakir Mohan, however, Gopabandhu Das came to be a political activist, a nationalist. After a brief foray into the Odia identitarian politics spearheaded by Madhusudan Das, with its demand for the unification of the Odia-speaking tracts across the three provinces, he threw himself into the Mahatma Gandhi-led freedom movement. He was with him in Kolkata in 1921, when, using the same Odia word, *arata* for charkha, Gopabandhu Das urged the Odias to return to the spinning wheel. He said:

Having understood well the benefit that may accrue if the *arata* is used in every household of Odisha, especially the famine-struck areas where it would help mitigate their misery, the *sabha* [Kalikata Odia Sabha] urges the men and women of Odisha to work the *arata*.[84]

Before this, even when he used coarse khadi, he seldom made a public cause of the charkha, unlike what Fakir Mohan attempted in the public sphere in 1908. In 1921, Gopabandhu Das spoke about the subject only after his mentor, Mahatma Gandhi, popularized the idea.

Mahatma Gandhi rightly acknowledges, long after the charkha and khadi had become 'metonymous' with his name, that 'The *charkha* is not my invention. It was there before . . . God whispered into my ear: "if you want to work through nonviolence, you have to

proceed with small things, not big".'[85] Continuing with Mahatma
Gandhi's attempts to mystify the khadi, Rajmohan Gandhi sees
connections between Kabir and Thiruvalluvar, weaver poets.[86] But,
surely, there are less mystifying ways of looking at Mahatma
Gandhi's sources.

III

I had begun this chapter hypothesizing how the large conclusions
scholars tend to draw on the basis of limited archives available to
them in colonial times could prove to be of dubious merit. This is
especially the case while theorizing the semiotic of or assigning
meanings to certain Gandhian tropes. The foregoing discussion
clearly shows the merit of the hypothesis. Of course, there is already
work afoot, and more and more archives are emerging, widening the
required database. One such in the relevant area, Tridip Suhrud's
Writing Life familiarizes the non-Gujarati readers with the work of
such important thinkers as Narmadashankar Lalshankar, Manibhai
Nabhubhai, and Govardhan Tripathy. Of particular relevance here is
the confessional autobiography of the second; for, Manibhai's
principal quest was towards finding 'a pure locus of love', to which
end he 'entered into relationship with some women, but that was
for the purpose of this quest and not out of any lust or desire'. But,
as Suhrud points out, it was only in 1930 that the custodian of his
autobiography acknowledged the existence of the text, but remained
unwilling to publish it[87] on the ground that, unlike the autobiographies
of De Quincey's or Mahatma Gandhi's, its publication would not
benefit anyone. This is a throwback on the entire Radhanath Ray
episode, and his regret that there was, in his time, no exemplary
book. It is no fault of the author, Manibhai, that his autobiography
appeared in 1979, and the publication record shows that it *succeeds*,
instead of preceding Mahatma Gandhi's *An Autobiography*.

Through this discussion, I hope to have shown how certain
practices and symbols which have become prominent and pan-
Indian only after their association with Mahatma Gandhi were
nonetheless available for retrieval, for those symbols and practices
were truly 'intimations', and were always inevitably indigenous and
pre-Gandhian. His triumph lay in his re-discovery of India after
decades of life away from it. These are examples of the way Mahatma
Gandhi appropriates and popularizes already available indigenous
modes of confessional-writing, or, even, everyday practices such as
that of weaving and clothing. Upon his return from South Africa, he
did not want to come across as an alienated Indian and tried to

adopt a cultural semiotic around himself, both in words and deed.[88] How successfully he did it comes across clearly in the way latter-day historians have identified those very symbols as 'Gandhian', nor can they be dissociated from the 'Mahatma' or the Great Soul. Nonetheless, and ironically enough, the honorific, 'Mahatma' was a common appellation for any great man. Not only many great personalities or benefactors of society—contemporary or otherwise— were customarily referred to as 'Mahatma' (such as Mahatma Ram Mohan Rai, Mahatma Vidyasagar, even Mahatma John Beames, as the British Administrator, was called by Fakir Mohan). But now it is and can only be applied to Mahatma Gandhi. Similarly, older practices that he adopted got stuck with his name and cannot be unstuck now.

Notes

1. Richard Grenier, *Commentary*, 1 March 1983, pp. 59–72. See, <https://www.commentarymagazine.com/articles/the-gandhi-nobody-knows/>, accessed 1 November 2016.
2. *The Little Magazine*, vol. 1, no. 1, 2000, pp. 38–41.
3. *The Guardian*, 17 October 2003, <https://www.theguardian.com/world/2003/oct/17/southafrica.india>, accessed 12 September 2014.
4. Ibid.
5. Ibid.
6. Emma Tarlo, 'Khadi', 2014. <http://www.soas.ac.uk/ssai/keywords/file24807.pdf>, accessed 24 February 2014.
7. Dipesh Chakrabarty, *Habitations of Modernity: Essays in the Wake of Subaltern Studies; with a Foreword by Homi K. Bhabha*, Chicago: University of Chicago Press, 2002, p. xxiii.
8. Ibid., p. 60.
9. Ibid.
10. Sarala Devi was born in Kolkata in 1872 to Janakinath Ghosal (a Congress man) and Swarnakumari Devi (an early Bangla novelist). The latter was the daughter of 'Maharshi' Debendranath Tagore, a Brahmo leader and older sister of Rabindranath Tagore. She died in 1945.
11. Rajmohan Gandhi, *Mohandas: A True Story of a Man, His People and an Empire* (2006), Middlesex: Penguin, 2007, p. 229.
12. Literary historians of Odisha describe Radhanath Ray (1848–1908) as the first and most important modern poet. He remained at the centre of Odia literary culture from the mid-nineteenth century until his death, and his reputation as the preeminent poet of his time has never been seriously questioned. A Bengali, born and brought up in Balasore in north Odisha, he quickly rose to fame in the 1870s as a poet and public figure. His first collection of poetry was in Bangla, but all his subsequent publications were in Odia. The colonial governors had

honoured him with the title Rai Bahadur. Bhudev Mukhopadhyay (1827–94), whom Partha Chatterjee calls 'the most brilliant rationalist defender of "orthodox" tradition', had come to know Radhanath Ray during his visits to Odisha in his official capacity as the inspector of schools. As a deputy school inspector under the Raj, Radhanath Ray had already been embroiled in controversies. During the years 1878–9, Bhudev commended his learning, and 'rejoiced to find that [Radhanath Ray] was as well a Sanskrit as an English scholar . . .' (Durgacharan Ray, *Radhanath Jibani*, Cuttack: Friends Publishers, 1941, p. 100). The two had an endearing relationship until Bhudev's death.

13. Saraswati Nagendrabala (1878–1906) was the daughter of Nrityagopal Sarkar and was married at the age of ten to Khagaendranath Mitra (Mustophi). From the age of thirteen she began to live with her husband. She taught herself several languages including Odia. Her work *Naridharma* published in 1900, which Judith Wall discusses at some length is a celebration of traditional marriage and family as well as nationalism.

14. Adikand Sahoo, *Radhanath Granthabali,* Cuttack: Vidya Prakashan, 2002, pp. 592–7.

15. Chakrabarty, *Habitations of Modernity,* p. 61.

16. Ibid.

17. Prasanna Kumar Mishra and Debendra Kumar Dash, *Kabibar Radhanath Granthabali*, Cuttack: Grantha Mandir, 1998.

18. This was deleted in the later editions.

19. Gangadhar Meher (1862–1924) was himself a poet of eminence and he was a weaver by caste. Hailing from a background of abject poverty, his schoolteachers had advised him to attend school for half a day, and in the other half, to weave and make some money to alleviate his family.

20. Sahoo, *Radhanath Granthabali*, p. 643.

21. Ibid., p. 644.

22. *Naridharma* is a conduct treatise written by Saraswati and is discussed by Judith Walsh. For more about Saraswati, see Judith E. Walsh, *Domesticity in Colonial India: What Women Learned When Men Gave Them Advice*, Maryland: Rowman & Littlefield Publishers, 2004.

23. Ibid.

24. In 1882, Bhudev invited Radhanath Ray to stay with him at Hooghly and liked him so much that he went to the extent of admitting that he would have given his daughter in marriage to Radhanath Ray, had he been a brahman, even as a second wife (Ray, *Radhanath Jibani*, p. 101).

25. Mishra and Dash, *Kabibar Radhanath Granthabali*, p. 434.

26. Sahoo, *Radhanath Granthabali*, pp. 596–7.

27. The title was '*Atmakathara Kiyadanmsa*' or 'A Portion of the Autobiography'.

28. It appears under diverse titles in different newspapers and periodicals.

29. Ray, *Radhanath Jibani*, pp. 492–3.

30. Gandhi, *Mohandas*, p. 229.

31. Ibid., pp. 228–9.
32. Ibid.
33. Ibid., p. 233.
34. Ibid.
35. Ibid.
36. Ibid., p. 232.
37. Ray, *Radhanath Jibani*, pp. 493–4.
38. Gandhi, *Mohandas*, p. 232.
39. Ibid.
40. Ibid.
41. His body and mind were wrecked by an acutely guilt-ridden conscience. His son took a lot of trouble over comforting Radhanath Ray, even taking him to the river Kathjodi for 'hydropathy'. He went to the extent of writing to the lieutenant governor of Bengal, begging forgiveness. But, while Radhanath Ray thought it necessary to expiate his wrongdoing against his wife, he never thought of doing any justice to the woman who had given her all to him. While unilaterally accusing Saraswati when she was not there to defend herself, he never felt any qualms or pangs of conscience. The most questionable aspect of his conduct towards her was that he confessed his sin levelling all kinds of serious charges against her after her death. While Radhanath Ray received nothing but accolades for his brave confession, for having come clean, and in a way retained his untarnished image as a sage-like character, there was none to defend Saraswati. So much so, very few biographical notes even mention that she committed suicide, let alone go into the reasons thereof.
42. Mishra and Dash, *Kabibar Radhanath Granthabali*, p. 339.
43. Ibid., p. 344.
44. He even composed a few poems on the same subject such as *Sati* 'Satiprati Satidrohi Patira Ukti', or 'Words of an Unfaithful Husband for his Chaste Wife' (*Utkal Sahitya*, 1909) and 'Nibedana', or 'A Supplication' (*Utkal Sahitya*, 1911), in Mishra and Dash, *Kabibar Radhanath Granthabali*, p. 484.
45. Ibid.
46. For a discussion of a quasi-feminist angle, see Brajanath Rath, '. . . As Radhanath got busy trying to clear his conscience, exorcising the "spell" of the now dead Nagendrabala, in the last few years of her life she suffered silently, unless, one reads her 1902 poem, "The Thief" (in Bangla) as a prescient response to his accusations, an uncanny anticipation of Radhanath's Confession:

Are you alone righteous and pure, and am I alone the thief?
Have you not stolen my heart's treasure by hacking the gate of my life?
Have you not stolen my all? Have you not plundered everything I had?
I do whatever you do, my friend and the love of my life?
Yet, you accuse me in different ways for loving you!

Though a thief yourself, you call yourself a saint; and I am branded a thief?

Having found you I loved you, is that all my fault?

As king you are happily seated on the throne of my heart!

If having been a thief, one becomes a king, God save the perfect thief!'

47. See Tanika Sarkar, who tries to 'place ideas about Hindu conjugality at the very heart of militant nationalism', which, in turn, she sees in as 'a moment of absolute and violent criticism of foreign rule . . . in the late 1880s and early 1890s'; Tanika Sarkar, *Hindu Wife, Hindu Nation: Community, Religion, and Cultural Nationalism*, Delhi: Permanent Black, 2001, p. 191.

48. Sarkar, *Hindu Wife, Hindu Nation*, p. 198.

49. Gandhi, *Mohandas: A True Story of a Man*, p. 233.

50. Radhanath Ray told all his close confidants such as Gourishankar Ray, editor of *Utkal Dipika*, and Shashibhusan, his son, who tried to stop him from such a 'foolish' act that he just could not help it, quoting, 'If he did not atone for the sin through a public confession my pain will not subside'. Interestingly enough, he consulted his close Brahmo friends, Madhusudan Rao and Biswanath Kar (Ray, *Radhanath Jibani*, p. 492). The public confession was sent out for printing to Gourishankar Ray; one hundred copies each in Bangla and Odia were sent to all the newspapers of Odisha and Bengal as well to all friends. He sent a humble prayer to the lieutenant governor of Bengal. These appeared in different titles, presumably provided by the editors themselves. A few of the reverential responses have been published in *Radhanath Jibani* showing the increased respect with which Radhanath Ray was now viewed after the confession was published. One correspondent, seemingly of Vaishnava persuasion, drawing Radhanath Ray's attention to the example of Vilwamangala of the fourteenth century from Kerala, who had an illicit relationship with a prostitute, but repentantly withdrew to become a great Vaishnava saint (see Ray, *Radhanath Jibani*).

51. It is interesting to note that Biswanath Kar, writing in his *Utkal Sahitya* column 'Bibidha Prasanga', says how a Christian missionary met Radhanath Ray to congratulate him on his public confession and how he offered a long prayer to Christ (Ray, *Radhanath Jibani*, p. 513). He seems to misremember Milton's *Paradise Lost* and, instead of the term 'Umpire Conscience' he uses the term, 'Detective Conscience'. He also quotes St. Augustine and shows his familiarity with the Christian practice of confession, thus confirming Radhanath Ray's deliberate avoidance of the Christian sources.

52. I have made liberal use of material from Natabar Samantaray. See, Natabar Samantaray, *Odiya Sahityara Itihasa*, Bhubaneswar: Bani Bhavan, 1964; 2nd edn., 1983, p. 324.

53. Ibid.

54. Michel Foucault, Luther H. Martin, Huck Gutman and Patrick H. Hutton, *Technologies of the Self: A Seminar with Michel Foucault*, Amherst: University of Massachusetts, 1988, pp. 16–17.

55. The English translation appeared in 1910. Of course versions of the same had appeared in *Indian Opinion* earlier 'yet he imagined energy—economic, political and psychological—flowing from "looms" plying in a number of homes' (Gandhi, *Mohandas*, p. 226).

56. One might recall that Fakir Mohan, like Radhanath Ray, was already a well-established litterateur and a public servant as well, not unlike many other Odia intellectuals who were to get involved in the creation of or amalgamation of the Odia-speaking tracts (like Madhusudan Das and Gopabandhu Das, to mention the most prominent ones). However, writers like Fakir Mohan believed in cultural nationalism and strove towards building a strong, modern Odia literary culture. He had already written the first Odia short story and the first successful novel, was soon to write the first Odia autobiography, but was unsure about the essay form. It is necessary to remind ourselves that the modern Odia essay, then about three decades in the making, had barely been perfected as a literary form. It was restricted to the magazines and newspaper culture, and was just about emerging as a literary genre. Unsurprisingly, Fakir Mohan's scepticism about his mastery over the form was apparent in the essay itself, 'I have been talking randomly, but dear reader, please rearrange my thoughts yourself, and you will understand the drift of my argument', he admits.

57. *Baleswer Sambad Bahika*, vol. 41, no. 10, 1908; see for etymology of the word from Sanskrit '*araghatta*', *Purnachandra Bhasakosha*, vol. I, p. 557. This is the Odia word for charkha (for etymology of charkha see, ibid., p. 2559).

58. Rebecca M. Brown, *Gandhi's Spinning Wheel and the Making of India*, London and New York: Routledge, 2010.

59. At this point, however, we might do well to remind ourselves that the movement itself was low-key in Odisha, in some places, even meeting with some opposition. Only a few instances can be found in the newspapers. Fakir Mohan is said to have delivered a speech in one public meeting in Balasore in 1905, though this is not mentioned in a more authentic edition of Fakir Mohan's *Granthabali*. In the absence of any evidence, and going by the intricate details of Fakir Mohan's argument, it might be safe to assume that he covers new ground. Purushottam Kar's history seems to be the only one which cites instances of meetings and rallies regarding swadeshi. But there were such cases as Pandit Nilakantha Das and the others wearing black badges when the people of Sambalpur were celebrating the introduction of Odia in place of Hindi in Sambalpur. Maybe, the launching of *Utkal Sammilani* had something to do with this indifference. This is recounted in the autobiography by Nilakantha Das's friend, Bharat Chandra

Nayak. See, Bharat Chandra Nayak, *Mor Purba Smruti Katha* (*Remembering my Past*), Cuttack: Self Published, 1996(?).

60. Lisa Trivedi, *Clothing Gandhi's Nation: Homespun and Modern India*, Bloomington & Indianapolis: Indiana University, 2007, p. 12.

61. This was a speech delivered at the Baleswar National Society's fourth annual conference on 7 July 1883 (Fakir Mohan, *Granthabali*, p. 412). This Society may have been a local branch of the 'national Society' of Nabagopal Mitra aka 'National Nabagopal'. He (1840–94) was an important early Bengali nationalist, best known as an organizer of the 'Hindu Mela'.

62. M.K. Gandhi, *Hind Swaraj and Other Writings*, ed. Anthony J. Parel, New Delhi and Cambridge: CUP, 1997; repr. 2009.

63. M.K. Gandhi, *An Autobiography or the Story of My Experiments with Truth*, tr. Mahadev Desai, Ahmedabad: Navajivan Trust, 1927, p. 407.

64. Ibid., p. 410.

65. Gandhi, *Mohandas*, p. 226.

66. Fakir Mohan, *Granthabali: Complete Works of Fakir Mohan Senapati*, ed. Debendra Dash, vol. 3, Cuttack: Grantha Mandir, 2008, p. 371.

67. Ibid.

68. Ibid.

69. 'According to Thomas Bowrey (1669–79), in Bengal 4 *cauris* made one *ganda*, 20 *gandas* one *pan*, and 16 *pans* one *kahana*. 2½ such *kahana*s (or 3,200 *cauri*s) went for a rupee'; Om Prakash, 'Co-existence of Standardized and Humble Money: The Case of Mughal India', <http://www.helsinki.fi/iehc2006/papers2/Prakash.pdf>, accessed 16 July 2012.

70. Ibid., p. 372.

71. Ibid.

72. Gandhi, *An Autobiography*, p. 410.

73. Gandhi, *Hind Swaraj and Other Writings*, p. 36.

74. Mohan, *Granthabali: Complete Works*, p. 372.

75. Ibid.

76. Trivedi, *Clothing Gandhi's Nation*, p. 24.

77. Fakir Mohan, *Granthabali: Complete Works*, p. 372.

78. I consider Fakir Mohan to be belonging, though not to the subaltern groups, at least to the non-elite, somewhat indeterminate class and an 'intermediate caste' in the way Sumit Sarkar describes the latter (see, Sumit Sarkar, 'The Conditions and Nature of Subaltern Militancy: Bengal from Swadeshi to Non-Cooperation, *c.* 1905–22', in *Subaltern Studies* III, ed. Ranajit Guha, New Delhi: OUP, 1994, pp. 272–3). Also see, Fakir Mohan's *Autobiography* for an appreciation of his class and caste plight in his childhood.

79. Samantaray, *Odia Sahityara Itihasa*, p. 375.

80. Sarkar, 'The Conditions and Nature of Subaltern Militancy', p. 274.

81. Ibid., p. 313. See *Dorai Charitmanas* where the charkha is seen as *sudarshan-chakra*.

82. Rabindranath Tagore, *My Remembrances*, 1917; quoted in John R. McLane, *The Political Awakening in India*, New Jersey: Prentice Hall, 1970, pp. 38–9.

83. Yogeshchandra Ray, *Ja Manepade* (2002) [What I Remember], tr. Rabindra Prasad Panda, Bhubaneswar: Lark Books, 2006, pp. 387, 391. He tells us 'I never bought foreign goods if I could find indigenous items: this was an old habit with me. I even started selling handloom items in Cuttack procuring them from Medinipur.' In September 1898, he set up, with the help of friends, a cooperative store. A signboard with the Odia name, 'Udyogi Samiti Bhandar', and inscribed below it in English 'Udyog Samiti Stores' was hung in front of the two-room store for indigenous clothing and other daily-use items. In 1905, there was a fresh wave of call for swadeshi. As early as 1890, he also discovered the indigenous art and science of colouring cotton cloth by Odia weaver women and launched his own experiments (pp. 350–5).

84. *Asha*, 12 September 1921.

85. Gandhi, *A True Story of a Man*, p. 226.

86. Ibid.

87. Tridip Suhrud, *Writing Life: Three Gujarati Thinkers*, Hyderabad: Orient BlackSwan, 2009, p. 85.

88. This was common strategy, practised during the period under scrutiny. I am not thinking of the hilarious cartooning of Indians getting in and out of Indian dhoti and donning European pants and suit before disembarking in England or vice versa (See illustration in Emma Tarlo, *Clothing Matters: Dress and Identity in India*, New Delhi: Penguin India (Viking), 1996, p. 54). I am thinking of how Mahatma Gandhi 'mastered sartorial matters' when he went to England so that he did not 'look a "barbarian in the eyes of the Englishman"' (ibid., p. 65). Though he quickly gave up his early attempts to learn French or dancing lessons or playing the violin, 'it was years before he cast off his Western appearances' (ibid., p. 66). He as quickly donned the Indian look as he had done the European clothes and manners. There is a picture of the suited Mahatma Gandhi with Kasturba, shortly before leaving South Africa (1914) and another when he appeared in public after he disembarked in Bombay a few months later (January 1915) dressed as a Kathiawadi peasant (ibid., p. 69). Around the same time, we have the supreme example of Eliot donning his bowler hat, 'brolly' in hand and Saville Rowe or Oxford Street suit passing off as an Englishman, and finally accepted as an iconic status soon after. Ezra Pound was critical of his fellow American poet's capacity to pretend to be dead like the opossum ('Ol' Possum'), but himself soon realizing the impossibility of being accepted as an English poet without flaunting the cultural semiotic of being a local.

7

Minute by Minute
Impossibility of a Conclusion

> Contemporary politics is not about 'truths' of history; it is about remembered pasts and the problems of fashioning a future based on collective memories.
>
> — ASHIS NANDY

The Introduction to the book begins with a select list of examples of controversies and proceeds to offer a tentative definition of the category, 'controversy'. It then explores whether the discursive entity called controversy could be treated as a genre and suggests that the genesis of this genre, as we now recognize it, coincides with the high-noon of modernity. I also try to highlight modernity's coevality with the nineteenth-century phenomenon of nationalism in India, and attempt to chart possible theoretical links between the emergence of the public sphere, print culture, and the rising incidence of this 'modern' discursive experience, which may have had implications for identitarian movements. During the course of analysing certain significant controversies across the five chapters, especially their cultural expressions and their contexts, we saw how these controversies were wrapped around questions of script-language, textuality and authorship, as well as representations of history. A few were also related to issues of sexuality, around representations of the body and the gendering of its embellishments, the semiotic and economy of clothing, forms of religious worship, etc. I hope I have shown the validity of the various hypotheses proposed in the Introduction. Also, we have seen in the chapters how none of the issues were limited to the immediate and seemingly innocuous level of discourse. They all had, directly or indirectly, much at stake— questions of identity, nation, and power of specific communities.

These controversies were enmeshed with issues of caste and religion but were directly related to the material conditions of communities who got involved in the controversies. Precisely because of such enmeshing, they keep resurfacing in postcolonial times. In attempting to sum up my chief arguments and see here interconnections between different controversies, I discover the impossibility of drawing any definitive conclusions. Instead in this last and concluding chapter, I wish to suggest the manner in which the seemingly disconnected controversies exist in dialogue with each other and each one of them helps us understand the others better.

Along with identifying their archaeological heritage, diverse linguistic communities were helped by British scholars and cultural historians to unearth, date, and evaluate literary texts from the early vernacular millennium. Soon the 'learned natives' joined hands with them and squabbles followed over the dating, authenticity, and identity of authors and texts, their print-worthiness, not to speak of the *ruchi parivartan* in matters of these texts vis-à-vis an imbibed sense of morality. In all these, the intervention of the new 'knowledges of power', and modernization of traditional knowledge is discernible. While these are discussed at some length in the chapters, what is also taken up for discussion by way of setting up a contrast is a limited but significant attempt to resist such modernization of knowledge as the continuity of indigenous knowledges was sought to be upheld. The clash of tradition and modernity, especially whenever tradition took a beating, resulted in controversies. As the colonial powers tried to tighten their grip over this major 'dependency', the newly emerged intelligentsia also started regrouping (especially following 1857) to forge anti-colonial and later nationalist goals. These developments had implications for cultural practices too.

For, nationalism, Ernest Gellner says, is the 'congruence between culture and power'.[1] Taking this formulation further, G. Aloysius says that nationalism, both as an ideology and a movement, has two referral points, 'one external and the other internal. The external reference is to other cultures, nations and nation states, which are perceived as obstacles in the way of one's own nationalism. . . . The internal dimension of the culture-power fusion is what constitutes the specifically modern element in the notion of the nation. Here the reference is to culture's own past as the other'.[2] This is evident in the analysis provided across the chapters. Though none of these chapters deal directly with the Babri Masjid controversy, I wish to invoke the subject here which seems to have lasted a century and a half, if not more, affecting the lives of most (and causing the death of many) Indians. Its relevance to the many issues discussed already can hardly be overestimated. As Roma Chatterji says, '[t]he demolition of the Babri Masjid in the controversy over sacred spaces is surely considered a "critical event" in [Veena] Das's sense [of the term] that many would argue it had put the whole nature of the Indian nation as a secular nation into question'.[3]

During the course of studying a narrowly local controversy over an unfinished epic called *Mahayatra*, I discussed two other controversies over sacred spaces: one local and lesser known (the Alekh attack on the Jagannath Temple) and the better known and long-drawn controversy in Bodh Gaya (involving two major religious communities, Hindus and Buddhists, but also featuring one Muslim individual, Hossain Baksh, who acted on the side of the Hindu priest). That by the beginning of the twentieth-century Buddhist presence in the Indian public sphere had diminished to negligible dimensions is borne out by the fact that the momentous controversy in Bodh Gaya is seldom talked about in any context of controversy over sacred places. Many Buddhist monuments have been appropriated by Hindu modes of worship without causing a flutter of protest. Such is the dominance of Muslims as a relatively powerful minority that the category 'minority' community has become synonymous with Muslims. Not even the fact that Buddhists and Jains also had intermittently staked their claims on the territory in Ayodhya-Faizabad, is deemed newsworthy. Truly enough, as late as 2011, tucked away in an obscure corner of a newspaper, a report said, 'The Buddha Education Foundation has filed a Special Leave Petition against the Ayodhya-Babri Masjid verdict given by the Lucknow Bench of the Allahabad High Court on 30 September 2010. In its petition, the BEF says that the real claimants of the disputed land in Ayodhya are Buddhists and the followers of Dr. B.R. Ambedkar.'[4]

At this point I wish to invoke Ahmad again for he draws a parallel between India and the early twentieth-century Italian context:

'Culture' . . . has been a rather fatal ingredient in the hundred-odd years of our communal history. . . . Muslim communalism [Syed Ahmad Khan et al] has always been based on a certain nostalgia for the Moghul imperium, the princely state and the specialness of the Persianized culture of upper class Muslims. . . . But the idea that 'culture'—indeed spirituality—is the special 'national' vocation of the Indian has led an even more powerful life in the history of Hindu communalism. Already by the middle of the 19th century, well before Bankim or Aurobindo or Vivekananda bestowed the idea with such hallowed respectability, so numerous were its purveyors that Madhusudan Dutt was constrained to denounce openly a certain cluster of them, in a felicitous phrase, 'Ram and his rabble'.

Ahmad seems to confuse 'rabble' with the 'purveyors' of spirituality as culture. Michael Madhusudan Dutt was simply referring to the 'banar sena' or the army of monkeys and the pro-Rama crowd. Also, for some reason, Ahmad seems to go soft on the course of action that Syed Ahmad Khan proposes. Though he mentions here a time frame, 'hundred-odd years of communal history', Ahmad does not explain such temporal delimitation of 'our communal history', and allows the time frame for the 'hundred-odd years of our linguistic history'[5] in the quoted passage to go unexplained. The fact of the matter is that the 'rabble' was transformed literally to demolish the Babri structure in the name of Rama's birthplace.

As we have already seen, Indian linguistic and literary cultures have been inseparable. These in turn have been enmeshed in our communal history. Ahmad quickly draws a connection between these. Since he was writing in the immediate aftermath of the Babri Masjid demolition, Ahmad further argues that '[t]he Fascist intellectual appears among us today in the garb of the traditional intellectual, invoking and appropriating the classical text, refashioning the old Brahmanical world into a new kind of marketable Hinduism, which is then asserted against our own modern traditions of secularity, socialism, rationality, religious tolerance, and plurality'.[6] Here, I wish to take on Ahmad for his use of the loaded phrase, 'our own modern traditions of secularity, socialism, rationality, religious tolerance, and plurality', complete with its first person, plural possessive pronoun, used obviously for emphasis. One wonders whether the confidence is misplaced. After all, all these categories and values are elements of imbibed modernity too. Where they are indigenous, they are heavily tempered by colonial modernity. The foregoing chapters have clearly established that the controversies leading to serious linguistic, communal and caste conflicts, all owed their genesis and continuity to these new knowledges of power, purportedly necessary for pluralism, secularity, and tolerance. Their effect as indeed their original purpose, as the twin Minutes of Macaulay and Canning[7] show, were far from salutary. When colonial governmentality tried to discipline the natives in times of controversy and conflict, worse consequences followed. The circuitous logic employed in the court case of Anagarika Dharmapala that has already been examined in Chapter 3 is a case in point. In the context of the Babri Masjid legal battles, if the aim was to break the real or imagined stranglehold of brahmanical, Sanskritic-Hindu, casteist status quo, and usher in progress, quite the contrary followed. As Deepak Mehta has presented in his study of the legal wrangling over Babri Masjid-Ram Janmabhoomi, 'the status quo' itself kept changing.

When the battles over Urdu/Perso-Arabic and Nagri/Hindi were yet to heat up, when the philologists and linguists were already busy with their researches, which, as we have seen in Chapter 1, precipitated the 'walls of words', another controversy was brewing thanks to the intervention of the other new science, Archaeology. Thirty years after Macaulay's Minute had given fillip to the fostering of the researches on the Indian scripts and languages discussed in the first chapter, yet another Minute by Lord Canning gave rise to the latter. This was the 'Minute by the Right Hon'ble the Governor General of India in Council on the Antiquities of Upper India dated 22nd January 1862', in which the author (Lord Canning, who had by then quelled the 'Mutiny') said, 'It is true that in 1844, on a representation from the Royal Asiatic Society, and in 1847, in accordance with detailed suggestions from Lord Hardinge, the Court of Directors gave a liberal sanction to certain arrangements for examining, delineating, and recording some of the chief antiquities of India'. He then bemoans the fact that after a few lackadaisical steps, the scheme was lost sight of after two or three years. In his Minute, therefore, he grants the memorandum submitted by Cunningham, who during the next three years or so conducts an extensive archaeological research and submits the *Four Reports*.[8] The Minute mentions that, it was the 'duty of the Government' to investigate and place on record, 'for the instruction of the future generations, many particulars that might still be rescued from oblivion, and throw light upon the early history of England's great dependency and Englishmen are led to give more thought to India than such as barely suffices to hold it and govern it'.[9]

Somehow, the mention of Babri-Faizabad always figures in the national imagery, not in terms of the numerous Buddhist ruins, but only as the silhouetted image of three domes on which weapon wielding Hindus seem to be gesticulating in warlike postures. The picture conjures up what must have been a replica of the image of a century-and-a-half ago when the first recorded dispute took place. As per British administrative records, armed Hindu ascetics occupied the 'birth place of Rama' in 1853. This was followed by a Muslim offensive, leading to compromise. I refer to the Minute because, in the years that followed, it open the floodgates and lead to a massive amount of archaeological findings of which the natives were until then blissfully ignorant. Of course, until these reports were published, travel accounts of Xuanzang existed, which Cunningham uses. But, they were accounts which were not passed around as 'scientific' or 'objective' knowledge. Between Xuanzang and Cunningham, successive history-hungry Europeans had converted oral accounts of folk-memory into written documents. A few interesting aspects of the *Four Reports* are as follows (and I am restricting my discussion to the portions of the reports on Faizabad and Ayodhya):

1. Though Ramkot is mentioned, there is no mention of the Masjid domes.
2. There is more emphasis on Hindu and Buddhist relics than any of the Moghul period.
3. Though one of the two disputes (1853, 1885) had already taken place, Cunningham does not mention any of it in his *Reports*.

Surprisingly enough, Cunningham does not mention any of the European scholars who attributed the demolition of the Rama temple to the period of Babur. For, by then Joseph Tiefenthaler, who visited the site during 1766–71 had suggested the mosque's connection to the birthplace of Rama. Written in French, this latter observation would have remained obscure had Johann Bernoulli not translated his account from French into English, and included it in his 1788 publication. According to this account, either Aurangzeb or Babur had demolished the Ramkot fortress. A mosque was constructed in its place, though the Hindus continued to use the mud platform that was supposed to be the birthplace of Rama. In 1810, Buchanan visited the site, and stated that the structure destroyed was a temple dedicated to Rama, during Babur's time. Cunningham, most likely willfully, ignores this in his reports. But by then, these reports must have circulated and incited the Hindu ascetics to storm the mosque in 1853.

Nonetheless, the following extract from Cunningham's reports is worth quoting because of its relevance to our context, and if only because the detailed studies of the history of the controversy somehow do not make use of it:

Thus, Ramkot, or Hanuman Garhi, on the east side of the city, is a small walled fort surrounding a modern temple on the top of an ancient mound. The name Ramkot is certainly old, as it is connected with the traditions of the Mani Parbat . . .; but the temple of Hanuman is not older than the time of Aurangjb. . . . [A]bout one quarter of a mile distant [from near the Ashok Bat (or griefless Banyan)] in the very heart of the city, stands *Janam Asthan*, or 'Birth-place temple' of Rama.

These detailed reports, rather than what the Allahabad judgement has pointed out about past practice of sharing the site by both Hindus and Muslims,[10] must have ensured that the local folklore/ history got disseminated among the 'learned natives' and because of the aura of positivism they gave rise to controversies, which in turn fuelled religious nationalism. We have already examined how similar scientific and philological enquiries into questions of language, dialect, script, etc., which had resulted in numerous controversies across north and east Indian territories, were also steadily giving rise to linguistic nationalism. Meanwhile, many more claimants to the site have been reported; many more scholars and officials have suggested different dates. Though no one claims any record of any date when the Rama temple was built (not even the report of the Archaelogical Survey of India), the dates for the Masjid have been shifted backward and forward.

This bears a close similarity with the more inocuous controversy over the dating of Sarala Das and another cultural controversy as to whether Jayadev, the twelfth-century poet of the famous and popular *Gitagobinda*, was an Odia or Bengali. The latter having had a tradition since the nineteenth century of dating him and locating his birth in a place called Kenduli Sasan in Odisha.[11] In his comment on Michael Madhusudan Dutt, Bankimchandra Chattopadhyay had used a hyperbole to say that there were 'two great Bengali poets since the beginning of Bangla poetic tradition—Jayadev was one and it was Michael Madhusudan Dutt now'.[12] Let it be said here that *Gitagobinda* had been a shared inheritance well into the eighteenth century, i.e. until William Jones's translation appeared (1792). Once it fell into the hands of Europeans, curiosity about the poet spread among scholars and by mid-nineteenth century, Bengali nationalists such as Bankimchandra Chattopadhyay claimed Jayadeva to be a Bengali poet, along with the Maithili poet, Vidyapati. As we have seen in the first chapter, the tug-of-war over language-dialect (Hindi, Nagari, Mithilakshar, Odia and Bengali, etc.), the claims of the respective linguistic communities, especially in their studies of their languages, script, and later, the writing of literary history heated up. In the specific instance of Jayadeva, one of the earliest literary historians, M.M. Chakarvarty identified him as a Bengal-born

Bengali poet, much to the chagrin of Odia nationalists. The controversy refuses to die down even after the government of Odisha staged a cultural coup of sorts when the postal department literally gave the Odia, Jayadeva, a stamp of its approval by issuing a postage stamp to commemorate the Odia poet, a stamp that was released by the Odisha chief minister, whose alleged Odia-illiterarcy is itself a controversy that has dogged him. Popular culture in India has not helped matters at all, and has led people to comical situations. The 16 April 2007 episode of the popular Indian TV game show *Kaun Banega Crorepati (KBC III)* mentioned Jayadeva as the court poet of King Lakshmanasena of Bengal. This triggered an immediate volley of protests by the culture-aware people of Odisha. Shah Rukh Khan, the game show's host, was denounced for spreading false information. The then government of Odisha also demanded an apology and claimed that the game show 'mutilated historical facts' and 'hurt the feelings of the people of Odisha'. I have quoted the Odia historian Krishnachandra Panigrahi's irked response in the third chapter on the Sarala Das controversy. Surprisingly enough, though for eight centuries no dispute over the identity of Jaydeva is known to have existed, suddenly in the twentieth-century Odias and Bengalis began wrestling over the claim and counterclaim of whether Jayadeva too belonged to their region, thanks to the impact of the European practice of biographies, fact-finding, and archival research. Every now and then, newspapers in Odisha come up with arguments and counterarguments, though Sudipta Kaviraj has categorically called him an Odia poet that ought to have settled the matter once and for all.

One of the reasons why controversies over Sarala Das and Jayadeva (and, of course, that of the Ram Janmabhoomi) have proliferated is because the claims and counterclaims require evidence and proof, which are hard to come by, and therefore any conclusion or closure of the controversy is well-nigh impossible, and as long as identity related politics is privileged there is no reason to hope that such controversies can be laid to rest. One is reminded of 'Benford's Law of Controversy'. Cast in the form, almost a parody, of a physical law, this law 'propounded' by Gregory Benford states that 'Passion is inversely proportional to the amount of real information available'.[13] The higher the level of ignorance, the greater is the passion (in any given controversy). While these narratives complicate the debate around whether or not the concept of nations pre-existed colonization,[14] they certainly reveal patterns in internal, pre-colonial hegemonies, cultural productions, and reproductions of which undergo modifications on impact of the moment of colonization and modernity. In the case of the issue of the Babri Masjid, the matter is far more complicated. Whereas, the Masjid structure is a part of historical fact, it is pitted against claims over the birth of a personality, whose historicity cannot be proved with the tools of archaeology. Even the pre-existence of a Hindu structure defies scientific enquiry. This explains why these controversies have arisen only after the intervention of colonial modernity. As has been argued by historians of the dispute, even the judges who are expected to be 'objective' and 'scientific' tend to bow to supernatural powers and invoke faith and belief rather than law. The contradiction can be traced back to the discipline of history-writing that we have seen seriously challenged not only in the imaginative literature such as that of Radhanath, but also in the early histroies of Fakir Mohan, and Bhudev's stubborn refusal to toe the line of European historiography. We have seen Fakir Mohan's decisive statement on this, 'we do not know from where [Bentley Sahib] got the evidence of all this; but his words cannot be trusted more than those in the *Purana*'.[15]

Shifting the focus to another of my concerns in the book, I have briefly mentioned the relatively milder form of hostile reception of Michael Madhusudan Dutt's subversive reinvention of the *Ramayana* and that of Radhanath Ray's Odia reinvention of the *Mahabharata*. It might be more profitable to compare the *Mahayatra* controversy with the storm that Nabinchandra Sen's work on the historical subject of the Battle of Plassey kicked up in the Bangla public sphere. More pertinent because both are 'literary things' that are caste in the form of history. In the case of Nabinchandra Sen's work, the subject was just about one hundred years old, and 'historical'. In the case of Radhanath Ray's narrative, though the frame narrative is from the mythological, *Mahabharata*, many of the details were supposed to be historical facts, including the circumstances of Buddhism and the caste system, etc. What Rosinka Chaudhuri says about the controversy over Nabinchandra Sen's *Palasseyr Youddhya* is equally applicable to the *Mahayatra* controversy, Nabinchandra's work, she says, 'confounded the public because it contained at once both the logic of narrativity and the appearance of truth, thus resembling, in its essential poetic structure, the new discourse of history'.[16] The fact of the matter is that Dutt's work was still seen as a piece of literature and not history, whereas both Nabinchandra's work and Radhanath's unfinished epic dealt with explicitly historical subjects, even when Radhanath's carried a mythical frame narrative.

Michael Madhusudan Dutt's highly subversive *Meghnadhbadh Kavya* may not have upset too many people, but similar 'distortions' are claimed to be 'hurting the religious sentiments' of many believers. For example, recently, the withdrawal of an essay by A.K. Ramanujan on alternative versions of the *Ramayana* from the University of Delhi syllabus is a proof of the recalcitrance of controversies of the kind discussed, in the book, to die down. In an interview, Romila Thapar has tried to answer some of the questions that the controversy had raised. In an interview published in *The Hindu* she says, 'I think there's a political background to it because the initial attack against this essay [in 2008] was led by the ABVP which made sure that TV cameras had begun to roll when they carried out the attack, so that it would be properly recorded'.[17] This latter (reference to the media) reinforces my argument in the Introduction about the role of the media-modernity nexus in the propagation of controversies. Thapar further states that the 'demand was that this hurt the sentiments of the Hindu community and therefore it should be withdrawn'.[17] This again is the recasting of Fakir Mohan's observation regarding *Meghnadbadh Kavya* discussed in the chapter on *Mahayatra*, 'Through civil wars and diverse atrocities the Hindu has lost all; but no one can touch the Hindu's proudest monuments. The foundation of this pride lies in the Hindu heart. Any attempt to distort these icons will naturally hurt the Hindu heart. That is why we have said all these things about *Meghnadbadh*.'[18]

We return briefly to the subject of the last chapter dealing with the two texts, one each of Radhanath Ray and Fakir Mohan, and one of its concerns, tradition *v.* modernity. It might be worth our while to invoke Marx on India in relation to Fakir Mohan's ideas already discussed 'Arata' at this juncture. Analysing the traditional Indian economy, Marx claims, 'spinning and weaving are carried on in each family as subsidiary industries'. He goes on to opine that, '[s]ide by side with the masses thus occupied with one and the same work', dozens of individuals carry out a kind of division of labour, 'Brahman who conducts the religious services; the school master who on the sand teaches the children reading and writing; the calendar Brahman or astrologer who makes known the lucky or unlucky days for seed time and harvest . . ., the barber . . . the washer man, . . . here and there the poet, who in some communities replaces the silversmith, in others the school master . . .'. He speaks of the difference between the British rule and the earlier conquests, 'All the civil wars, invasions, revolutions, conquests, famines, strangely complex, rapid and destructive as their successive action in Hindostan may appear, did not go deeper than its surface. England has broken down the whole framework of Indian society . . .'.[19] Thus, for Ahmad to run down 'tradition' as fascism ('our own modern traditions of secularity, socialism, rationality, religious tolerance, and plurality') is to be such a radical Marxist as to forget Marx himself, on India.

In the context of the foregoing discussion, Nandy's formulation (as discussed by Dipesh Chakrabarty)[20] of the idea of 'critical traditionalism' can be invoked for a better understanding and contextualization of the two texts I mention above. On the face of it, the texts in focus there seem to belong to vastly different, mutually exclusive discursive domains—Radhanath Ray's confession seems deeply concerned with questions of the self, and Fakir Mohan's seems entirely concerned with the public good. But, the manner in which Radhanath Ray articulates his innermost trepidations turns the moment of confession away from interiority to the public domain, and as such, it is no less concerned with public good than Fakir Mohan's. After all, Radhanath Ray bemoans the absence of exemplary, admonitory 'book' which would have saved him from 'slipping'. He was determined to leave behind such a monitory text for posterity. Nandy's leading examples of 'critical traditionalism' are those of Gandhi and Tagore. But many other lesser lights too continued to view traditional practices with respect. Through their work, they also offer critiques of modernity whenever they find aspects of it unhelpful and are critical of traditions whenever they found tradition obscurantist. I would like to rephrase Nandy's formulation and call this attitude 'strategic traditionalism' in the sense in which Spivak uses the term 'strategic essentialism'. I do this advisedly since the first term, in the context under discussion, appears to be an innocent and intuitive resistance, whereas both Radhanath Ray and Fakir Mohan, and the others (much before Gandhi), were invoking traditions with suitable modifications for strategic reasons. Thus, Radhanath, even when he is aware of European modes of confession, cites from traditional Sanskritic wisdom in spite of being aware of social ills of traditional Hindu practices. He shuns any thoughts of conversion into Christianity or Brahmoism. He critiques Brahmanism through historicization of the advent of Buddhism and its decline in his epic, *Mahayatra*. While glorifying the Arya traditions, he blames Brahmanism for the decline of Hindusism and Aryadharma.

One of the problems that researchers encounter when they embark on the task of historicizing Indian literary-culture is the paucity of instances from numerous vernacular archives. I have tried to suggest that the way to circumvent the problem is by exploring and making available diverse discrete archives scattered across diverse linguistic cultures of India through mutual translations. Speaking of the problem in South Asian studies (though of an earlier period), Pollock has recently argued how

A good deal of this scholarship has been both substantively and theoretically exciting and provocative and has changed the way we understand the transformative interactions between India and the West, starting from the consolidation of British power in the subcontinent around 1800. But as many of its practitioners would be ready to admit, colonial studies has long been skating on the thinnest ice, given how far it presupposes knowledge of the precolonial realities that colonialism encountered and how little such knowledge we actually possess.

Currently, during the period relevant to our discussion, the English archive is limited to Bangla, English, and a modicum of Hindi. Even these are around the best-known among figures in the dominant linguistic groups such as Gandhi, the Nehrus, the Tagores, Bankimchandra Chattopadhyay (1838–94), Bharatendu (1850–85) and others. Surely, there are other important but obscure personalities and their untranslated works which could prove revealing in certain contexts. In the chapter on Gandhi vis-à-vis khadi and the confessional mode of writing, I tried to show, with the help of two examples from colonial Odisha, just how accurate Pollock's observation is but also how instead of developing a pessimistic view, one should work towards bringing to light the many discrete archives inaccessible to the world of scholarly scrutiny in various vernacular cultures in India. This alone can provide the necessary corrective to many of our blemished cultural histories.

Pollock further suggests how, 'we cannot know how colonialism changed South Asia if we do not know what was there to be changed'. While wholeheartedly agreeing with this, one finds it difficult to uncritically accept another aspect of Pollock's position. He asks:

how South Asian knowledge and imagination lost, which in turn requires a better understanding of what exactly these forms of thought were, how they worked, and who produced them. To date, hypotheses on the demise of Indian science and scholarship with the advent of colonialism seem largely dependent on interpretations dominant since the time of Max Weber, which takes for granted the presumed uniqueness of Western rationality, technology, rights bearing citizenship, or capacity for capitalism —in short, Western, the inevitability of its eventual global conquest.

In this aspect of Pollock's position, I identify two problematic formulations that are relevant to our concern here. One is the assumption that there was 'demise of Indian science and scholarship with the advent of colonialism'. I have tried, in the relevant chapter, to suggest through examples that the 'demise' has not been conclusive. The second is about the assumption that the colonized people were a homogeneous whole, i.e. they all equally internalized the Western discourses of modernity. In consequence, the question of colonial modernity is addressed from the usual perspective of impact and response, i.e. first defined as a Western phenomenon that was transplanted in India and responded to and spread by the educated natives. One can understand why this is so—the dramatis personae concerned were mostly English educated, and it is believed that there was a trickle-down effect of modernity.[21]

True, many of the Odia writers like Radhanath Ray, Madhusudan Rao, Biswanath Kar, Gopalachandra Praharj and others who lived around the same time and within the administrative zone of the Bengal Presidency were among the more 'enlightened' of the emergent intelligentsia, Radhanath Ray being the most erudite of the lot. But there were, surely, those others who were untouched by the Western discourse of modernity. I am thinking here of relatively obscure Odias like the Kondh poet-saint Bhima Bhoi and home-grown scientist, Samanta Chandrasekhar Harichandan Mahapatra aka Pathani Samanta, one of the last indigenous astronomers to arrive at scientific conclusions totally devoid of Western education. The former, considered by some to be a neo-Buddhist,[22] spoke up against social injustice, religious bigotry, and caste discrimination, though in no way influenced by the reformation movement then sweeping through many parts of India under the influence of colonial modernity. Samanta Chandrasekhar too, totally ignorant of 'modern scientific' methods, used many improvisations of traditional instruments, worked during the heyday of British colonialism, and produced his treatise in immaculate Sanskrit verse (*Siddhant Darpan*).[23]

At the end, perhaps, we need to reiterate the axiomatic proposition guiding the narratives throughout the book, that there exists an inextricable link between the coordinates of an argument and issues of identity or nationalism. In the case of many of the controversies, major or minor, brought into focus in the chapters, the actions or words of a single individual motivated by some personal-ideological predilection trigger off a chain of reactions and counter points, because the same words or actions are seen in terms of othering by a dominant community or as impacting adversely on the nationalist or identitarian aspirations, on an iconic figure or on the image of the hegemonized community or nation. In the very proposition of the thesis inheres its antithesis, and by the time a synthesis emerges through historical processes, the latter acquires the status of yet another thesis due to shifts in historical circumstances of the nation-subject or subject-nation; and the resulting instability of the synthesis ensures the longevity of the controversy in question, albeit in altered forms.

Notes

1. Ernest Gellner, *Nations and Nationalism*, New York: Cornell University Press, 1983, p. 1.
2. G. Aloysius, *Nationalism without a Nation in India*, New Delhi: OUP, 1997, p. 15.
3. Roma Chatterji, ed., 'Introduction', in *Wording the World: Veena Das and Scenes of Inheritance*, New York: Fordham University Press, 2015. Also see, Deepak Mehta, 'The Ayodhya Dispute: Law's Imagination and the Functions of the Status Quo', in *Wording the World: Veena Das and Scenes of Inheritance*, ed. Roma Chatterji, New York: Fordham University Press, 2015, pp. 273–87; and Peter van der Veer, *Religious Nationalism: Hindus and Muslims in India*, London: University of California Press, 1994.
4. Report in the *Sunday Guardian*, see, <http://www.sunday-guardian.com/investigation/buddhist-body-lays-claim-to-disputed-ayodhya-site>, accessed 25 September 2015.
5. Aijaz Ahmad, *Lineages of the Present*, London: Verso, 2000.
6. Ibid., p. 131.
7. The allusion here is both to the paradigm-changing Minute by Macaulay and to the lesser known Minute by Lord Canning discussed in this chapter. I also allude to W.B. Yeats's controversial stance in 'Easter', 1916:

> Hearts with one purpose alone
> Through summer and winter seem
> Enchanted to a stone
> To trouble the living stream.
> The horse that comes from the road,
> The rider, the birds that range
> From cloud to tumbling cloud,
> Minute by minute they change;
> A shadow of cloud on the stream
> Changes minute by minute;
> A horse-hoof slides on the brim,
> And a horse plashes within it;

The long-legged moor-hens dive,
And hens to moor-cocks call;
Minute by minute they live:
The stone's in the midst of it all.

The poet was often accused of ambivalent attitude towards Irish nationalism, which he shared with Tagore as has been discussed in the Introduction. See, W.B. Yeats, *Yeats: Selected Poetry*, ed. A. Norman Jeffares, London: Pan Books, 1974, pp. 93–5.

8. Alexander Cunningham, *Four Reports: Made During the Years 1862–63–64–65*, vol. I, Simla: Government Central Press, 1871.

9. Ibid., p. ii.

10. The judgement said, 'That much before 1855 Ram Chabutra and Seeta Rasoi had come into existence and Hindus were worshipping in the same. It was very very unique and absolutely unprecedented situation that in side the boundary wall and compound of the mosque Hindu religious places were there which were actually being worshipped along with offerings of Namaz by Muslims in the mosque'. See, <http://timesofindia.indiatimes.com/india/Text-of-Allahabad-high-court-order-on-Ayodhya-dispute/articleshow/6659163.cms>, accessed 14 October 2015.

11. Sealy quotes Bankimchandra Chattopadhyay praising Michael Madhusudan Dutt by comparing him with the twelfth-century Bengali poet, Jayadeva.

12. Ibid.

13. Gregory Benford, *Timescape*, London: Hachette, 2011. Benford is professor of Physics and a science fiction-writer, *Timescape* being one of his novels.

14. Tagore dwelt on the subject in many of his lectures and articles, and his nuanced understanding of nationalism of course did not meet with the approval of the colonized brethren, Mahatma Gandhi excepted. See, Ashis Nandy, *The Illegitimacy of Nationalism: Rabindranath Tagore and the Politics of Self*, New Delhi: OUP, 1994.

15. See Chap. 3, fn. 72.

16. Rosinka Chaudhuri, *The Literary Thing: History, Poetry and the Making of a Modern Cultural Sphere*, New Delhi: OUP, 2011, p. 237.

17. Thapar, *The Hindu*, 28 October 2011.

18. 'Kavi Michael Madhusudan Dutt and Meghnadhbadh Kavya', *Fakir Mohan Granthabali*, vol. 3, Cuttack: Granth Mandir, 2008, p. 362.

19. Karl Marx, *Capital*; extract reprinted in McLane, *The Political Awakening in India*, pp. 93–5.

20. Gayatri Chakravorty Spivak, 'Subaltern Studies: Deconstructing Historiography', in *In Other Worlds: Essays in Cultural Politics*, ed. Ranajit Guha and Gayatri Chakravorty Spivak, Oxford: OUP, 1988, pp. 197–221.

21. Tanika Sarkar critiques such ideas, especially of Partha Chatterjee, who 'postulates a process of percolation: the idea that western cultural

forms filter down through a bourgeois poet and modernize the indigenous-popular'. See, Tanika Sarkar, *Wives, Saints Designing Selves and Nations in Colonial Times,* Ranikhet: Permanent Black, 2009, p. 270.

22. Bhima Bhoi (1850–95). See, Nagendranath Basu, *Buddhism and its Followers in Orissa,* Calcutta: Self Published, 1911, p. 154.

23. Also known as Pathani Samant (1835–1904), who had not had an iota of Western education. He was first called an 'astrologer', then an 'astronomer', and finally recognized as a scientist. See, Yogeshchandra Ray, *Ja Manepade,* 2002 [What I Remember], tr. Rabindra Prasad Panda, Bhubaneswar: Lark Books, 2006, pp. 332–49; and Chandrasekhar Mishra, *Samanta Chandrasekhar (Life Story),* Cuttack: Satyabadi Press, 1932.

Appendix

These documents were made available to the author by the late Brajanath Rath from the latter's personal collection in Balasore.

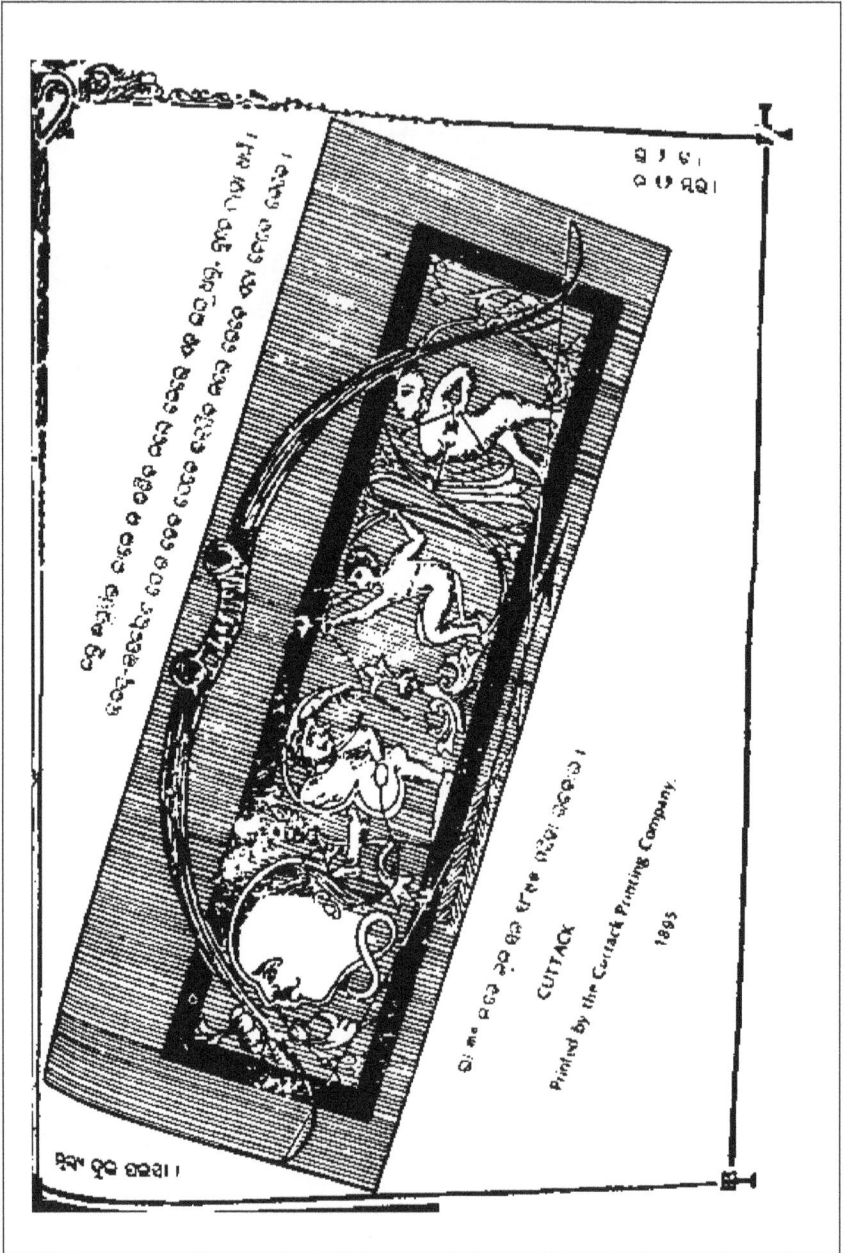

Masthead of the little magazine *Indradhanu* which was engaged in a fierce debate with its rival *Bijuli* during the ancient *v.* modern debate.

ସରଳ ବ୍ୟାକରଣ ।

ଶ୍ରୀ ଫକୀର ମୋହନ ସେନାପତି

ପ୍ରଣୀତ ।

SIMPLE GRAMMAR

IN ORIYA,

BY

FHUKEER MOHUN SENAPUTY

Balasore.

CALCUTTA :

PRINTED AT THE BAPTIST MISSION PRESS

1866.

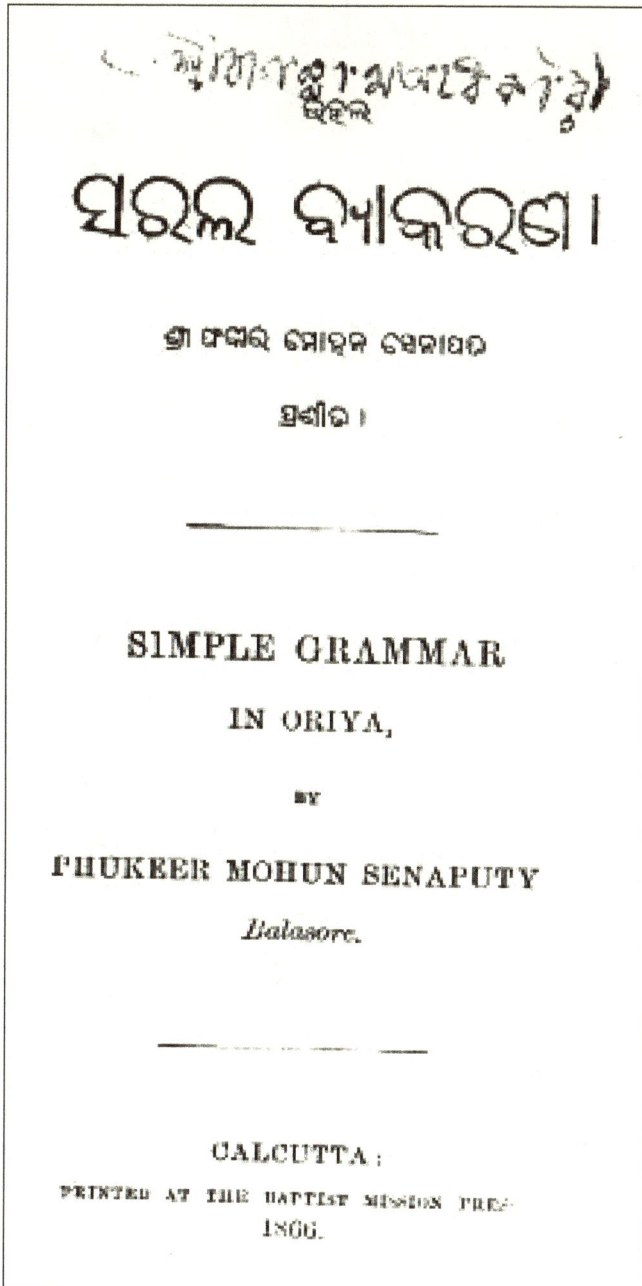

The first Odia grammar textbook prepared by Fakir Mohan Senapati (1866) in close imitation of its Bangla counterpart.

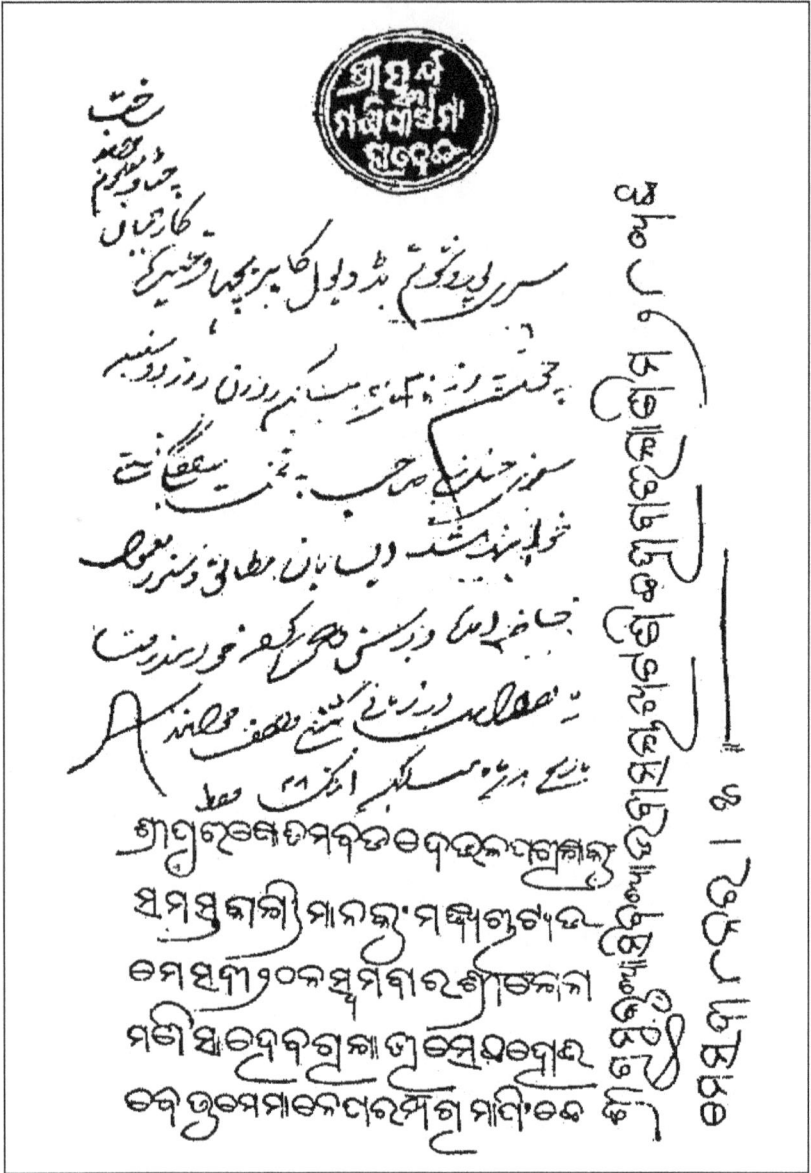

Formal royal, bilingual (Odia and Persian) invitation from the Queen of Puri, 'Suryamani Patamahadei' dated 1 May 1882. It says, 'The parichha of the temple of Lord Jagannath and other servitors are hereby informed that the coronation of Jagannath Jenamani will take place on Monday, the 20th day of Mesha. You are all required, as custom demands, to present yourselves before His Majesty.' It is noteworthy here that Persian was as yet not associated with the Muslims. No punctuation marks were in vogue in the writing of the Odia sentences.

Basant-Gatha, a popular collection of Odia devotional poetry by Madhusudan Rao, a Brahmo convert.

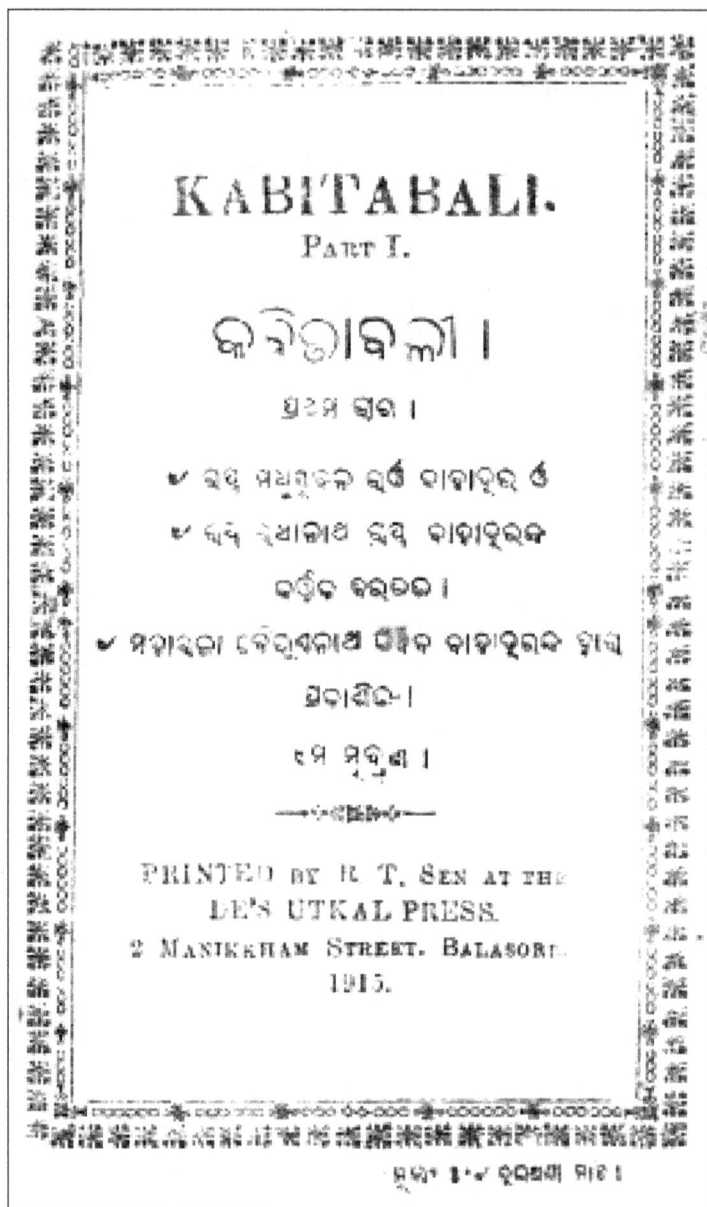

The ninth edition of *Kabitabali* Part I (1915), one of the earliest Odia textbooks jointly composed by Madhusudan Rao and Radhanath Ray.

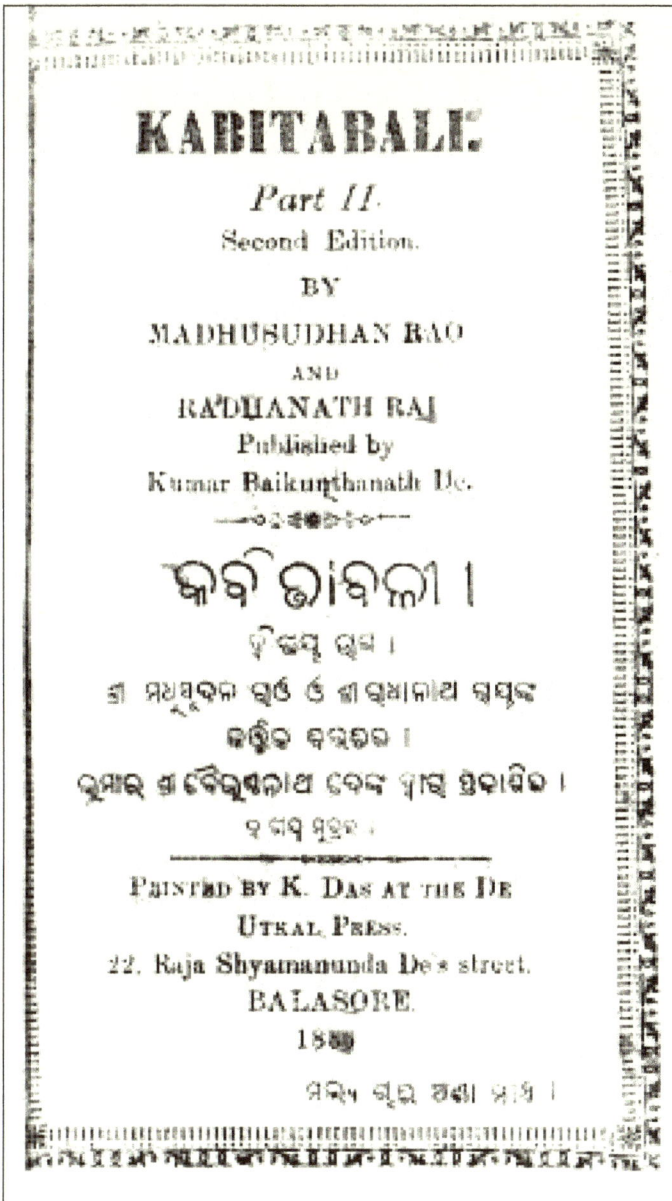

The fifth edition of *Kabitabali* Part II (1885), one of the earliest Odia textbooks jointly composed by Madhusudan Rao and Radhanath Ray.

লেখাবলী।

শ্রীরাধানাথ রায় বিরচিত।

হেয়ার প্রেস।

৪৬ নং বেচু চাট্যর্য্যের ষ্ট্রীট, কলিকাতা।

মূল্য ৵• পাঁচ আনা মাত্র।

One of Radhanath Ray's first collections of writing called *Lekhabali*, which was in Bangla.

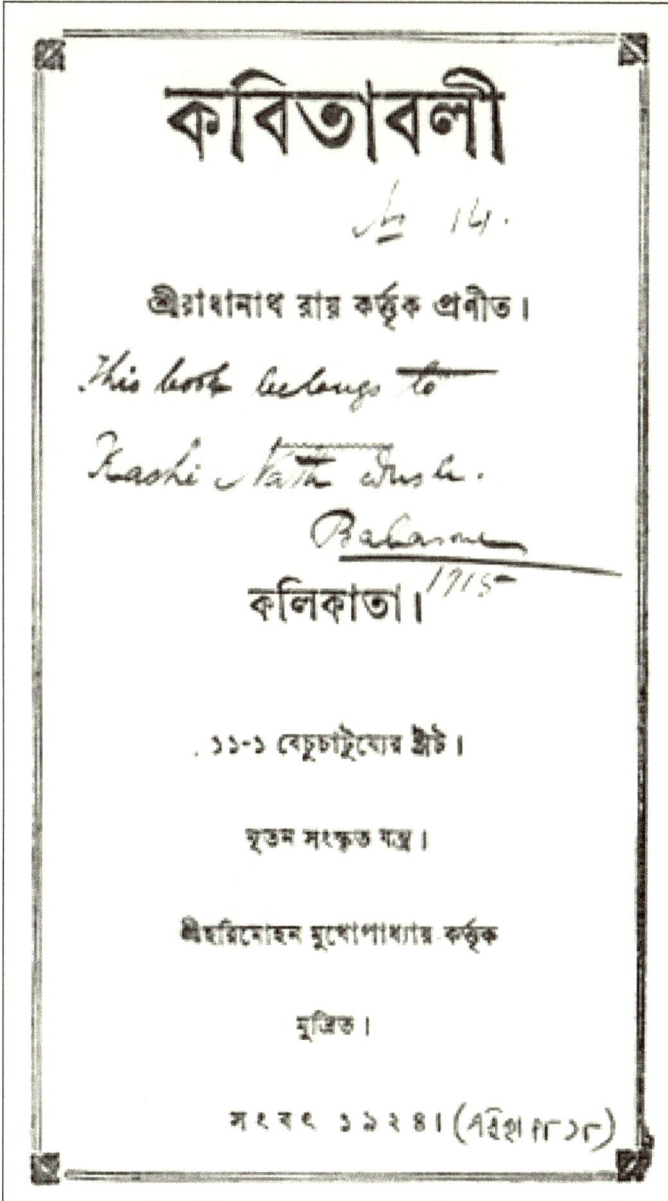

The first poetry collection by Radhanath Ray, which was in Bangla (1868).

Bibliography

Acharya, Pyari Mohan, 'Bhumika' [Foreword], in *Odishara Itihas*, Cuttack: Cuttack Printing Company, 1879, pp. 1–3.

———, *Odishara Itihas*, Cuttack: Cuttack Printing Company, 1879, pp. 23–4.

Achebe, Chinua, 'An Image Of Africa: Racism In Conrad's *Heart of Darkness*', *Massachusetts Review*, vol. 18, 1977, pp. 782–94.

Ahmad, Aijaz, *In Theory: Classes, Nations, Literatures*, Delhi: OUP, 1992.

———, *Lineages of the Present*, London: Verso, 2000.

Aloysius, G., *Nationalism without a Nation in India*, Delhi: OUP, 1997.

Anderson, Benedict, *Imagined Communities: Reflections on the Origin and Spread of Nationalism*, London: Verso, 1983.

Aquil, Raziuddin and Partha Chatterjee, eds., *History in the Vernacular*, Ranikhet: Permanent Black, 2008.

Bal, Nandakishor, '2nd Khanda [Part II] Chhāndamālā', *Utkal Sahitya*, vol. 3, no. 10, 1899, pp. 220–9.

Basu, Nagendranath, *Buddhism and its Followers in Orissa*, Calcutta: Self Published, 1911.

Bauer, J. Edgar, 'The Sexologist and the Poet: On Magnus Hirschfeld, Rabindranath Tagore, and the Critique of Sexual Binarity', *Rupkatha Journal on Interdisciplinary Studies in Humanities*, vol. 2, no. 4, 2010; special issue on Rabindranath Tagore, ed. Amrit Sen, <http://rupkatha.com/v2n4.php>, accessed 12 September 2012.

Beames, John, 'On the Arabic Element in Official Hindustani, Part II', *Journal of the Asiatic Society*, pt. I, no. 3, 1867, pp. 146–8.

———, *A Comparative Grammar of the Modern Aryan Languages of India*, London: Turner & Co., 1872.

———, *Essays on Orissan History and Literature*, ed. Kailash Pattanaik, Jagatsinghpur: Prafulla, 2004.

———, *Memoirs of a Bengal Civilian*, London: Chatto & Windus, 1961.

Benford, Gregory, *Timescape*, London: Hachette, 2011.

Benjamin, Walter, 'Art in the Age of Mechanical Reproduction', in *Illuminations: Essays and Reflections*, tr. Harry Zohn, New York: Knopf Doubleday Publishing Group, 1968, pp. 218–55.

Bentley, John, *A Historical View of the Hindu Astronomy, from the Earliest Dawn of that Science in India to the Present Time*, London: Smith, Elder, & Co., 1835.

Blackburn, Stuart and Vasudha Dalmia, eds., *India's Literary History: Essays on the Nineteenth Century*, Delhi and Ranikhet: Permanent Black, 2004.

Boulton, John, 'Sarala Dasa: His Audience, His Critics and His Mahabharata', in *Essays on Oriya Literature*, compiled and with an afterword by Ganeswar Mishra, Prafulla Pathagara, 2003, pp. 7–38.

Bourdieu, Pierre, et al., *The Rules of Art: Genesis and Structure of the Literary Field*, tr. Susan Emanuel, California: Stanford University Press, 1996.

Brown, Rebecca M., *Gandhi's Spinning Wheel and the Making of India*, London and New York: Routledge, 2010.

Buitenen, J.A.B. van, tr. and ed., *The Mahabharata*, Chicago and London: University of Chicago Press, 1973.

Caldwell, Robert, *A Comparative Grammar of the Dravidian or South Indian Family of Languages*, London: Williams and Norgate, 1856.

Chakrabarty, Dipesh, *Habitations of Modernity: Essays in the Wake of Subaltern Studies; with a Foreword by Homi K. Bhabha*, Chicago: University of Chicago Press, 2002.

Chatterjee, Partha, *The Nation and its Fragments: Colonial and Postcolonial Histories*, Princeton: Princeton University Press, 1993.

———, 'Nationalist Thought and the Colonial World: A Derivative Discourse?', in *The Partha Chatterjee Omnibus: Comprising Nationalist Thought and the Colonial World, The Nation and its Fragments, and A Possible India* (II), New Delhi: OUP, 1999.

———, *The Partha Chatterjee Omnibus: Comprising Nationalist Thought and the Colonial World, The Nation and its Fragments, and A Possible India* (II), New Delhi: OUP, 1985; repr. 1999.

———, 'Introduction', in *History in the Vernacular*, ed. Raziuddin Aquil and Partha Chatterjee, Ranikhet: Permanent Black, 2008, p. 18.

Chatterji, Roma, ed., 'Introduction', in *Wording the World: Veena Das and Scenes of Inheritance*, New York: Fordham University Press, 2015.

Chattopadhyay, Bankimchandra, 'The Bengali Language: The Language of Writing', tr. Gautam Chakravarty, *Indian Literature*, vol. LVII, no. 3, May/June 2014, pp. 26–33; originally published in *Bangadarshan*, 1285 Jaishta (May 1879).

Chaudhuri, Amit, ed., 'Introduction', in *The Picador Book of Modern Indian Literature*, London: Picador, 2001, pp. xvii–xxxii.

Chaudhuri, Pramatha, 'Sabuja patrera mukhapatra' [Sabuj Patra's Manifesto], in Nana-katha [Miscellany], Calcutta: Self Published, 1919, pp. 109–10.

Chaudhuri, Rosinka, *The Literary Thing: History, Poetry And The Making Of A Modern Cultural Sphere*, New Delhi: OUP, 2014, pp. 234–40.

Choubey, Gautam, 'Hindi Prose and Gandhian First Principles: Issues of

Agency, Community and Justice (1915–48)', Unpublished Ph.D. dissertation, University of Delhi, 2016.

Classical Odia in Historical Perspective, Department of Culture: Government of Odisha, 2015.

Cunningham, Sir Alexander, *Four Reports: Made During the Years 1862–63–64–65*, vol. I, Simla: Government Central Press, 1871.

———, *Mahabodhi or the Great Buddhist Temple under the Bodhi Tree at Buddha-Gaya*, London: W.H. Allen & Co., 1892.

Dalmia, Vasudha, *The Nationalisation of Hindu Traditions: Bharatendu Harischandra and Nineteenth Century Banaras*, New Delhi: Permanent Black, 2010.

Das, Gourangacharan, ed., *Artaballav Rachana Samagra*, vol. II, Cuttack: Ravenshaw College, 2015.

Das, J.P., *Puri* Paintings, New Delhi: Arnold-Heinemann, 1982.

———, 'Micchha Itihasa', in *Ama Odia Amara Odisha*, Bhubaneswar: Shikshasandan, 2016, pp. 116–22.

———, *Time Elsewhere*, tr. Jatindra K. Nayak, Delhi: Penguin, 2009.

Das, Kamala, 'Foreword', in *Our Favourite Indian Stories*, ed. Khushwant Singh and Neelam Kumar, eds., Delhi: Jaico, 2002, pp. 17–20.

Das, Nilakantha, *Odia Sahityara Krama Parinama* (1953), Cuttack: Grantha Mandir, 2011.

Das, S.K., *A History of Indian Literature, 1911–1956*, Delhi: Sahitya Akademi, 1995; repr. 2006.

Dash, Gaganendranath, '*Jagannātha* and Oriya Nationalism', in *The Cult of Jagannath and the Regional Tradition of Orissa*, ed. Anncharlott Eschmann, Hermann Kulke and Gaya Charan Tripathi, Delhi: Manohar, 1978, pp. 359–74.

———, *Odia Bhasha Charchara Parampara*, Cuttack: Institute of Odia Studies, 1983.

———, 'Sarala Mahabharata o Itihasa', in *Nirbachita Prabandha Samkalana*, Cuttack: Vidyapuri, 2005.

———, '*Soma-vamsi* Yayati in Tradition and Medieval Odia Literature', *Studies in History*, vol. 28, no. 2, 2012, pp. 151–77.

———, *Nirbachita Prabandha Samkalana*, Cuttack: Vidyapuri, 2005.

Davis, Horace B., *Towards a Marxist Theory of Nationalism*, New York: Monthly Review Press, 1978.

De, Esha Niyogi, 'Gender, Nation, and the Vicissitudes of *Kalpana:* Choreographing Womanly Beauty in Tagore's Dance Dramas', in *Rabindranath Tagore in the 21st Century: Theoretical Renewals*, ed. Debashish Banerji, New Delhi: Springer, 2015, pp. 157–71.

Dharwadker, Vinay, 'The Historical Formation of Indian-English Literature', in *Literary Cultures in History: Reconstructions from South Asia*, ed. Sheldon Pollock, New Delhi: OUP, 2003, pp. 199–270.

Dirlik, Arif, 'Rethinking Colonialism: Globalisation, Postcolonialism and the Nation', *Interventions*, vol. 4, no. 3, 2002, p. 434.

Dirks, Nicholas, *Castes of Mind: Colonialism and the Making of Modern*

India, Princeton and Oxford: Princeton University Press, 2001, pp. 154–6.

Dutt, Michael Madhusudan, *Meghnadbadh Kavya* (in Bangla), <http://www.banglainternet.com/pdf-legend/michael_madhusudan_dutt_meghnad_badh_kabya.pdf>, accessed 21 September 2015.

Eliot, T.S., *What is a Classic?*, Orlando: Mariner Books, 1975.

Fallon, S.W., *English-Hindustani Law and Commercial Dictionary*, Banaras: Medical Hall Press, 1879.

Farmer, Brett, *Spectacular Passions: Cinema, Fantasy, Gay Male Spectatorship*, Durham: Duke University Press, 2000.

Faruqi, Shamsur Rahman, 'A Long History of Urdu Literary Culture, Part I: Naming and Placing a Literary Culture', in *Literary Cultures in History: Reconstructions from South Asia*, ed. Sheldon Pollock, New Delhi: OUP, 2003, pp. 805–63.

Fergusson, James, 'Preface', in *Archaeology In India, With Especial Reference to the Works* of *Babu Rajendralal Mitra*, London: Trubner & Co., 1884.

Foucault, Michel, Luther H. Martin, Huck Gutman and Patrick H. Hutton, *Technologies of the Self: A Seminar with Michel Foucault*, Amherst: University of Massachusetts, 1988.

Fraser, Nancy, 'Rethinking the Public Sphere: A Contribution to the Critique of Actually Existing Democracy', *Social Text*, nos. 25–26, 1990, pp. 56–80.

Gandhi, Leela N., 'Indo-Anglian Fiction: Writing India, Elite Aesthetics, and the Rise of the "Stephanian" Novel', *Australian Humanities Review*, no. 8, November 1997.

Gandhi, M.K., *An Autobiography or the Story of My Experiments with Truth*, tr. Mahadev Desai, Ahmedabad: Navajivan Trust, 1927; repr. 1999.

———, *Hind Swaraj and Other Writings*, ed. Anthony J. Parel, New Delhi and Cambridge: CUP, 1997; repr. 2009.

Gandhi, Rajmohan, *Mohandas: A True Story of a Man, His People and an Empire*, 2006, Middlesex: Penguin, 2007.

Ganguly, Kisari Mohan, tr., *The Mahabharata of Krishna-Dwaipayana Vyasa*, translated into English prose from Sanskrit, New Delhi: Munshiram Manoharlal, 1998.

Geertz, Clifford, *The Interpretation of Cultures: Selected Essays*, New York: Basic Books, 1973.

Gellner, Ernest, *Nations and Nationalism*, New York: Cornell University Press, 1983.

Ghosh, Rituparno, *Chitrangada: The Crowning Wish* (2012 Bangla Feature Film with English subtitles).

Ghosh, Shohini, 'Forbidden Love and Passionate Denial: A Dialogue in Queer Love and Domesticities', in *Handbook of Gender*, ed. Raka Ray, New Delhi: OUP, 2012, pp. 428–52.

Goyanka, Kamal Kishore, ed., *Premchand ki Hindi-Urdu Kāhāniyan*, New Delhi: Bharatiya Jnanpith, 1990.

Grierson, George A., 'A Plea for the People's Tongue', *The Calcutta Review*, vol. LXXVI, 1880, pp. 151–68.

Guillory, John, 'The Sokal Affair and the History of Criticism', *Critical Inquiry*, vol. 28, no. 2, 2002, pp. 470–508.

Gupta, Balmukund, 'Hindī mein bindī (1900)', <http://www.columbia.edu/itc/mealac/pritchett/00urduhindilinks/shacklesnell/308gupta.pdf>, accessed 12 August 2015.

Guruge, Ananda W.P., *Return to Righteousness: A Collection of Speeches, Essays, and Letters of the Anagarika Dharmapala*, Colombo: Government Press, 1965.

Habermas, Jürgen, 'The Public Sphere', *New German Critique*, vol. 3, 1974, pp. 49–55.

Halhed, Nathaniel Brassey, *A Grammar of the Bengal Language*, Bengal: CUP, 1778.

Higl, Andrew, *Playing the Canterbury Tales: The Continuations and Additions*, Surrey: Ashgate, 2012.

Hill, Kenneth, <http://woolfandwilde.com/2009/07/the-day-judy-garland-outed-me/>, 2009, accessed 12 November 2013.

———, <http://woolfandwilde.com/2013/02/im-not-coming-with-you/>, 2013, accessed 12 November 2013.

Hunter, W.W., *Odisha or the Vicissitudes of an Indian Province under Native and British Rule*, London: Smith, Elder & Co., 1872.

Jha, Jata Shankar, *Beginning of Modern Education in Mithila: Selections from Educational Records, Darbhanga Raj, 1860–1930*, Patna: K.P. Jayaswal Research Institute, 1972.

Jussawalla, Adil, *New Writing in India*, Harmondsworth: Penguin, 1974.

Jussawalla, Adil and Eunice de Souza, eds., *Statements*, Mumbai: Orient Longman, 1977.

Kar, Purushottam, *Indian National Congress and Orissa, 1885–1936*, Cuttack: Kitab Mahal, 1987.

Kaviraj, Sudipta, *The Unhappy Consciousness*, New Delhi: OUP, 1995.

———, 'The Two Histories of Literary Culture in Bengal', in *Literary Cultures in History: Reconstructions from South Asia*, ed. Sheldon Pollock, New Delhi: OUP, 2003, pp. 503–66.

———, 'Writing, Speaking, Being: Language and the Historical Formation of Identities in India', in *Language and Politics in India*, ed. Asha Sarangi, New Delhi: OUP, 2009, pp. 312–50.

Kinnard, Jacob N., 'When Is The Buddha Not the Buddha? The Hindu-Buddhist Battle over Bodhgaya and its Buddha Image', *Journal of the American Academy of Religion*, vol. 66, no. 4, 1998, pp. 817–39.

Kristeva, Julia, *The Powers of Horror: An Essay on Abjection*, tr. Leon S. Roudiez, Oxford: Columbia University Press, 1982.

Kumar, Lalit, 'Literary Cultures in North Bihar: The Coming of Print in Mithila', Unpublished Ph.D. dissertation, University of Delhi, 2016.

Lamos, Colleen, 'The Ethics of Queer Theory', in *Critical Ethics: Text,*

Theory and Responsibility, ed. Dominic Rainsford and Tim Woods, London: Macmillan, 1999.

Long, Revd James, 'Notes and Queries suggested by a visit to Orissa in January 1859', *Journal of the Asiatic Society of India*, vol. 28, no. 3, 1859, pp. 189–90.

MacGregor, Stuart, 'The Progress of Hindi, Part I: The Development of a Transregional Idiom', in *Literary Cultures in History: Reconstructions from South Asia*, ed. Sheldon Pollock, New Delhi: OUP, 2003, pp. 912–57.

Mahey, Arjun, 'Epic Mediations: Text, Book, and Authority in the Organization of the *Mahabharata*', in *Reflections and Variations on the Mahabharata*, ed. T.R.S. Sharma, New Delhi: Sahitya Akademi, 2009, pp. 165–386.

Mansinha, Mayadhar, *History of Odia Literature*, New Delhi: Sahitya Akademi, 1962.

Mayo, Katherine, *Mother India*, London: Jonathan Cape, 1927.

McLane, John R., ed., *The Political Awakening in India*, New Jersey: Prentice Hall, 1970.

Meher, Gangadhar, *Kichak Badh* (1904); repr. in *Gangadhar* Granthabali (1951), 3rd edn., Berhampur: Das Brothers, 1961, pp. 129–64.

Mehta, Deepak, 'The Ayodhya Dispute: Law's Imagination and the Functions of the Status Quo', in *Wording the World: Veena Das and Scenes of Inheritance*, ed. Roma Chatterji, New York: Fordham University Press, 2015, pp. 273–87.

Milton, John, *History of Great Britain*, MDCLXXI, London: St. Paul's Church-Yard, 1671. See, <http://www.ebay.com/itm/John-Milton-The-History-of-Britain-1671-Second-Edition-Frontispiece-No-Reserve-/222089316462?rmvSB=true>, accessed 10 May 2016.

———, *Paradise Lost*, ed. Thomas Newton, London: J. and R. Tonson and S. Draper, 1750, Book X.

Mishra, Chandrasekhar, *Samanta Chandrasekhar (Life Story)*, Cuttack: Satyabadi Press, 1932.

Mishra, Krishna Bihari, *The Origin and Growth of Hindi Journalism in Kolkata*, Kolkata: Press Club, 2005.

Mishra, Prasanna Kumar and Debendra Kumar Dash, eds., *Kabibar Radhanath Granthabali*, Cuttack: Grantha Mandir, 1998.

Mitchell, Lisa, *Language, Emotion, and Politics in South India: Making of a Mother Tongue*, Bloomington and Indianapolis: Indiana University Press, 2009.

Mitra, Rajendralal, 'On the Origin of the Hindavi Language and Its Relation to the Urdu Dialect', *Journal of the Asiatic Society*, no. V, 1864, p. 50.

———, *The Antiquities of Orissa*, vol. 1, Calcutta: Baptist Mission Press, 1875.

———, *The Antiquities of Orissa*, vol. 2, Calcutta: W. Newman & Co., 1880.

————, *Indo-Aryans: Contributions towards the Elucidation of Their Ancient and Mediaeval History*, 2 vols., Calcutta: W. Newman, 1881.

————, *The Sanskrit Buddhist Literature of Nepal*, Calcutta: Asiatic Society of Bengal, 1882.

Mohanty, Bansidhar, *Odiā Bhāshā Āndolana*, 2nd edn., Cuttack: Sāhitya Sangraha Prakāshana, 2001.

Mohanty, Gopinath, 'Sarala Dasnka Ghara Keunthi?', *Jhankara*, vol. 8, no. 2, 1957, pp. 249–58.

————, 'Sarala Dasnka Samaya O Sabhaparva', *Jhankara*, vol. 5, no. 4, 1958, pp. 363–71; cont. in vol. 9, no. 5, pp. 433–50 and vol. 9, no. 6, pp. 430–7.

Mohanty, Jatindra Mohan, *History of Odia Literature*, Bhubaneswar: Vidya Prakashan, 2006.

Mohanty, Nivedita, *Oriya Nationalism: Quest for a United Orissa, 1866-1956*, revised and enlarged edn., Jagatsinghpur: Prafulla, 2005.

Mohanty, Surendra, *Odiya Sahityara Kramabikasha*, Cuttack: Agraduta, 1978.

Mohapatra, Animesh, 'The Local and the Global in Oriya Public Sphere: 1866–1948', Unpublished Ph.D. dissertation, University of Delhi, 2016.

Mohapatra, Bishnu, 'Ways of Belonging: The Kanchi Kaveri Legend and the Construction of Oriya Identity', *Studies in History*, vol. 12, no. 2, 1996, pp. 203–21.

Muhammad, Shan, ed., 'Introduction', in *The Aligarh Movement: Basic Documents (1864–1898)*, Meerut: Meenakshi Prakashan, 1978, pp. i–xv.

————, ed., *The Aligarh Movement: Basic Documents (1864-1898)*, Meerut: Meenakshi Prakashan, 1978.

Mukerjee, Ashutosh, comp., *Odia Sahitya Parichaya*, Calcutta: Baptist Mission Press, n.d., p. 85.

Naipaul, V.S., *An Area of Darkness*, London: A. Deutsch, 1964.

Nandy, Ashis, 'Preface', in *The Illegitimacy of Nationalism: Rabindranath Tagore and the Politics of Self*, New Delhi: OUP, 1994, pp. i–iii.

————, *The Illegitimacy of Nationalism: Rabindranath Tagore and the Politics of Self*, New Delhi: OUP, 1994.

Nayak, Bharat Chandra, *Mor Purba Smruti Katha (Remembering my Past)*, Cuttack: Self Published, 1996(?).

Nayak, Jatindra Kumar, *The Historical Novel in Oriya*, Cuttack: Cuttack Students' Store, 1982.

Nayak, Labanya, *Odia Charita-Sahitya*, Cuttack: Friends Publishers, 1988.

Orsini, Francesca, *The Hindi Public Sphere, 1920–1940: Language and Literature in Age of Nationalism*, New Delhi: OUP, 2002.

Paige, D.D., ed., 'Letter to Homer Pound, 1913', in *The Selected Letters of Ezra Pound: 1907–1941*, London: Faber and Faber, 1950; repr. 1982, pp. 14–15.

Pal, Bipin Chandra, *Memories of My Life and Times*, Calcutta: Modern Book Agency, 1932; repr. 2004.

Panigrahi, Krishnachandra, 'Sarala Sahityara Rachannakala O Aitihashika Chitra', *Jhankara*, vol. 8, no. 5, 1956, pp. 1–10.

———, 'Sarala Sahityara Rachannakala O Aitihashika Chitra', *Jhankara*, vol. 9, no. 9, 1957, pp. 825–36.

———, *Mo Samayara Odisha* (*Odisha of My Time*), Cuttack: Kitab Mahal, 1978.

Pati, Biswamoy, *Situating Social History: Orissa (1800–1997)*, New Delhi: Orient BlackSwan, 2001.

Pollock, Sheldon, ed., *Literary Cultures in History: Reconstructions from South Asia*, New Delhi: OUP, 2003.

———, *Forms of Knowledge in Early Modern Asia: Explorations in the Intellectual History of India and Tibet, 1500–1800*, Durham and London: Duke University Press, 2011.

Prakash, Om, 'Co-existence of Standardized and Humble Money: The Case of Mughal India', <http://www.helsinki.fi /iehc2006/papers2/ Prakash.pdf>, accessed 16 July 2012.

Premchand, ed., 'Rastrabhasa Hindi aur Uske Samasyaen', in *Kuch Vichar: Sahitya aur Sambandhi Kuch Vichar*, New Delhi: Bharatiya Granth Niketan, 1990.

———, 'Urdu, Hindi aur Hindustani', in *Kuch Vichar: Sahitya aur Sambandhi Kuch Vichar*, New Delhi: Bharatiya Granth Niketan, 1990, p. 117.

———, *Kuch Vichar: Sahitya aur Sambandhi Kuch Vichar*, New Delhi: Bharatiya Granth Niketan, 1990.

Radice, William, tr., *The Poem of the Killing of Meghnad*, New Delhi: Penguin India, 2010.

Rai, Alok, *Hindi Nationalism*, New Delhi: Permanent Black, 2000.

Rai, Amrit, *Premchand: A Life*, tr. Harish Trivedi, New Delhi: People's Publishing House, 1982.

———, *A House Divided: The Origin and Development of Hindi/Hindavi*, Delhi: OUP, 1984.

Rajan, B., *Under Western Eyes: India from Milton to Macaulay*, Durham: Duke University Press, 1999.

Rajguru, Shyamsundar, 'Shudramuni Sarala Das (the *Mahabharata*-writer)', *Utkal Sahitya*, vol. 7, no. 4, 1903, pp. 112–15.

Ramanujan, A.K., *Speaking of Siva*, Middlesex: Penguin, 1978.

Rath, Brajanath, 'Kavivara Radhanathanka Pranaya Prasanga', in *Sachitra Vijaya*, Bhubaneswar: Anupam Bharat, January–February 1998, pp. 53–5.

Ray, Durgacharan, *Radhanath Jibani* (1941), Cuttack: Friends Publishers, 1998.

Ray, Yogeshchandra, *Ja Manepade* (2002) [What I Remember], tr. Rabindra Prasad Panda, Bhubaneswar: Lark Books, 2006.

Raza, Zafar, *Premchand, Urdu-Hindi Kathākār*, Allahabad: Lokbharti Prakashan, 1993.

Report in the *Sunday Guardian*, see, <http://www.sunday-guardian.com/investigation/buddhist-body-lays-claim-to-disputed-ayodhya-site>, accessed 25 September 2015.

Rushdie, Salman, *Midnight's Children*, London: Vintage, 1981.

———, *Step Across the Line: Collected Non-Fiction 1992–2002*, London: Jonathan Cape, 2002.

Rushdie, Salman and Elizabeth West, eds., 'Introduction', in *The Vintage Book of Indian Writing, 1947–1997*, London: Vintage, 1997, pp. ix–xxii.

Suhrud, Tridip, *Writing Life: Three Gujarati Thinkers*, Hyderabad: Orient BlackSwan, 2009.

Sahoo, Adikand, *Radhanath Granthabali*, Cuttack: Vidya Prakashan, 2002.

Sahoo, Karunakar, ed., *Bhaktakabi Bhimabhoi Granthabali*, Cuttack: Dharmagrantha Store, 2011.

Said, Edward, *Culture and Imperialism*, London: Chatto & Windus, 1993.

Samantaray, Natabar, 'Panchasakha: A Myth?', in *Adhunika Odia Sahityara Bhittibhumi*, Cuttack: Friends Publishers, 1964.

———, *History of Modern Odia Literature*, Cuttack: Self Published, 1963.

———, *Odia Sahityara Itihasa (1803–1920)*, Bhubaneswar: Bani Bhavan 1964; 2nd edn. 1983.

Sāralā Mahābhārata, Cuttack: Sarala Sahitaya Samsada, 2007.

Sarkar, Sumit, 'The Conditions and Nature of Subaltern Militancy: Bengal from Swadeshi to Non-cooperation, *c*.1905-22', in *Subaltern Studies III*, Ranajit Guha, New Delhi: OUP, 1998, pp. 271–320.

———, *The Swadeshi Movement in Bengal: 1903-1908*, New Delhi: People's Publishing House, 1973.

Sarkar, Tanika, *Hindu Wife, Hindu Nation: Community, Religion, and Cultural Nationalism*, Delhi: Permanent Black, 2001.

———, *Wives, Saints Designing Selves and Nations in Colonial Times*, Ranikhet: Permanent Black, 2009.

Satapathy, Nityananda, *Hey Sathi Hey Sarathi*, Cuttack: Grantha Mandir, 1st edn., 1969; 2nd revised edn., 1976; 3rd edn., 1989.

Sen, Prabodh Chandra, *India's National Anthem*, Calcutta: Visva-Bharati, 1972.

Senapati, Fakir Mohan, 'Foreword', in *Chha Mann Atha Guntha (Six Acres and a Third)*, 1902; repr. in *Granthabali: Complete Works of Fakir Mohan Senapati*, ed. Debendra Dash, vol. 3, Cuttack: Grantha Mandir, 2008, p. 17.

———, *Chha Mann Atha Guntha (Six Acres and a Third)*, 1902; repr. in *Granthabali: Complete Works of Fakir Mohan Senapati*, vol. 3, ed. Debendra Dash, Cuttack: Grantha Mandir, 2008, p. 17.

———, *Sabhapati Abhibhasan*, 1914; repr. in *Granthabali: Complete Works of Fakir Mohan Senapati*, ed. Debendra Dash, vol. 3, Cuttack: Grantha Mandir, 2008, p. 423.

———, *Autobiography* repr. in *Granthabali: Complete Works of Fakir Mohan Senapati*, ed. Debendra Dash, vol. 3, Cuttack: Grantha Mandir, 2008.

———, *Granthabali: Complete Works of Fakir Mohan Senapati*, vol. 3, ed. Debendra Dash, Cuttack: Grantha Mandir, 2008.

———, *Lachhama*, tr. Chandan Das, New Delhi: Three Rivers Publishers, 2013.

Shandilya, Krupa, 'The Widow, the Wife and the Courtesan: A Comparative Study of Social Reform in Premchand's *Sevasadan* and the Late-Nineteenth Century Bengali and Urdu Novel', *Comparative Literature Studies*, vol. 53, no. 2, 2016, pp. 272–88.

Sharma, Pandey Bechan 'Ugra', *Chocolate and Other Writings on Male Homoeroticism*, Translated from Hindi and with and Introduction by Ruth Vanita, Delhi: OUP, 2009.

Sharma, T.R.S., ed., *Mahabharata in Reflections and Variations on the Mahabharata*, New Delhi: Sahitya Akademi, 2009.

Shastri, H.P., 'Introduction', in *Buddhism and its Followers in Orissa*, ed. Nagendranath Basu, Calcutta: Self Published, 1911, pp. 1–28.

Singh, Bachchan, *Hindi Sahitya ka Doosra Itihas*, tr. Gautam Choubey, Delhi: Radhakrishna Prakashan, 2014.

Sinha, Mrinalini, ed., 'Introduction', in *Selections from Mother India*, New Delhi: Women's Press, 1998, pp. 1–74.

———, 'Rhetoric Agency and the Sarda Act', in *Gender, Sexuality and Colonial Modernities*, ed. Antoinette Burton, London and New York: Routledge, 1999, pp. 207–21.

Spivak, Gayatri Chakravorty, 'Subaltern Studies: Deconstructing Historiography', in *In Other Worlds: Essays in Cultural Politics*, ed. Ranajit Guha and Gayatri Chakravorty, Oxford: OUP, 1988, pp. 197–221.

———, *Death of a Discipline*, Columbia: Columbia University Press, 2003.

Sukthankar, V.S., et al., eds., *The Critical Edition of the Sanskrit Text*: the *Mahabharata for the First Time Critically Edited*, 19 vols., Poona: BORI, 1939–59.

Sutton, Amos, 'Preface', in *An Introductory Grammar of Oriya Language*, Calcutta: Baptist Mission Press, 1831, pp. ii–iv.

Tagore, Rabindranath, *Rabindra Rachanabali*, Calcutta: Saraswati Press, 1961.

———, *Chitra*, New York: Macmillan, 1914.

———, *My Remembrances*, 1917; quoted in John R. McLane, ed., *The Political Awakening in India*, New Jersey: Prentice Hall, 1970.

———, 'Meghanadavadha kavya' (The Slaying of Meghanada), in *Rabindra-racanavali, Acalita Samgraha* (The Collected Works of Rabindranath Tagore: Out-of-Print Material), Calcutta: Visva-Bharati, 1962; first published in Bharati, August 1882.

————, '"Chitrangada" Giti Natya' (Odia), in *Panchanatika*, tr. Prabhat Mukhopadhyay, New Delhi: Sahitya Akademi, 1970.

————, 'Giti Natya', in *Chitrangada*, tr. Anandi Charan Chatterjee (Odia), Balasore: Subarnashree, 2011.

————, *Tagore's Dance Drama Omnibus*, tr. Utpal K. Banerjee, Delhi: Niyogi Books, 2013.

Tagore, *Streer Patra* (*The Wife's Letter*), tr. Prasanjit Gupta, <http://www.parabass.com/translations/stories/Streer Patra1.html>, accessed 28 May 2015.

Tarlo, Emma, 'Khadi', 2014. <http://www.soas.ac.uk/ssai/keywords/file24807.pdf>, accessed 24 February 2014.

————, *Clothing Matters: Dress and Identity in India*, New Delhi: Penguin India (Viking), 1996.

Trivedi, Harish, 'The Progress of Hindi, Part 2: Hindi and the Nation', in *Literary Cultures in History: Reconstructions from South Asia*, New Delhi: OUP, 2003, pp. 958–1022.

Trivedi, Lisa, *Clothing Gandhi's Nation: Homespun and Modern India*, Bloomington and Indianapolis: Indiana University Press, 2007.

Vanita, Ruth, 'Introduction', in *Chocolate and Other Writings on Male Homoeroticism*, ed. Pandey Bechan 'Ugra', Delhi: OUP, 2009, pp. 1–30.

Vedvyas, 'Adi Parva', in *The Mahabharata of Krishna-Dwaipayana Vyasa*, tr. Pandit Ramnarayan Dutt Shastri Pandeya, Gorakhpur: Gita Press, 1989.

Veer, Peter van der, *Religious Nationalism: Hindus and Muslims in India*, London: University of California Press, 1994.

Walsh, Judith E., *Domesticity in Colonial India: What Women Learned When Men Gave Them Advice*, Maryland: Rowman & Littlefield Publishers, 2004.

————, *How to be the Goddess of your Home: An Anthology of Bengali Domestic Manuals*, Delhi: Yoda Press, 2005.

Wesley, John, 'Preface', in *Principles of a Methodist*, London: R. Hawes, 1746; repr. 2010, pp. 1–32.

Williams, Raymond, *Culture and Materialism*, London: Verso, 1988, p. 38; repr. 2005.

Winthrop, John, *Models of Christian Charity*, quoted in Sacvan Bercovitch, *The American Jeremiad* (1978), London: University of Wisconsin Press, 2012.

Yashaschandra, Sitanshu, 'From Hemacandra to *Hind Svaraj*: Region and Power in Gujarati Literary Culture', in *Literary Cultures in History: Reconstructions from South Asia*, ed. Sheldon Pollock, New Delhi: OUP, 2003, pp. 567–611.

Yeats, W.B., *Yeats: Selected Poetry*, ed. A. Norman Jeffares, London: Pan Books, 1974.

Newspapers and Periodicals

Asha
Baleswer Sambad Bahika
Jhankara
Imprint
Indradhanu
Journal of Contemporary Thought
Marie Claire
Mukura
Quarterly Review
Sambalpur Hiteisini
Sunday Guardian
The Hindu
The Little Magazine
The New Yorker
The Telegraph
The Times of India
Utkal Dipika
Utkal Sahitya
Utkala Darpana

Index